Public-Sector Labour Relations
in an Era of Restraint
and Restructuring

Public-Sector Labour Relations in an Era of Restraint and Restructuring

Edited by

Gene Swimmer

OXFORD
UNIVERSITY PRESS

OXFORD

UNIVERSITY PRESS

70 Wynford Drive, Don Mills, Ontario M3C 1J9
www.oupcan.com

Oxford University Press is a department of the University of Oxford.
It furthers the University's objective of excellence in research, scholarship, and education
by publishing worldwide in

Oxford New York

Athens Auckland Bangkok Bogotá Buenos Aires Calcutta
Cape Town Chennai Dar es Salaam Delhi Florence Hong Kong Istanbul
Karachi Kuala Lumpur Madrid Melbourne Mexico City Mumbai
Nairobi Paris São Paulo Singapore Taipei Tokyo Toronto Warsaw

with associated companies in Berlin Ibadan

Oxford is a trade mark of Oxford University Press
in the UK and in certain other countries

Published in Canada
by Oxford University Press

Copyright © Canadian Policy Research Networks 2001

The moral rights of the author have been asserted

Database right Oxford University Press (maker)

First published 2001

Canadian Cataloguing in Publication Data

Main entry under title:

Public-sector labour relations in an era of restraint and restructuring

Includes bibliographical references.
ISBN 0-19-541591-4

1. Collective bargaining — Government employees — Canada. 2. Employee-management
relations in government — Canada. 3. Civil service — Canada. 4. Industrial relations —
Canada. I. Swimmer, Gene R., 1946– .

HD8005.6.C3P835 2000   331.89'04135263'0971   C00-931286-2

1 2 3 4 - 04 03 02 01

This book is printed on permanent (acid-free) paper ∞.
Printed in Canada

Contents

Abbreviations

AMAPCEO	Association of Management, Administrative and Professional Crown Employees of Ontario
ATA	Alberta Teachers Association
AT&U	Alberta Transportation & Utilities
AUPE	Alberta Union of Provincial Employees
BCGEU	British Columbia Government Employees' Union
BUO	Bargaining Unit Overhaul Project (Ont.)
CAW	Canadian Auto Workers
CBRS	Canadian Bond Rating Service
CCF	Co-operative Commonwealth Federation
CECBA	Crown Employees Collective Bargaining Act (Ont.)
CHCG	Canadian Health Care Guild
COLA	cost-of-living allowance
CPI	consumer price index
CRP	Civilian Reduction Program (Can.)
CSC	Civil Service Commission (NS)
CUPE	Canadian Union of Public Employees
DBRS	Dominion Bond Rating Service
EDI	early departure incentive (Can.)
ERI	early retirement incentive (Can.)
FOS	Final Offer Selection (Man.)
FTA	Canada-United States Free Trade Agreement
FTE	full-time equivalent
GDP	gross domestic product
GSB	Grievance Settlement Board (Ont.)
HRDC	Human Resources Development Canada
HRF	Human Resource Factor (Ont.)
HRM	human resources management
HRP	Human Resources Plan (Ont.)
ILO	International Labour Office
JAC	Joint Adjustment Committees (Can.)
JSSC	Joint System Subcommittee
MASH	municipalities, academic institutions, schools, and hospitals
MGEA	Manitoba Government Employees' Association
MGEU	Manitoba Government Employees' Union
MLA	Member of the Legislative Assembly

MP	Member of Parliament
NDP	New Democratic Party
NJC	National Joint Council
NPM	new public management
NSGEU	Nova Scotia Government Employees Union
NSTU	Nova Scotia Teachers Union
NUPGE	National Union of Public and General Employees
OBU	One Big Union
OECD	Organization for Economic Co-operation and Development
OFL	Ontario Federation of Labour
OHS	Occupational Health and Safety (NS)
OMA	Ontario Medical Association
OPS	Ontario Public Service
OPSEU	Ontario Public Service Employees Union
OPSSU	Ontario Public Service Staff Union
PIPSC	Professional Institute of the Public Service of Canada
PQ	Parti Québécois
PSERA	Public Service Employee Relations Act (Alta)
PSLRA	Public Service Labour Relations Act (BC)
PSSRA	Public Sector Staff Relations Act (Can.)
QWL	quality of working life
RCMP	Royal Canadian Mounted Police
RJO	reasonable job offer
SCA	Social Contract Act (Ont.)
SNA	System of National Accounts
SSEA	Social Sciences Employees Association
SNAA	Staff Nurses Association of Alberta
TAP	Telecommunications Access Partnership (Ont.)
TVO	Television Ontario
UCS	Universal Classification System (Can.)
UN	United Nations
UNA	United Nurses of Alberta
VLT	video lottery terminal
VSIP	Voluntary Separation Incentive Program (Man.)
WFAD	Workforce Adjustment Directive (Can.)

Chapter 1

Public-Sector Labour Relations in an Era of Restraint and Restructuring: An Overview

Gene Swimmer

The 1990s will probably go down as the most stressful decade for public-sector industrial relations since the inception, 25 years earlier, of collective bargaining for public-sector workers. Fuelled by a combination of high deficits that dictated spending restraint and, in some cases, a change in philosophy about the efficacy and role of government in society, virtually all senior levels of government across Canada took action to reduce their compensation bill. This was certainly not the first time that the federal and provincial governments felt the need to restrain public-sector compensation, but this decade is set apart as much by the policy tools used to obtain the desired outcomes as by the outcomes themselves. Instead of achieving restraint at the bargaining table, governments increasingly have relied on the threat and/or use of legislation to override collective agreements. It is ironic that as governments increasingly attempt to emulate private businesses in their management techniques, they have largely abandoned the private-sector model of collective bargaining.[1] By 1997, most governments had slashed their workforces, leaving the survivors of downsizing to endure salary freezes or cuts, despite increased workloads.

This book is a collection of case studies focusing on labour-management relations in six public administration jurisdictions. The Canadian Policy Research Network commissioned the research on the provinces of Nova Scotia, Ontario, Manitoba, Alberta, British Columbia, and the Canadian federal government. The studies all involved primary research, including extensive interviews, and were conducted by academics with industrial relations expertise. Each chapter includes an explanation of the jurisdiction's fiscal and political environment, followed by an in-depth account of how the government attempted to restrain and/or restructure its public service and how the unions responded. Although the cases focus on the public service, as opposed to education, health, and municipal services, most provincial governments attempted to reduce compensation in the broader public sector, making it necessary for some authors to include these groups in their discussions. The final chapter of this volume places the Canadian experience within a broader international context and synthesizes the issues addressed in the individual cases.

This introductory chapter begins with an explanation of the competing views of what has happened to public-sector collective bargaining during the past decade. This is followed by a discussion of the perceived need for public-sector restraint and restructuring across the provincial and federal governments and of the policy instruments at their disposal to restrain public-sector compensation. Next, each of the case studies is summarized and supplemented with information on the five provinces not examined in-depth. These data serve as the basis for an analysis of the restraint processes and outcomes across all 11 civil service jurisdictions. The chapter concludes with some reflections about the future of labour-management relations in the public sector.

Models of Public-Sector Bargaining

It has been argued that the most important factor distinguishing public-sector collective bargaining from the private sector is politics (Swimmer and Thompson, 1995: 2). Governments focus primarily on public opinion and the likelihood of re-election rather than on profit maximization, as is the case in the private sector. Simultaneously, civil service unions use the strike weapon to create public pressure on governments rather than to penalize their employer financially.[2] As a result, public-sector labour relations outcomes are the product of both economics and politics. Another distinctive aspect of the public sector is the dual role of governments as both employer and protector of the public interest. During the past decade, these roles were constantly in conflict as governments attempted to address what were generally perceived as serious deficit and debt problems.

Two schools of thought have emerged in the academic literature concerning the trends in public-sector labour relations. The pessimistic view is associated with the work of Panitch and Swartz (1993) and Warrian (1996). According to Panitch and Swartz, the 1990s represent the culmination of governments' assault on trade union freedoms begun 20 years ago. Rather than weaken public-sector unions through permanently removing their rights, governments have increasingly resorted to ad hoc legislation temporarily suspending collective bargaining to address the problems of inflation (in the 1980s) or deficits (in the 1990s). They believe that this policy of 'permanent exceptionalism' has effectively ended the era of free collective bargaining in the public sector. Warrian argues that the Wagner model of collective bargaining, characterized by fragmented bargaining units, separation of employer and employee interests, and narrow job classifications, is inconsistent with the recent economic imperatives and organizational environment of the public sector. The system must be transformed or governments will simply get out of the business of providing services, relying instead on contracting and privatization. The more optimistic view, associated with

Thompson (1998), is that the basic parameters of the public-sector labour relations system remain intact. Although there has been substantial government intervention into collective bargaining, it represents a measured response to a specific economic problem, rather than reflecting dissatisfaction with the labour relations process. One of the goals of this research project is to shed some light on this debate.

Deficits and Debts

Large annual budget deficits were a common problem across the federal and all provincial governments during the early 1990s. Table 1.1 presents the absolute size of these deficits from 1988 to 1997, while Table 1.2 expresses the deficits as a percentage of provincial (or federal) gross domestic product (GDP), thus allowing for cross-jurisdictional comparisons.[3] To a certain extent, the increased indebtedness was a response to the business cycle, with tax revenues falling and social welfare expenditures increasing as a result of the 1990–1 recession. In addition, the federal government's decisions to cap or reduce its transfer payments to provinces and to change unemployment insurance regulations, reducing benefits, had the effect of off-loading some of the federal deficit to the provinces. Specifically, cash grants to the provinces for social programs were effectively reduced by $6 billion (or 37 per cent) between the 1995–6 and 1997–8 fiscal years (Phillips, 1995: 22). As a result, most provinces saw their deficits more than double between 1991 and 1993, whether measured in absolute or relative terms. For example, the average provincial deficit increased from 1.4 per cent to 3.3 per cent of provincial GDP.

At the same time, more than a decade of government deficits and high interest rates generated mounting accumulated debt levels. Between 1975 and 1988 the federal debt increased from $27 billion to $305 billion.[4] Tables 1.3 and 1.4 present the absolute and relative debt figures for the provinces and the federal government. Provincial debts climbed steadily between 1988 and 1996, with big jumps between 1992 and 1994, reflecting the large deficits in that period. Although there is wide variation among provinces, the average debt increased from about 24 per cent to almost 37 per cent of GDP. The federal debt ratio was even higher, increasing from 50 per cent to 70 per cent over the same time frame. A few provinces had their credit worthiness downgraded by bond-rating services and many business groups and politicians warned that, unless governments took action, federal and provincial credit ratings could be reduced further, leading to even higher debt servicing costs. The extent to which these concerns were legitimate, rather than a convenient basis for corporate lobbying, is debatable, but the public accepted the view that debt and deficits had to be addressed.

There are basically two ways to reduce deficits and debt: increase revenues by raising taxes or decrease expenditures by cutting costs or services. The former was generally ruled out by governments as not politically feasible. The con-

Table 1.1: Government Deficits or Surpluses ($ millions)

Fiscal Year Ending	Nfld	PEI	NS	NB	Que.	Ont.	Man.	Sask.	Alta	BC	Federal
1988	-187	-20	-236	-255	-1,902	-1,740	-155	-537	-1,010	175	-27,631
1989	-138	-8	-287	-34	-2,404	-819	27	-498	-1,952	1,015	-26,829
1990	-82	-6	-701	15	-2,433	1,081	-216	-741	-2,486	659	-28,001
1991	-230	-14	-307	-160	-3,788	-2,344	-270	-322	-1,143	-234	-31,859
1992	-274	-54	-524	-336	-5,231	-10,812	-435	-1,646	-2,130	-1,943	-37,971
1993	-311	-80	-834	-335	-6,274	-12,109	-683	-360	-3,855	-1,646	-39,195
1994	-134	-78	-612	-263	-6,225	-10,481	-571	-713	-1,006	-606	-41,674
1995	-3	-13	-231	-56	-6,839	-8,737	62	433	714	-102	-37,234
1996	69	20	-72	66	-4,305	-6,141	138	38	739	-14	-32,250
1997	37	9	24	130	-4,131	-5,406	73	318	322	432	-13,525

Note: Deficits are designated with negative signs.
Source: CANSIM matrices 00155, 2780, 2782-91

Table 1.2: Government Deficits or Surpluses as a Percentage of Gross Domestic Product

Fiscal Year Ending	Nfld	PEI	NS	NB	Que.	Ont.	Man.	Sask.	Alta	BC	Federal	Provincial average*
1988	-2.31	-1.10	-1.56	-2.08	-1.35	-0.69	-0.73	-2.90	-1.62	0.26	-4.52	-1.41
1989	-1.62	-0.40	-1.78	-0.26	-1.62	-0.30	0.12	-2.55	-2.97	1.36	-4.09	-1.00
1990	-0.93	-0.31	-4.19	0.11	-1.59	0.39	-0.93	-3.57	-3.48	0.84	-4.13	-1.37
1991	-2.51	-0.65	-1.76	-1.19	-2.43	-0.84	-1.17	-1.55	-1.60	-0.29	-4.66	-1.40
1992	-2.96	-2.49	-2.95	-2.42	-3.32	-3.82	-1.85	-8.00	-2.95	-2.24	-5.44	-3.30
1993	-3.28	-3.42	-4.64	-2.29	-3.88	-4.20	-2.87	-1.66	-4.96	-1.80	-5.41	-3.30
1994	-1.36	-3.25	-3.34	-1.71	-3.72	-3.48	-2.29	-3.08	-1.22	-0.61	-5.43	-2.41
1995	-0.03	-0.52	-1.23	-0.35	-3.95	-2.78	0.24	1.76	0.84	-0.10	-4.62	-0.61
1996	0.69	0.74	-0.38	-0.41	-2.45	-1.90	0.50	0.14	0.82	-0.01	-3.89	-0.14
1997	0.34	0.31	0.12	0.76	-2.33	-1.56	0.25	1.13	0.32	0.40	-1.58	-0.03

*Unweighted average of the 10 provinces.

Source: CANSIM matrices 00155, 2780, 2782–91, 2612–19, 6949, 6547; 1997 GDP data from Statistics Canada, *Canadian Economic Observer: Statistical Summary*, Catalogue no. 11–010 (Jan. 1999), 58.

Table 1.3: Government Debt ($ millions)

Fiscal Year Ending	Nfld	PEI	NS	NB	Que.	Ont.	Man.	Sask.	Alta	BC	Federal
1988	4,626	417	3,543	4,626	40,388	31,804	6,531	4,073	(-664)	2,326	305,438
1989	5,028	468	3,611	4,769	42,256	32,659	5,988	4,378	1,221	1,342	333,519
1990	5,202	523	4,615	4,292	44,708	37,683	6,094	4,996	3,512	620	362,920
1991	5,468	648	4,892	4,463	45,586	40,966	6,349	5,239	2,342	932	395,071
1992	5,639	700	5,431	5,010	52,011	51,261	7,115	8,647	4,152	3,308	428,682
1993	6,804	760	6,884	5,329	59,941	63,797	8,137	9,391	7,646	5,178	470,046
1994	7,401	921	8,381	5,711	68,112	77,052	9,266	10,974	9,346	5,464	513,219
1995	7,910	1,078	9,419	5,937	77,005	86,045	9,281	11,083	8,513	7,980	550,685
1996	7,888	1,045	8,917	5,743	80,312	97,016	8,918	11,046	7,084	8,166	578,718
1997	7,780	1,021	8,627	5,570	84,976	104,163	8,571	9,776	4,022	7,510	588,465

Source: CANSIM matrices 3199, 3202–11

Table 1.4: Government Debts as a Percentage of Gross Domestic Product

Fiscal Year Ending	Nfld	PEI	NS	NB	Que.	Ont.	Man.	Sask.	Alta	BC	Federal	Provincial Average*
1988	57.22	23.14	23.43	37.70	28.73	12.56	30.77	22.03	(1.07)	3.39	49.93	23.79
1989	58.98	24.49	22.50	36.78	28.52	11.83	26.68	22.42	1.86	1.79	50.83	23.59
1990	58.91	26.22	27.60	32.68	29.19	13.58	26.25	24.07	4.92	0.79	53.52	24.42
1991	59.51	30.89	28.10	33.06	29.30	14.71	27.59	25.33	3.28	1.14	57.82	25.29
1992	61.05	32.05	30.56	36.04	33.05	18.13	30.36	42.02	5.74	3.82	61.37	29.28
1993	71.61	32.69	38.35	36.44	37.06	22.11	34.22	43.17	9.83	5.68	64.84	33.12
1994	75.40	38.68	45.78	37.10	40.71	25.61	37.11	47.36	11.29	5.54	66.87	36.46
1995	77.97	43.02	50.14	36.71	44.49	27.40	35.46	45.14	10.03	7.83	68.26	37.82
1996	78.35	39.46	47.37	35.66	45.79	30.03	32.62	41.78	7.87	7.88	69.81	36.68
1997	71.51	34.69	42.45	32.65	45.84	30.01	29.31	34.59	3.98	6.87	68.74	33.19

*Unweighted average of the 10 provinces.
Source: CANSIM matrices 3199, 3202–11, 2612–19, 6949, 6547; GDP data from Statistics Canada, *Canadian Economic Observer:
Statistical Summary*, Catalogue no. 11–010 (Jan. 1999), 58.

ventional wisdom in the early 1990s was that the Canadian public would not accept tax increases, given stagnant (or falling) real incomes and rapid tax increases in the recent past.[5] In addition, governments feared that higher taxes would lead, in the newly globalized economy, to a flight of private-sector capital investment (and potentially jobs) to another province or country. Greater competition among governments to attract capital was actually moving towards lower corporate taxes and less regulation.

With revenue enhancement unlikely, governments were obliged to focus on reducing expenditures through a combination of providing less public services and/or lowering the costs of a given service. Belman and Gunderson (1996) argue that the prevailing North American economic environment was conducive to lowering the quantity for public services. Reducing business regulation to attract capital translated into fewer public employees needed to administer the regulations. Stagnant real incomes, combined with greater income inequality, also affected service demand:

> While the growing portion of the population at the bottom of the distribution may have considerable need for public services, their incomes cannot provide the tax revenues required to support such services. The growing portion of the high-income population has the financial resources to pay for the public services, but may see little benefit from taxes for services they are unlikely to access. . . . Demand from the higher end of the income distribution for public services may come in the form of services to protect their position (e.g., police and prisons), but even these can be purchased privately (e.g., security systems and safe suburbs). (Belman and Gunderson, 1996: 5)

On the other hand, an aging population should lead to greater demands for health services while the increased number of single-parent families and two-earner families should increase demands for publicly provided child care. On balance, it is clear that the mix, if not the overall volume, of public services demanded was changing during this period.

At the same time, a new view of government was emerging across Western countries. It originated with the 1979 election of Margaret Thatcher as Prime Minister of the United Kingdom:

> She was adamant that three dimensions of British government be reformed. First, the power of the civil service was to be diminished to make the state apparatus more responsive to political direction. Second, private sector management practices were to be introduced to promote economy and efficiency in government. And third, the freedom of individual citizens was to be enhanced to counter the dominance of state control over the design and delivery of public services. (Aucoin, 1995)

Over the next decade, these precepts became the basis of new public management (NPM) policies, which became popular with governments across the political spectrum trying to restrain public spending.[6] According to NPM, governments should focus on policy formation and regulation ('steering the boat') and leave program delivery ('rowing') to the private sector, which was deemed to be inherently more efficient than the public sector. These new doctrines imply a leaner public sector that relies on alternate service delivery systems (including private-sector partnerships), information technology, and performance measurement to ensure efficiency. Simultaneously, the quality of services provided to the public should be enhanced through greater decentralization of authority and accountability (Thomas, 1996).

A survey conducted by the Organization for Economic Co-operation and Development (OECD) gives an indication of the appeal of NPM. All but two of the 25 countries responding were involved in a major human resource management reform initiative between 1989 and 1992. Of these, nine reported a policy to limit the size of the public service, 10 reported key privatization initiatives, and seven reported the development of 'agencies' (OECD, 1993: 13–15).

In this environment, it is not surprising that all Canadian senior governments focused on reducing the costs of public services, and given the labour-intensive nature of public service provision, that focus narrowed to controlling labour costs. Senior governments' expenditures on employee compensation have both a direct and indirect component, with the indirect component being substantially greater. The direct component represents employees on the government's payroll providing governmental administration, which amounted to about 10 per cent of federal government expenditures and about 9 per cent of provincial expenditures.[7] In addition, provinces indirectly or directly pay all salaries at public hospitals, which amounted to about another 9 per cent of provincial expenditures. These are lower bound estimates because all governments have another workforce, employed in a variety of contracting arrangements. Finally, through transfers to municipalities and school boards, provinces indirectly pay some or all of education and local government salaries. The federal government makes similar transfer payments to provincial governments for the provision of social programs, which can be used by provinces to pay public-sector salaries (these funds were dramatically reduced in the mid-1990s).

Restraint Policy Options

Assuming governments are committed to reducing labour costs, a number of alternatives are potentially available. One set of actions are clearly management's unilateral right. Governments can reduce expenditure on management personnel, employment contracting, and personnel policies not covered by collective agreements. In addition, politicians can decide to cut specific types of programs or services, thereby reducing the number of employees required (whether the employees can be laid off would depend on the collective agreement language).

With respect to direct and indirect unionized employees, there are three possible approaches, none of which are mutually exclusive (see Fryer, 1995). The government can be adversarial, demanding employee concessions at the bargaining table. It can threaten that it will contract out, privatize, or discontinue programs if its demands are not met (the public-sector equivalent of shutting the plant and moving capital elsewhere). If necessary, the government must be prepared to withstand a strike over its position. With regard to its indirect compensation component, the adversarial government strategy is even more straightforward: reduce transfer payments to hospital and school boards and other levels of government, and force these junior employers to demand concessions from their own unions at the bargaining table. Alternatively, a government can adopt a co-operative approach, 'opening the books' to union officials to establish the extent of the financial problem and then jointly attempting to resolve it. Some possible solutions include compensation concessions in return for early retirement incentives and other forms of work sharing, greater employee input into decision-making, and/or enhanced job security. In terms of indirect employees, governments could facilitate co-operative bargaining in health, education, and welfare by using its expenditure and legislative powers. For instance, a provincial government could offer special grants to school and hospital boards to facilitate downsizing through early retirement incentives. Both options are identical to private-sector alternatives, and as in the private sector the co-operative approach is relatively rare.[8]

The final option, and the most popular among governments in the last decade, is to change compensation and working conditions unilaterally through legislation (this option is not available to private employers). The legislative option has been used in two ways: passing a law to impose compensation restrictions or threatening to introduce specific legislation if concessions are not accepted at the bargaining table. Direct and indirect government employees can be dealt with simultaneously, because the jurisdiction of the threatened or actual law can include boards, state enterprises, and municipalities. The province then reduces transfers to these junior jurisdictions to capture the compensation savings.

From a management perspective, there are important trade-offs among these strategies. Unilaterally cutting executive salaries or consulting contracts lends greater credibility to requests for compensation reductions from unionized personnel but could precipitate an exodus of talented managers to the private sector. The major benefit of the adversarial approach is that it preserves the collective bargaining process, regardless of how extreme management's concession demands may be. Therefore, it is more politically acceptable for centre-left governments. The legitimacy of a negotiated settlement is also inherently greater than one unilaterally imposed, and this legitimacy helps to mitigate the negative impact of concessions on employee morale. On the downside, hard bargaining takes a long time (with existing conditions of employment continuing in the interim) and may lead to strikes. The low inflation rates of the past decade exacerbate these risks, as inflation cannot be counted on to reduce automatically real public-sector compensation. Employers may require actual concessions rather than just a freeze, and these are more difficult for unions to accept, thus increasing the likelihood of a work stoppage. Finally, in those jurisdictions where disputes are resolved by arbitration, rather than the right to strike, demanding concessions at the bargaining table may be doomed to failure, particularly if arbitrators tend to favour the status quo or only incremental changes.[9]

While the co-operative approach is even better in terms of political legitimacy and employee morale, the process is bound to be slow, and with no guarantee of success, if the unions do not choose to buy in. In contrast, legislation is fast and dependable. Although it will likely unleash the wrath of union leaders and rank-and-file employees, the legislative approach will be applauded by the business community and financial markets as signalling commitment to restraint, and it may not be a difficult sell to the public at large.

If the government makes overtures to reduce compensation, unions must choose how to respond.[10] Unions could try to turn public attention to other ways of attacking the deficit, from increasing taxes to reducing contracting out. This kind of campaign would be expensive and require development of coalitions beyond the labour movement (such as social welfare interest groups) to have any hope of success. Some unions are not comfortable or experienced with these more political initiatives and would naturally rely on collective bargaining. The government's popularity and the extent to which public opinion has coalesced around expenditure restraint would also affect the feasibility of such a strategy.

On the collective bargaining front, a union must decide whether to refuse to discuss compensation concessions, to stall (agreeing to address the issue, but being unprepared to move), or to negotiate compensation restraint seriously. Certain unions may not engage in concession bargaining for ideological reasons. Maintaining such a strategy, however, would be an open invitation for the government to legislate. In the case of stalling, the union may be buying time for its public relations campaign to work and/or trying to force the government to act unilaterally. With unions being democratic organizations, it is much easier for a union leader to denounce the government for imposing concessions than to agree to them voluntarily. This is particularly true if there are potential leadership challenges and/or imminent union elections. On the other hand, many union officials would argue it is better to mitigate the impact of concessions on the membership through negotiations than to have the government legislate its demands. Other things being equal, a union ought to be more willing to engage in such concession bargaining when a left-of-centre political party is in power because real financial need, rather than a hidden ideological agenda, would be driving the government demands.

The degree of financial hardship among provinces (and the federal government) should determine management's goals with respect to concessions, but other factors could also be important. A government with a conservative ideology could use the deficit as an excuse for reducing public services and/or weakening public-sector unions. The content of management's concession proposals should then affect the restraint option adopted by a government and the union response. Presumably, the more stringent the proposals are, the less likely it is that a union would voluntarily agree to the terms at the bargaining table. Anticipating this fact, a government requiring substantial compensation savings would be more likely to opt for the legislative route.

These possible government restraint strategies and union responses must be compared with what has happened in recent years. The next section summarizes the actual process and content of compensation restraint for five provinces and the federal government. This information is then supplemented with an overview of what occurred in the remaining provinces. Despite the variety of political and economic environments, the most common government strategy has been legislation. In the less common scenario, where a government attempted to negotiate, unions generally have been prepared or resigned to accept some form of concessions.

An Overview of the Case Studies

Nova Scotia

In Chapter 2, Terry Wagar describes how Nova Scotia public employees were repeatedly subjected to the legislative approach. In 1991, the Conservative government of David Cameron passed a law to impose a two-year freeze on public compensation (defined broadly to include provincial, education, health, and municipal employees). Public-sector unions and opposition parties were irate because the government made no attempt at consultation. As the freeze was expiring, Nova Scotia went to the polls. The public sector unions campaigned actively to unseat the Conservatives, which helped give the Liberals a majority under John Savage. Shortly after his election, Savage met leaders of the Nova Scotia Government Employees Union (NSGEU) to discuss compensation rollbacks in the form of unpaid days. The NSGEU indicated they would consider the proposal in return for job security. Rather than negotiate, the government legislated all public employees to take approximately five days off between 1 November 1993 and 31 March 1994, which amounted to a 2 per cent pay cut (government transfer payments to municipalities, schools, and hospitals were simultaneously reduced by 2 per cent to retain the $40 million savings at the provincial level). The Savage government subsequently imposed a 3 per cent salary reduction coupled with a three-year compensation freeze for all public employees until November 1997, stating that the province's financial crunch made collective bargaining untenable. Public-sector unions felt betrayed by the Liberals, who had attacked the previous government's control legislation and assured the unions that the lack of consultation surrounding the unpaid leave legislation would not be repeated. In part due to the unions' media campaign against the government, the Liberals' popular support dropped markedly and remained low until Savage resigned and was replaced by Russell MacLellan. In 1997, the NSGEU prepared to bargain for the first time since 1989. Negotiations were ongoing at the time of the 1998 provincial election. The Liberals were able to maintain a minority government position (although the NDP won as many seats). Shortly after the election, an agreement was reached to reinstate the 3 per cent salary rollback and then increase salaries by about 4 per cent over two years.

Provincial government employment also fell, slowly between 1991 and 1996, after which there was a dramatic decline of 3,000 (or 28 per cent). In reality, the major share of the downsizing resulted from health employees being moved from the province to employers covered by private-sector legislation (they were still represented by the NSGEU, with the same collective agreements). Most real employment reductions were managed through attrition, thanks to hiring freezes, employee transfers, and voluntary separation packages.

The decade of government restraint has taken its toll on employee morale and job satisfaction. Nonetheless, a positive relationship emerged between the NSGEU leadership and the MacLellan Liberal government, which appeared to be committed to the joint consultation and the collective bargaining process. Wagar concludes that while the Cameron and Savage governments' restraint initiatives played a role in achieving a balanced budget, they failed most of the tests of effective restructuring programs. Virtually no labour consultation occurred, insufficient attention was given to 'survivors' of restructuring, and there was little evidence of a well-planned government strategy.

Ontario

Joseph Rose, in Chapter 3, characterizes provincial labour relations in Ontario as moving from 'softball' to 'hardball' as the NDP and then the Conservative governments attempted to reign in public spending. During the transition, these governments moved from co-operation to legislation, and then to adversarial collective bargaining. The NDP government of Bob Rae came to power in 1990, just as Ontario went into a severe recession. The government's original decision to 'spend its way out of the recession', combined with falling tax revenues from the shrinking private economy, led to a soaring budget deficit, which reached $10.9 billion in 1991–2 compared to $3 billion the previous year. In early 1992, the government and the Ontario Public Service Employees Union (OPSEU) agreed to a two-year contract, which included a minimal salary increase, flexible work arrangements, and guaranteed job security, which the NDP hailed as a model of restraint for the public sector at large. A year later the government, with OPSEU's formal blessing, amended the law governing Crown employees to substitute the right to strike (subject to provision of emergency services) for interest arbitration.

As the recession continued to push up deficits (a $17 billion deficit was forecast for the 1993–4 fiscal year), the Rae government realized it had to take drastic action to curtail spending. The government called for special province-wide 'Social Contract' negotiations in eight public-sector jurisdictions (including provincial, hospital, and municipal workers) aimed at reducing compensation for three years in return for job security. When the voluntary negotiations broke down, the NDP passed legislation that effectively reduced public-sector compensation by 4 per cent for three years through unpaid leave days. Organized labour viewed the Social Contract as an attack on free collective bargaining, made even more pernicious by the fact that it was legislated by one of their own. The loss of political and financial support from the labour movement contributed to the NDP's third-place finish in the 1995 election.

The Conservatives under Mike Harris successfully ran on a campaign of income tax cuts, smaller government, and a balanced budget. The Harris government, intent on downsizing and privatization, used a mixture of legislation and hard bargaining to reach its goal. First, union successor rights provisions were removed from Crown employees, which meant the government could privatize without transferring the union's representation or the existing collective agreement terms to the new employer. In the 1995 OPSEU negotiations, the government demanded that job security guarantees be removed. After a five-week strike, the parties agreed to a four-year deal with no salary increase, removal of the guaranteed job offer for surplus employees in return for better severance payment and transfer rights, and a government commitment, in cases of privatization, to make a reasonable effort to ensure that employees are offered jobs with similar terms by the new employer. This latter clause has been the subject of several grievances and, as a result of arbitral decisions, has become a substantial impediment to privatization.

Nonetheless, the Harris government succeeded in downsizing the provincial government by about 20 per cent (about 14,000 jobs) between 1995 and 1997, in the process reducing the number of provincial ministries from 28 to 19. As a result of the government's top-down decision-making and general disdain for OPSEU, a climate of mistrust and insecurity has developed among union officials and employees.

Rose believes that even though the provincial economy and fiscal situation have improved, with the Conservatives being re-elected in 1999 there is little likelihood that the downsizing of the provincial public service will be reversed or that relations between the parties will improve.

Manitoba

In Chapter 4, Paul Phillips and Carolina Stecher document provincial government labour relations since 1988 when the Manitoba Conservatives, led by Gary Filmon, formed a minority government (ending the NDP rule that extended for most of the previous two decades). By 1991, Filmon was re-elected with a one-vote majority and the recession had converted a healthy budget surplus into a growing deficit. The government responded by legislating a retroactive freeze on provincial civil service compensation from September 1990 to September 1991. Deficits continued to rise, which led the government, in 1993, to pass a law allowing public-sector employers (broadly defined) to assign up to 15 annual days off without pay for the next two years. These 'Filmon Fridays' had the effect of removing most of the wage increases that the Manitoba Government Employees' Union (MGEU) had negotiated in its 1991–4 contract with the province, as well as allowing the government to limit its health, education, and social transfers.

Following Filmon's election to a third term in 1995, now with a solid majority, the provincial government changed from a legislative to hard-bargaining approach and was able to get the MGEU to agree to two successive agreements that froze salaries and continued 10 unpaid days per year. In both rounds government negotiators made it clear that monetary limits were established by the Finance Minister in the budget and that cabinet would not accept any encroachment on management rights. In the 1996–7 round of negotiations, the MGEU leaders became so fed up with the process that they held a strike vote to back up their position. Only 43 per cent voted in favour of striking, partially because a strike might be illegal (disputes are supposed to be resolved by arbitration). As a result the union had no alternative but to accept management's offer.

Between 1993 and 1997, the government reduced provincial administrative employment by almost 3,000 (about 18 per cent). Although the contractual job security provisions proved to be minimal, the government and the MGEU co-operated to set up adjustment committees to oversee the limited early retirement program and to encourage transfers of surplus employees to vacant positions. Nonetheless, hundreds of employees were actually laid off, while the survivors faced heavier workloads.

The government and the MGEU returned to normal bargaining in 1997 and reached a three-year agreement calling for small annual pay increases and a phase-out of unpaid days by 1999. Both MGEU leaders and the Civil Service Commission agree that the bargaining relationship has continued on a professional and non-confrontational level throughout the period, although there is some evidence that union members are more negative about the labour relations climate.

Phillips and Stechner conclude that the recession and the public concerns over government deficits provided the Filmon government with a convenient rationale to downsize the public sector, cut transfers to other levels of government, and reduce provincial salaries. These measures fit well into Filmon's right-of-centre agenda to make the province more attractive to business investment.

Alberta

Yonatan Reshef, in Chapter 5, focuses on Alberta, which has been characterized as one of Canada's most conservative provinces. Ralph Klein, leader of the Conservatives, was elected in 1993, promising to balance the budget without higher taxes and to eliminate the provincial debt by 2010. Union leaders warned that the new government was headed for a massive labour conflict if it did not compromise. In the ensuing years, no such conflict materialized, despite substantial layoffs and salary rollbacks.

The government began its assault on public expenditure by announcing that salary budgets for provincial administration, health, education, and municipalities were being cut by 5 per cent. As a result all public employees were expected to accept voluntarily a 5 per cent compensation cut in 1994, followed by a two-year salary freeze, with the exact details of the reduction to be determined by the parties. The government backed up its adversarial bargaining approach with massive budget cuts to government departments and transfer payments. Even with the wage rollback, all public employers would be instituting layoffs. The Alberta Union of Provincial Employees (AUPE) agreed to a three-year contract in 1994 that rolled back salaries by 2.3 per cent and generated another 2.7 per cent in compensation savings by employees accepting seven days of unpaid leave (four days being statutory holidays). Despite these concessions, full-time provincial employment fell by over 6,600 (a 24 per cent reduction) over the same period.

By 1996 the various restraint measures reduced Alberta's spending per capita to the lowest level of any province, and by 1998 the government was forecasting a surplus of $2.73 billion ($2.6 billion was used to pay down the provincial debt). Given the bright financial picture, the AUPE was intent on recouping the salary it had given up. As of September 1999, all but one AUPE provincial unit had reached agreement that reinstated the 5 per cent in stages by 1 January 1998 and increased salaries by 2.25 per cent (the first raise since 1992), plus a 2 per cent lump-sum bonus in September 1998. Not surprisingly, the labour relations climate has suffered, with union officials quite pessimistic about their ability to work constructively with the government or the senior bureaucrats.

Reshef concludes that there were several reasons why the AUPE and other public-sector unions were so ineffective in resisting the 'Klein Revolution'. While the union membership was extremely afraid of layoffs, they agreed with the government's argument that expenditure cuts were needed. In addition, union leaders were unprepared for the rapid pace of government initiatives and were never able to articulate a different vision for how financial problems could be solved (i.e., through increased revenues), with the result that the government successfully marginalized them as another 'special interest group'. Finally, the government used the prevailing 'business union' philosophy to its own advantage. Allowing the compensation rollback to be negotiated kept the union leadership busy with how to obtain the least painful deal through collective bargaining, and consequently they did not focus on challenging the program itself.

British Columbia

Mark Thompson's description in Chapter 6 of labour-management co-operation in the British Columbia public sector stands in stark contrast to the other cases in this volume. When the NDP formed the government in 1991, Premier Mike Harcourt immediately terminated the formal wage control program that had existed during most of the Social Credit government's rule; in its stead, he called for meetings between senior management and public-sector union leaders to improve relations. Although the NDP was beholden to organized labour for electoral support, the government was sensitive to the charge that it could not effectively manage provincial finances. To that end, Harcourt appointed a commission to examine ways of improving the public service delivery. The commissioner's recommendations, which were generally adopted by the government, called for a more direct provincial role in public-sector bargaining and greater worker empowerment in the delivery of public services.

The British Columbia Government Employees' Union (BCGEU), which represents almost the entire provincial civil service, understood that co-operating with the government to improve the efficiency of service delivery would protect its members if and when a right-wing government replaced the NDP. The union and the government developed a 'Partnership Agreement' to increase efficiency through an elaborate system of joint committees. Results were disappointing and the Agreement was eventually abandoned by the parties.

With the provincial economy worsening and demands that the NDP make good on its election promise to balance the budget, in early 1998 the government announced that it could not afford any public sector salary increases for two years. The statement was worded so as not to be construed as an imposed wage control. Bargaining would continue and the government promised dual-track negotiations involving possible public policy changes that would be favourable to a specific union, once conventional bargaining was completed.

After a short round of negotiations the BCGEU agreed to the government's two-year salary freeze, to be followed by a 2 per cent raise in 2001. The second track of these negotiations led to enhanced job security and pensions, plus a new plan for 'gain-sharing'. Ministry-based joint committees would be responsible for identifying operational efficiencies, with the savings shared equally between the parties.

During the NDP rule, provincial civil service employment actually increased in absolute terms until 1996, when jobs were cut in non-social service ministries through attrition and early retirement packages. The first agreement negotiated between the BCGEU and the NDP government increased salaries by about 4 per cent more than the BC average over the 1992–5 period. Though justified as a way of making up for the decade of wage controls, the settlement was criticized by some as a political payback. Subsequent settlements were at or below the average.

Thompson attributes the relatively favourable labour relations process and outputs to a shared goal of the NDP and the BCGEU to demonstrate that public services can be provided efficiently. This could enhance the NDP's chances of being re-elected and of having provincial employment conditions survive a change in government. Both sides want to avoid the Ontario experience, where a confrontation between the NDP and organized labour helped to establish a right-wing provincial government.

Federal Government

Gene Swimmer and Sandra Bach, in Chapter 7, focus on the federal government's restructuring in the 1990s, which relied heavily on the legislative approach. Facing a much larger government deficit than expected in 1991, the Mulroney Conservative government established a wage guideline of 3 per cent over the next two years that would be enforced by legislation to roll back excessive arbitration awards and/or to end strikes. In fact, the Public Service Alliance of Canada, the largest union representing federal public employees, had its members legislated back to work with an imposed salary settlement coincident with the guideline. However, shortly after the 1991 strike, the government agreed to guaranteed job security for all its regular employees. With the Conservatives' fiscal problems worsening, in late 1992 the government used legislation to extend existing federal agreements for another two years.

When the Liberals under Jean Chrétien were elected in 1993, public-sector union leaders expected a return to bargaining. Instead, the Liberal Finance Minister, Paul Martin Jr, announced in his 1994 budget that salaries would be frozen and contracts extended for two more years. Another part of the Liberal government's plan to reduce the deficit involved a comprehensive review to determine which federal programs could be terminated or provided by a different agency. It became clear to the government that the existing job guarantees could interfere with this program review. After secret negotiations with the public service unions failed, the government used legislation to suspend job security in departments facing major program (and staff) reductions, in return for lucrative employee buyout packages. By 1998, the Liberals, through a combination of legislation and collective bargaining under the legislative threat, succeeded in permanently watering down the job guarantees granted by the Mulroney Conservative government. The first real negotiations since 1989 began in 1997, and most groups reached agreements calling for salary increases of 4–5 per cent over two years, which did not reflect a catching up for six years of wage controls.

Between 1993 and 1998, federal public service employment fell by 53,000 (22 per cent). About 10,000 of these jobs were devolved to other service providers, with employees simply shifting from one employer (the government) to another in the private or non-profit sectors. Nonetheless, this still represents a massive downsizing that was accomplished with hardly any layoffs because the buyouts were generous, the government allowed job swapping, and the unions co-operated with management to implement the program smoothly.

Swimmer and Bach conclude that the restructuring and downsizing were much more successful in terms of output than process. The government eliminated the deficit, layoffs were minimized, and workers did not have their wages reduced. On the other hand, it has become clear that neither the current nor the previous federal governments have cared about the legitimacy of the collective bargaining process.

The Situation in Other Provinces

Table 1.5 provides a summary of restraint processes and policies in all eleven jurisdictions.[11] Like Nova Scotia, other Atlantic provinces relied heavily on legislative approaches to restrain compensation. The Liberal government in Newfoundland imposed a one-year wage freeze in 1991. Two years later, the Liberals made public-sector compensation restraint the centrepiece of their re-election campaign. Following victory at the polls, the Liberals used a mixture of actual and threatened legislation to get the provincial employees' union to accept wage freezes for three more years, as well as unpaid leave days and reductions in employer pension contributions. In 1998, after a year of hard bargaining, the parties reached a settlement, which provided for no salary increase between 1996 and 1998, followed by a staged 7 per cent raise over the next three years. During the 1991–7 period provincial public service employment fell by about 1,500 or over 18 per cent.

The Prince Edward Island provincial employees' union accepted a 6 per cent salary cut for four months in return for six vacation days. The 1991 settlement was obtained under the clear threat of wage control legislation from the Liberal government. Following re-election in 1994, the Liberals passed a law imposing a 7.5 per cent reduction in all public-sector salaries. The salary was reinstated in the two-year collective bargaining agreement reached in 1996. Since 1992 provincial employment has fallen by 18 per cent.

The New Brunswick Liberal government's 1991 foray into restraint was a one-year legislated wage freeze for all public-sector employees. A year later an innovative restraint bill was passed to give public employees a choice of extending their collective agreements for two years with salary increases of 1 per cent in 1992 and 2 per cent in 1993 or bargaining as usual. This less coercive plan backfired from the government's perspective, as almost all unions chose to bargain and it was faced with a province-wide strike by public employees (although provincial public service employees were not involved). Nonetheless, since 1994 there have been no legislative threats to public-sector bargaining. Typical settlements in the 1994–6 round called for a salary freeze in 1994, followed by staggered increases amounting to 7–8 per cent over the next two years. Several bargaining units agreed to new contracts that increased salaries by 4.5–5.75 per cent over the 1996–2000 period. Provincial government employment fell by approximately 2,600 (or 22 per cent) between 1991 and 1997.

The approach to restraint in Quebec changed with the government in power. The Liberals used legislation to extend collective agreements for up to three years (until 1993) and then imposed a two-year wage freeze plus a 1 per cent overall reduction in public-sector payrolls. With the election of the Parti Québécois, the strategy changed to bargaining (first co-operative, then more adversarial), largely reflecting the new government's and the unions' joint commitment to Quebec sovereignty. The 1 per cent payroll reduction was rescinded in 1995 and the parties agreed to increase salaries by about 2.5 per cent, over three years. When ris-

Table 1.5: Compensation Restraint Measures for Provincial and Federal Civil Service Employees

Province	Government in Office	Process	Restraint Outcomes	Relative Debt and Deficit*	Dispute Resolution
Newfoundland	Liberal	Legislative and adversarial bargaining	1991 – wage freeze: 1 year 1993 – suspension of govt. pension contributions; wage freeze: 1 year 1994 – 1 per cent reduction in govt. pension contributions and 1.5 leave days without pay per year; wage freeze: 2 years	Above average debt; above average deficit in 1991 improving to below average by 1994	Limited strike, subject to essential service provision
Nova Scotia	Conservative	Legislative	1991 – contract extension with compensation freeze: 2 years	Average debt, above average deficit	Arbitration
	Liberal (since 1993)	Legislative	1993 – 5 leave days without pay: 1 year 1994 – 3 per cent salary cut for all employees earning over $25,000: 3 years	Above average debt and deficit	
PEI	Liberal	Legislative and adversarial bargaining	1992 – negotiated 6 per cent reduction for 4 months in return for 6 extra vacation days following year 1994 – 7.5 per cent wage rollback for all public-sector employees	Average debt; below average deficit in 1991 worsening to above average by 1994, then improving to below average	Arbitration

Province	Party	Bargaining	Events	Fiscal situation	Strike rights
New Brunswick	Liberal	Legislative and adversarial bargaining	1991 – wage freeze: 1 year 1992 – union choice of 2-year contract extension with 1 per cent, 2 per cent wage increases or regular collective bargaining 1994 – agreements reached with all union groups, calling for no salary increase in 1994, followed by 7–8 per cent raise over the next 3 years	Above average debt, improving to average by 1994; below average deficits	Limited strike, subject to essential service provision
Quebec	Liberal	Legislative	1992 – contract extension with compensation freeze until July of the following year 1993 – wage freeze plus measure to be negotiated to reduce annual payroll by 1 per cent: 2 years	Average debt; average or above average deficits	Strike**
	Parti Québécois (since 1994)	Co-operative and adversarial bargaining	1995 – 1 per cent reduction in public-sector payroll abandoned; salaries increase by .5 per cent lump sum in 1996, followed by 2 per cent raise over the next two years 1997 – government calls for contract reopener to reduce salaries by 3 per cent; after many threats from both sides, parties agree to voluntary pre-retirement plan to reduce employment costing $2.5 billion, paid for by government (one-third) and pension plan surplus (two-thirds); salaries unchanged	Average debt increasing to above average by 1996; above average deficits	

Table 1.5 continued

Province	Government in Office	Process	Restraint Outcomes	Relative Debt and Deficit*	Dispute Resolution
Ontario	New Democrat	Co-operative first, then legislative	1992 – negotiated small salary increase (3 per cent over 2 years) in return for guaranteed job security 1993 – 4 per cent reduction in annual public-sector compensation for employees earning above $30,000, partially paid for by about 6 days off without pay per year: 3 years	Below average debt; below average deficits worsening to above average by 1993	Limited strike, subject to essential service provision
	Conservative (since 1995)	Legislative and adversarial bargaining	1996 – amended legislation to remove successor rights and wind-up pension provisions to ease privatization 1996 – after 5-week strike, union agrees to removal of guaranteed job security in return for some protection against privatization and greater bumping rights and severance payments; no wage increases: 2 years	Below average debt worsening to average; above average deficits	
Manitoba	Conservative	Legislative and adversarial bargaining	1991 – contract extension with wage freeze: 1 year 1993 – 10 unpaid days: 2 years 1995–6 – parties agree to 2 contracts, no wage increase, and 10 unpaid days: 3 years	Average debt; average or below average deficits	Arbitration

Saskatchewan	New Democrat	Adversarial bargaining and co-operative	1993 – after 6 months of rotating strikes, union agreed to contract retroactive to 1991, with a 2.5 per cent cost-of-living increase in the last year of contract: 4 years 1995 – mutual gains bargaining used to reach agreement with annual salary increases of 1 per cent for 3 years, job guarantee for one year, and establishment of departmental union management committees: 3 years	Average or above average debt; deficits varying from above average to below average	Strike**
Alberta	Conservative	Adversarial bargaining	1994 – employees agreed to 2.8 per cent temporary wage cut in return for 7 days unpaid leave, plus 2.3 per cent permanent wage cut: 3 years	Below average debt; deficits worsening to above average in 1993, then improving to below average by 1994	Arbitration
British Columbia	New Democrat	Co-operative	1994 – parties negotiated a 'Partnership Agreement' to work jointly at improving work organization and public service delivery; in return, union agreed to wage increase of 2.5 per cent over 4 years 1998 – parties agree to 2-year wage freeze, followed by 2 per cent in year 3; instituted joint committees to identify efficiencies and equally share the savings	Debts below average; deficits below average	Strike**

Table 1.5 continued

Province	Government in Office	Process	Restraint Outcomes	Relative Debt and Deficit*	Dispute Resolution
Federal	Conservative	Legislative and adversarial bargaining	1991 – guideline of 3 per cent over 2 years set by government; legislated end of strike and imposed settlement: 2 years 1993 – agreements extended with wage freeze: 2 years	Debt and deficits are not comparable in magnitude to provinces	Union choice of arbitration or limited strike, subject to essential service provision
	Liberal (since 1993)	Legislative and adversarial bargaining	1995 – agreements extended with wage freeze: 2 years 1995 – guaranteed job security removed in return for lucrative buyouts: 3 years 1996 – interest arbitration suspended: 2 years		

*Based on deficits and debt as a percentage of provincial GDP (presented in Tables 1.2 and 1.4), provinces were classified on an annual basis into below average, average, or above average. Below average was defined as more than 20 per cent below the annual unweighted provincial average for deficit or debt, average was between 20 per cent below and 20 per cent above the mean, and above average was more than 20 per cent above the mean.

**General labour legislation may require essential services to be continued during a strike.

Sources: Fryer (1995); Swimmer (1996); NUPGE (1997, 1998).

ing deficits forced the government to reduce expenditures, the goal was reached through negotiations with unions. In 1997, the government initially demanded that the existing collective agreements be reopened so that salaries could be rolled back. After several months of hard bargaining, including threats from both sides, the government agreed to abide by the existing contracts, in return for staff reductions generated by a $2.5 billion pre-retirement program, mainly financed by pension fund surpluses. Employment in provincial administration actually rose until 1994, after which it fell by 12,000 workers (or 14 per cent).

The NDP government in Saskatchewan took office in 1992 and was immediately confronted with how to restrain civil service compensation without compromising its commitment to free collective bargaining. The government adopted an adversarial approach that led to six months of rotating strikes. Eventually both sides accepted the recommendations for settlement proposed by a conciliation officer, which involved a modest wage increase (2.5 per cent) towards the end of a four-year contract. In the next round, the parties adopted mutual gains bargaining techniques to arrive co-operatively at an agreement that increased salaries by 3 per cent over three years, guaranteed jobs for one year, and established departmental union management committees to increase employee involvement in decision-making. The provincial civil service was fairly stable under NDP rule until 1996, when 1,600 jobs were eliminated (a 12 per cent reduction).

In June 1998, the parties reached a new three-year agreement that will increase salaries by 6 per cent over the next three years and guarantee jobs of all permanent employees. A new classification system will also be introduced to reduce the number of classifications from 440 to 13 and eliminate gender-based salary discrimination.

Factors Affecting the Choice of Restraint Process

Based on the information summarized in Table 1.5 for 15 governments[12] in power, it is possible to examine the impact of several factors on the type of compensation restraint processes used. One is immediately struck by the popularity of the legislative option. Eleven governments relied on legislation, either exclusively (four) or in conjunction with adversarial bargaining (seven), while only four governments relied exclusively on bargaining (sometimes adversarial, other times co-operative).

Political ideology appears to be an important factor in choosing restraint procedures. Three of the four governments led by left-of-centre political parties (the NDP in Saskatchewan and BC and the PQ in Quebec) avoided legislation. The sole exception, where the Ontario NDP government legislated its 'Social Contract', followed a failed attempt at sector-wide co-operative negotiations. There was little difference in the use of legislation between the two mainstream political parties. Liberals and Conservatives threatened or actually passed legislation restraining public-sector compensation in 10 of the 11 situations where they formed the government (the Alberta Conservatives were the only exception).

It was also expected that the existence of arbitration as the dispute resolution process would make reliance on bargaining less attractive. The data are somewhat supportive: in four of the five jurisdictions where arbitration was automatic or could be selected by the union, the government used legislation. The federal Conservatives specifically warned that legislation would be used to overturn any arbitration award exceeding the maximum salary increase, and their Liberal successors suspended arbitration for the latest round to ensure that adversarial bargaining would be possible. The fact that Alberta could rely on bargaining despite the presence of arbitration may be explained by its legislative criteria, which greatly limit interest arbitrators' discretion.[13]

The severity of the fiscal problem should be a factor propelling governments towards legislation, which is a quicker and more predictable fix. In these circumstances, it may also be easier to sell the legislative option to the public. There are several ways of measuring severity. Provinces were classified in terms of the relative size of their debt and deficits as a percentage of GDP. Provincial jurisdictions were ranked annually as having below average (more than 20 per cent below the unweighted provincial mean), average (within 20 per cent of the mean), or above average (more than 20 per cent above the mean) debt and deficits. As Table 1.5 indicates, relative debt levels were reasonably helpful in explaining the process choice. Three of the four provinces with relatively worse debt loads opted for legislation (Saskatchewan was the exception), while two of the three provinces (Alberta and British Columbia) with lower than average debt relied on bargaining. The Ontario NDP government opted for a mix of bargaining and legislation, despite its relatively favourable debt position.

The results regarding relative deficits are about as revealing. Legislative action was applied in six of the 10 situations where provinces were experiencing worse than average deficit problems. Two governments with relatively better deficit positions (New Brunswick and Manitoba) also resorted to legislation. Three of the four governments that maintained public-sector bargaining (the Quebec PQ, Saskatchewan, and Alberta) had higher than average deficits, which implies that it was possible to generate restraint without resorting to legislation.

Impact of Restraint and Restructuring on Civil Service Employment

Restructuring and restraint since 1991 have clearly taken a toll on provincial and federal employment. Table 1.6 presents total employment in provincial and federal administration from 1991 to 1997. This data set was constructed using information from Statistics Canada and specific government jurisdictions to exclude direct providers of education, health, or social welfare services, even if the provincial or federal government was their formal employer (Peters, 1999). In that way, cross-jurisdictional comparisons are more relevant.[14] Overall, provincial civil service employment fell by 41,600, or 15 per cent (the federal reduction was

Table 1.6: Federal and Provincial Administration Employees, 1991–1997 (000s)

	Nfld	PEI	NS	NB	Que.	Ont.	Man.	Sask.	Alta	BC	Federal	All Provinces
1991	8.1	2.4	10.4	11.7	76.3	86.4	13.2	11.2	33.6	26.1	313.1	279.5
1992	7.7	2.7	10.3	10.1	70.9	93.4	14.4	10.5	32.6	33.7	307.6	286.3
1993	8.1	2.6	9.6	9.5	77.2	83.2	15.8	11.5	32.8	32.6	315	282.9
1994	7.5	2.6	11.8	11.6	84.3	91.1	15.2	11.5	33.1	38.1	296.4	306.9
1995	6.9	2.4	9.1	11.2	71.5	76.2	13.3	11	24.2	37.9	283	263.7
1996	7.7	2.2	9.5	10	70.5	72.8	13.7	11.7	24.7	37.9	287.4	260.7
1997	6.6	2.2	10.4	9.1	72.1	61.9	12.9	10.1	20.5	32.2	269	237.9
% change 1991–7	–18.5%	–8.3%	0.0%	–22.2%	–5.5%	–28.4%	–2.3%	–9.8%	–39.0%	+23.4%	–14.1%	–14.8%
% change from peak	–18.5%	–18.5%	–11.8%	–22.2%	–12.2%	–33.7%	–18.4%	–12.2%	–39.0%	–15.5%	–14.6%	–22.5%

Source: Peters (1999).

Table 1.7: Federal and Provincial Administration Employees per Thousand of Population

	Nfld	PEI	NS	NB	Que.	Ont.	Man.	Sask.	Alta	BC	Federal	Unweighted Average*
1991	13.99	18.41	11.37	15.71	10.81	8.30	11.91	11.18	12.99	7.75	11.19	12.14
1992	13.28	20.63	11.21	13.51	9.98	8.85	12.95	10.47	12.40	9.74	10.86	13.10
1993	13.96	19.67	10.40	12.68	10.78	7.79	14.14	11.44	12.30	9.15	10.99	13.02
1994	13.04	19.47	12.74	15.45	11.70	8.43	13.54	11.39	12.26	10.38	10.22	12.60
1995	12.14	17.81	9.81	14.90	9.88	6.96	11.79	10.85	8.85	10.04	9.65	11.15
1996	13.72	16.18	10.20	13.28	9.70	6.57	12.09	11.48	8.90	9.79	9.70	11.05
1997	11.92	16.11	11.12	12.08	9.87	5.51	11.34	9.88	7.25	8.14	8.98	10.20
% change 1991–7	−14.8%	−12.5%	−2.3%	−23.1%	−8.7%	−33.6%	−4.8%	−11.6%	−44.2%	+5.1%	−19.7%	−16.0%
% change from peak	−14.8%	−21.9%	−12.7%	−23.1%	−15.6%	−37.7%	−19.8%	−13.9%	−44.2%	−21.6%	−19.7%	−22.1%

*Unweighted average of all eleven jurisdictions.
Source: Peters (1999); CANSIM Matrices.

14 per cent). There were substantial variations in employment across provinces and time. British Columbia provincial employment actually increased by over 20 per cent[15] while Nova Scotia and Manitoba reduced employment less than 3 per cent over the period. At the other extreme, Alberta cut employment by almost 40 per cent while Ontario and New Brunswick experienced reductions in excess of 22 per cent. Using 1991 as the starting point is somewhat arbitrary, and in most jurisdictions employment actually increased until 1993 or 1994. The drops in employment are much more dramatic when calculated from their peak to 1997 (which was also the trough in all but two jurisdictions). The overall provincial decline over this shorter period was 22.5 per cent, with the smallest reductions occurring in Nova Scotia, Quebec, and Saskatchewan (all at about 12 per cent) and the largest occurring in Ontario (34 per cent) and Alberta (39 per cent).

These numbers may underestimate the extent of restraint applied to civil service administration because they ignore population increases. Table 1.7 captures this relative impact by presenting the number of civil service administrative employees per thousand of population for each year and jurisdiction. The unweighted average decline in civil service employees per thousand of population was 16 per cent, a drop from about 12:1 to 10:1 during the 1991–7 period. As with absolute employment, the values varied across jurisdictions. The BC ratio actually increased by 5 per cent (compared to the 23 per cent increase in absolute civil service employment), while Nova Scotia and Manitoba experienced a decline of less than 5 per cent. Ontario and Alberta again exhibit the greatest contraction, with the ratio of civil service employees to population falling by 34 per cent and 44 per cent, respectively. For about half the jurisdictions, the employment-population ratio was at its maximum in 1991, while the ratio peaked in the remaining jurisdictions two or three years later. The average decline in employment from its maximum was 22 per cent. Viewed from this perspective, the smallest relative employment reduction occurred in Nova Scotia, at 13 per cent, while the largest reductions still were found in Ontario and Alberta (38 per cent and 44 per cent).

Taken together the data indicate substantial cuts in civil service employment for practically every jurisdiction during either the entire period or from peak values in the mid-1990s. In some cases, existing jobs were simply transferred from the civil service jurisdiction to another level of government or agency, or they were contracted out to the private sector; however, other employment reductions led to both greater workloads for current civil service employees and fewer services being provided.

The Trade-offs between Employment and Salary Concessions

It seems reasonable to presume that employment reductions and wage restraint would be substitutes from the perspective of a government attempting to reduce public-sector compensation. If wage concessions occur, there should be less need to reduce staff. Indeed, that is how the Ontario NDP government attempted to sell its Social Contract: unpaid days would allow for job security. Likewise, a government unable to negotiate wage concessions would be more inclined to reduce employment by cutting services or offloading the employees to another jurisdiction. Table 1.8 categorizes the 15 federal and provincial governments since 1991 by the extent of civil service employment reductions and wage concessions obtained. A three-way breakdown was developed (low, medium, high) for each variable. The employment reduction criteria were relatively straightforward, corresponding to whether the relative reduction in civil service employment, during the government's reign, was more than 20 per cent below the unweighted average reduction, within 20 per cent of the average, or greater than 20 per cent above the average.[16] The classification system for concessions was based on whether employees received salary increases during the relevant period (low), salaries were frozen (medium), or salaries fell either as straight reductions or through unpaid days (high). Although there is a subjective aspect to this breakdown, I believe it is not unreasonable.

The results for the six governments along the right to left diagonal are consistent with the view that the two policies were substitutes (italics in table). In particular, the Nova Scotia Liberals, PEI Liberals, and Manitoba Conservatives achieved high salary concessions and as a result were able to keep civil service employment reductions below average. On the other hand, the New Brunswick Liberals and federal Conservatives relied more on employment reductions than salary concessions. The federal Liberals fell in the middle in both categories.

Surprisingly, there do not appear to be trade-offs for the remaining nine governments. In particular, the British Columbia and Saskatchewan NDP governments exhibited lower than average salary concessions and/or employment cuts. The PQ government in Quebec also exhibited low salary concessions, while its employment reductions fell in the medium category.[17] While these were three of the four governments that refrained from using the legislative process to reduce compensation, it should not be assumed that bargaining is a less effective means to obtain salary concessions (Alberta generated major salary concessions through hard bargaining). These three governments' centre-left ideology likely led them to both a more politically correct process and less willingness to 'solve' the deficit problem by cutting expenditures.

The only exception was the Ontario NDP, which fell at the opposite extreme, with salary concessions and employment cuts above average (along with the Alberta Conservatives and Newfoundland Liberals). As Rose points out, massive deficit forecasts overwhelmed ideology in determining the NDP's policies. By the same token, it is easy to understand why the labour movement reacted so negatively.

There was also a difference between governments from the two centrist parties. Three of the five Conservative governments obtained high salary concessions or employment reductions without a corresponding trade-off in the other category, while only one of the six Liberal governments fits in the same category. Although party affiliation meant little in terms of restraint process, restraint outcomes under

Table 1.8: Trade-offs between Civil Service Employment Reductions and Salary Concessions

Employment Reductions	Salary Concessions		
	Low	Medium	High
Low	BC (NDP, 1991–7) Sask (NDP, 1992–7)	Que. (Liberal, 1991–4)	NS *(Liberal, 1993–7)* PEI *(Liberal, 1991–7)* Man. *(Conservative, 1991–7)*
Medium	Que. (PQ, 1994–7)	*Federal (Liberal, 1993–7)*	
High	*NB (Liberal, 1991–7) Federal (Conservative, 1991–3)*	NS (Conservative, 1991–3) Ont. (Conservative, 1995–7)	Nfld (Liberal, 1991–7) Alta (Conservative, 1991–7) Ont. (NDP, 1991–5)

the Liberals appear to be less restrictive than under the Conservatives. This is certainly consistent with Rose's and Reshef's accounts of the Ontario and Alberta Conservatives' evangelical fervour to reduce the size of government.

As mentioned in relation to the Ontario NDP government, the extent of the indebtedness problem should have affected the severity of restraint outcomes. Those jurisdictions with above average debts and/or deficits presumably would have higher salary concessions and employment reductions, and the reverse would be true for jurisdictions with below average indebtedness. Relative debt levels do not appear to be related in this way. Of the five governments corresponding to medium or high levels for both restraint outcomes, only one had above average debt, while three had below average debt. Similarly, only one of the four governments with lower concessions had below average debt (the others had average debt levels).

Relative deficits exhibit a somewhat clearer pattern. All five governments with high restraint outcomes had above average deficits at the start of the restraint initiatives, while two of the four governments with low outcomes had below average deficits for at least part of the restraint period. In summary, the results imply that the seriousness of the deficit problem (but not debt levels) influenced government perceptions about the extent of required restraint. These economic needs were either moderated or intensified by the government's political ideology.

Conclusions

Earlier in this chapter, I mentioned that there are optimistic and pessimistic assessments about whether public-sector labour relations have been transformed during the past decade. How does this current research relate to the debate? In line with the optimistic view that labour relations remain intact, the case studies do not indicate attempts by governments to attack the legitimacy of unions as organizations or to strip union rights permanently (the only possible exception was the Ontario Conservative government's legislative removal of successor rights from civil service unions). Some governments (e.g., Alberta) have attempted to portray unions as just another special interest group, but this is a long way from trying to bust unions as institutions. Aside from downsizing, provincial and federal civil service employees were left relatively unscathed. Although most jurisdictions froze or even reduced annual salaries, these restraint measures were temporary in that they had built-in sunset clauses or were eventually reversed through negotiations. It could also be argued that most governments downsized in a more humane manner than the private sector, relying more on attrition and resignation incentive programs than layoffs.

On the other hand, the almost ubiquitous use of legislation is consistent with pessimistic interpretations that public-sector collective bargaining is an endangered species. Only four of the 15 ruling governments were prepared to bring about labour relations change through adversarial or co-operative bargaining, as is the constraint in the private sector, without the luxury of changing the rules through legislation. Although some governments that resorted to legislation were not re-elected, e.g., the Nova Scotia and federal Conservatives and the Ontario NDP, there is little evidence that this policy was a major factor in their defeat. In each of these cases, the successor government was quick to continue the legislative approach. For some governments, like the Newfoundland Liberals, imposing conditions on public-sector unions was an extremely popular decision. Whether governments could have gotten away with this policy in earlier times or public opinion has recently changed is not clear, but the 'genie is now out of the bottle'. The entire political calculus of how a government should address public-sector labour relations has changed. Governments now have three viable alternatives: agree to union demands at the bargaining table, reach an impasse in bargaining and take their chances with the dispute resolution process (withstand a strike if necessary, or argue their case in front of an arbitrator as per the existing law), or simply impose their will on the union by legislation. With the political cost of legislation falling greatly, all governments, regardless of ideology, will be tempted to use that policy instrument to preserve their gains from the restraint period. Witness the recent use of legislation by the Saskatchewan NDP government to end a nurses' strike and impose a salary settlement (Killick, 1999).

Whether this situation represents a transformation or an evolution is a question of semantics, but public-sector labour relations have permanently changed. For those of us who view collective bargaining as an extension of legal 'due process' to the workplace, it is not a change for the better.

There is, however, a potentially more positive scenario for the future. First and foremost, governments must understand that there is another cost associated with rejecting the collective bargaining model—lost productivity from employees who become further demoralized. Given the downsizing across senior governments, many civil service employees are faced with higher workloads and will have to work harder and/or smarter to do their jobs effectively. Now that deficits have been tamed, government leaders must think of their employees as a source of value to be increased, rather than as a cost to be reduced, if they are truly committed to improving service to the public (another pillar of the 'new public management'). Given this mindset, it is arguably in the public employer's self-interest to reach bilateral agreement rather than legislate its will on unions. At the same time, public-sector unions have to come to terms with the new environment. Taking ideological positions, such as 'no concessions' ever, will guarantee unilateral government actions. Therefore, union leaders must reject the temptation to avoid accountability in favour of pragmatism. If both parties approach negotiations from these perspectives, jointly determined and mutually beneficial outcomes can be obtained.

Notes

1. This is not the first time that governments have used legislation to restrain public-sector salaries, although the controls were not as pervasive and comprehensive as in this period. Fears of inflation in the early 1980s led the federal government and five provinces to institute public-sector compensation controls; however, bargaining over non-monetary issues was often allowed to continue (Panitch and Swartz, 1993: 223–5).

2. In most situations a public-sector strike actually saves the employer money because salary costs are reduced during the strike, while revenues are not affected (in most situations the public does not pay directly for the public services).

3. According to Statistics Canada, these CANSIM data originate from federal and provincial public accounts and budgets, and are presented on a standardized financial management system basis. As a result, there are data differences between these series and the public accounts (http://datacentre.epas.utoronto.ca:/cgi-bin/cansim/cc_html?id = 2791). As most case study authors relied on their jurisdiction's public accounts and budget data, differences may exist between debt and deficit numbers presented in this chapter and the cases that follow.

4. For a discussion of the federal deficits and debt before 1990, see Gillespie (1991).

5. Between 1984 and 1991 Canadian total tax revenue as a percentage of gross national product increased from 33 per cent to 37.1 per cent, which constituted the biggest increase in tax burden for the 'Group of Seven' countries (Swimmer and Thompson, 1995: 16).

6. For an evaluation of NPM initiatives in the UK, Australia, New Zealand, and Canada, see Aucoin (1995). For a discussion of the US experience, see Osborne and Gabler (1992) and Doeringer et al. (1995).

7. The specific numbers for 1993 ranged from a low of about 8 per cent for Quebec, Ontario, Saskatchewan, and Alberta, 9–10 per cent for BC, Manitoba,

Nova Scotia, New Brunswick, Newfoundland, and the federal government, and 17 per cent for PEI. Statistics Canada (1998).

8. The adversarial and co-operative approaches represent the extreme cases, with actual bargaining relationships falling somewhere along this continuum.

9. Thompson (1998) estimates that 25 per cent of public-sector employees, broadly defined, are subject to interest arbitration.

10. Unions may never be given the opportunity to respond because a government could legislate without even attempting to consult its employee representatives.

11. This section is based on Fryer (1995), Swimmer (1996), and the National Union of Public and General Employees (NUPGE) (1997, 1998). I also want to acknowledge the help provided by the NUPGE research staff in providing information.

12. In this analysis, the re-election of a government with a new leader from the incumbent political party is considered to be a continuation of the same government.

13. As Reshef indicates, in Chapter 5, arbitrators in Alberta must consider the province's fiscal policies and wages and benefits in the non-union and union sectors when making an award.

14. The employment data presented here often differ from the numbers used by authors in the case studies which follow. Not only are health, education, and social service providers directly employed by some provincial governments, but the federal data presented here include armed forces and the RCMP employees working in administration, while the federal case study focuses on civilian employment.

15. The British Columbia data must be treated with some caution because the Social Credit government hired contractors in the 1980s (to exclude them from being counted as government employees). Subsequently, these individuals were deemed to be regular provincial government employees. See Chapter 6.

16. The comparison with the unweighted average for all jurisdictions was based on the specific years the government was in power, or from 1991 to 1997 for governments continually in office from before 1991.

17. It is quite possible that if our data included 1998, the Quebec PQ would have fallen in the high category for employment reduction, as the early retirement program kicked into high gear.

References

Aucoin, Peter. 1995. *The New Public Management—Canada in Comparative Perspective.* Montreal: Institute for Research on Public Policy.

Belman, Dale, Morley Gunderson, and Douglas Hyatt, 1996. 'Public Sector Employment Relations in Transition', in Belman, Gunderson, and Hyatt, eds, *Public Sector Employment Relations in Transition* (Madison, Wis.: IRRA), 1–19.

Doeringer, Peter, et al. 1996. 'Beyond the Merit Model: New Directions at the Federal Workplace?', in Belman, Gunderson, and Hyatt, eds, *Public Sector Employment Relations in Transition* (Madison, Wis.: IRRA), 163–96.

Fryer, John. 1995. 'Provincial Public Service Labour Relations', in Gene Swimmer and Mark Thompson, eds, *Public Sector Collective Bargaining in Canada: Beginning of the End or End of the Beginning?* (Kingston: IRC Press), 341–67.

Gillespie, W. Irwin. 1991. *Tax, Borrow and Spend: Financing Federal Spending in Canada 1867–1990*. Ottawa: Carleton University Press.

Killick, Adam. 1999. 'Saskatchewan nurses vow to stay on strike', *National Post*, 9 Apr., A1.

National Union of Public and General Employees (NUPGE). 1997. 'Collective Bargaining and Restructuring in the Provincial Public Sector', unpublished report, Dec.

———. 1998. 'Update: Collective Bargaining in the Provincial Public Sector', unpublished report, Dec. http://www.nupge.ca/Update1.html

OECD. 1993. *Public Management Developments—Survey 1993*. Paris: OECD.

Osborne, David, and Ted Gabler. 1993. *Reinventing Government: How the Entrepreneurial Spirit is Transforming the Public Sector*. New York: Plume.

Panitch, Leo, and Donald Swartz. 1993. *The Assault on Trade Union Freedoms: From Wage Controls to Social Contract*. Toronto: Garamond Press.

Peters, Joe. 1999. *Statistical Profile of Employment in Government*. Ottawa: CPRN.

Phillips, Susan. 1995. 'The Liberal Mid-Life Crises: Aspirations and Achievements', in Susan Phillips, ed., *How Ottawa Spends 1995–96: Mid-Life Crises* (Ottawa: Carleton University Press).

Swimmer, Gene. 1996. 'Provincial Policies Concerning Collective Bargaining', in Christopher Dunn, ed., *Provinces: Canadian Provincial Politics* (Peterborough, Ont.: Broadview Press), 351–78.

——— and Mark Thompson. 1995. 'Collective Bargaining in the Public Sector: An Introduction', in Swimmer and Thompson, eds, *Public Sector Collective Bargaining in Canada: Beginning of the End or End of the Beginning?* (Kingston: IRC Press), 1–19.

Statistics Canada. 1998. *Public Sector Employment and Wages and Salaries*, Catalogue no. 72–209. Ottawa: Statistics Canada.

Thomas, Paul. 1996. 'Visions Versus Resources in Federal Program Review', in Armelita Armit and Jacques Bourgault, eds, *Hard Choices or No Choices* (Toronto: Institute of Public Administration of Canada), 39–46.

Thompson, Mark. 1998. 'Public Sector Industrial Relations in Canada: Adaptation to Change', paper presented to the 11th Congress of Industrial Relations, Bologna, Italy, 22–6 Sept.

Warrian, Peter. 1996. *Hard Bargain: Transforming Public Sector Labour-Management Relations*. Toronto: McGilligan Books.

Chapter 2

Provincial Government Restructuring in Nova Scotia: The Freezing and Thawing of Labour Relations

Terry H. Wagar

Nova Scotia, like other jurisdictions across the country, faced the 1990s with a large and growing provincial debt and a recent history of budget deficits. As in other provinces, the government of the day embarked on a strategy of bringing in a balanced budget and reducing the provincial debt.

This chapter examines a number of industrial relations issues in the climate of restructuring that pertained to Nova Scotia in the 1990s. Particular attention will be directed to strategic decision-making, the impact on collective bargaining, and the nature of labour-management relations in the province. Although the focus of the chapter will be on the Nova Scotia civil service, some discussion of developments within the broader public sector is necessary.

Since 1990, both Conservative and Liberal governments have had an opportunity to try to get the provincial deficit under control. While a number of options were pursued, the one that dominated the industrial relations environment in Nova Scotia was the legislative approach. The Public Sector Compensation Restraint Act, introduced in 1991 by the Conservative government of Donald Cameron, and the Public Sector Compensation (1994–97) Act, a legislative initiative of the Liberal government of John Savage, in essence suspended collective bargaining on issues relating to compensation for public-sector employees (defined very broadly to include not only provincial government employees but also individuals employed in municipal government, police and fire services, education, and health care). In addition, there was major restructuring and amalgamation in municipal government, education, and health care.

After briefly summarizing the economic and political environment, I will trace the history of collective bargaining by Nova Scotia civil servants, document the province's deficit problem, discuss the wage restraint and rollback measures imposed by government, update the current situation, and examine the implications for public-sector bargaining in Nova Scotia.

The Economic and Political Environment

Nova Scotia is a province of about 950,000 people. The major industries include community, business, and personal services, trade, public administration, manufacturing and processing, and construction. Of the more than 32,000 businesses in the province, just under 75 per cent employ fewer than five workers (Nova Scotia Department of Finance, 1995). Approximately 460,000 Nova Scotians are members of the labour force and unemployment in the province is in the 11–12 per cent range.

Over the past 100 years Nova Scotians have elected either a Liberal or Progressive Conservative government, and in most instances the electorate has given the governing party more than one term in power. While the New Democratic Party has never governed the province, it fared very well in the March 1998 election and emerged as the official opposition party.

Historical Overview of Public-Sector Labour Relations

By the early 1930s there were approximately 1,600 civil servants in Nova Scotia and appointments were made largely on the basis of patronage. In 1935, Angus L. Macdonald's Liberal government introduced the Civil Service Act and a system for appointment to the civil service on the basis of merit. At the same time, the Civil Service Commission (CSC) was created to oversee the Act and assume responsibility for personnel management. While there was some modest decline in government paternalism, the culture within the public service was conservative. As Thomson (1989: 218) notes:

> the shadow of government paternalism persisted and contributed to the maintenance of a conservative ethic among civil servants as it was re-shaped by the new professional ideology of the CSC into a service ethic that was inimical to unionization. Unions were perceived as special self-interest groups while government workers were expected to serve all interests equally and neutrally.

The two decades following World War II witnessed considerable growth in the Nova Scotia public sector and the maintenance of traditional notions of job security for government employees. The postwar years were also characterized by growth in real wages, relatively favourable compensation, and the opportunity for advancement for qualified employees. As a consequence, civil servants were largely removed from the union movement and the militant struggles that occurred in the private sector.

With growth in public sector employment and the increasing role of government in society came the rationalization of the civil service. This led to major changes in the work environment and conditions of employment, resulting in substantial dissatisfaction among civil servants. In 1956, the Liberal government of Henry Hicks, by Order-in-Council, allowed the establishment of an association of Nova Scotia civil servants. Later that year, the Order-in-Council was passed as legislation by the Conservative government of Robert Stanfield (which had replaced the Hicks government in the fall of 1956), but there was no express provision for resolution of disputes. Two years later, the Nova Scotia Civil Service Association was formed, the first dues were established at 25 cents a month for each member, and the motto of the association ('Gaulinn Re Gaulinn' in Gaelic, translated as 'Shoulder to Shoulder') still exists today (Nova Scotia Government Employees Union, 1994).

Historically, public-sector workers were paid less than private-sector employees but often had better benefits and job security. The success of private-sector unions in securing greater benefits and job security protection, coupled with low rates of unemployment, began to erode some of the major advantages associated with government employment. However, the Nova Scotia Civil Service Association of 1958 was basically a 'company union' under the control of government and run largely by supervisory civil servants (Thomson, 1989; Nova Scotia Government Employees Union, 1994). In 1962 the Civil Service Act was revised to include a limited grievance procedure, and in 1967 the passage of the Civil Service Joint Council Act provided for a binding arbitration procedure.

In the late 1960s, a faction developed within the association favouring a movement away from joint consultation to free collective bargaining. However, the only mechanism for dispute resolution was binding arbitration (with the tripartite arbitration board being comprised of a member from the Civil Service Commission, a member from the Nova Scotia Civil Service Association, and a neutral chair). By 1970, dissatisfaction among civil servants was high due to the disparity in wage levels relative to the private sector and the increase in private-sector wages at a time civil servants were being asked to practise wage restraint as part of the anti-inflation program of the government (NSCSA Newsletter, 1969). Moreover, the Civil Service Commission expressed concern over the growing militancy of Nova Scotia government workers.

In 1971, an Order-in-Council amended the 1956 Order-in-Council, which had provided that the constitution of the Nova Scotia Civil Service Association could only be changed with the approval of government. Consequently, a new constitution was drafted, a dues check-off provision was established, and the association changed its name to the Nova Scotia Government Employees Association and claimed the right to organize employees of commissions and boards (under the jurisdiction of the Trade Union Act).

In the same year, the Nova Scotia government sought voluntary wage restraint, breaking the link between market prices and free collective bargaining, and 'making provincial government employees scapegoats in the battle against inflation' (Thomson, 1989). As well, there was concern within the association that the arbitration procedure was being manipulated by the government. Moreover, the Civil Service Commission was calling for change in the 'personnel management' function (and the collective bargaining process) to keep pace with the ongoing change in government management. However, most government employees supported the position that the right to strike contradicted the goal of providing service to the public.

The winter of 1972 witnessed the imposition of a 5 per cent wage ceiling on government employees. Liberal Premier Gerald Regan told the association executive that the province was poor and could not afford to give more—and he also stated that if the association challenged the 5 per cent ceiling at arbitration, he would remove the right to arbitration and give the association the right to strike. While this was a defining moment for the association, many on the executive viewed Regan's comment as a threat. At a fractious meeting of the executive committee, the president of the association, Alex Buchanan, resigned. However, executive secretary Tom Shiers mounted an effective campaign encouraging members to accept the 5 per cent ceiling, and in a referendum of the members more than 75 per cent voted to support the ceiling.

Subsequently, there was considerable discontent within the association, and in 1973 the structure and composition of the association was radically changed, with Cyril Reddy becoming president. Moreover, the association was confronting new challenges: 'They [the new executive] inherited a bargaining structure that was anachronistic and a bargaining climate that was propelling workers—especially public sector and white-collar workers—in the direction of labour militancy' (ibid., 238). February 1973 also witnessed the signing of the first written agreement between the association and Civil Service Commission.

The Nova Scotia Government Employees Association became affiliated with the Canadian Labour Congress in 1975, and in 1978 the Joint Council Act was replaced by the Civil Service Collective Bargaining Act (which will be subsequently discussed in more detail). In 1981 the constitution was rewritten and the name was changed to the Nova Scotia Government Employees Union. The 1970s and 1980s saw further growth and greater identification as a trade union. However, union militancy and the adoption of trade union values varied markedly within bargaining units and occupational groups. The most recent decade was characterized by considerable government intervention into the bargaining process, the suspension of collective bargaining for almost seven years, and the continued growth of the union.

Unlike some public-sector unions that represent only government workers, the Nova Scotia Government Employees Union has not limited its organizing efforts to the public sector. By the mid-1970s, the NSGEU represented non-public employees at the College of Cape Breton and laboratory technicians at the Halifax Infirmary; shortly after, it moved beyond the province to organize brewery and production workers in New Brunswick (Nova Scotia Government Employees Union, 1994). With the transfer of a significant number of health-care workers to the private sector in 1996–7, the NSGEU now has the balance of its members in the trade sector—as of October 1998, 5,909 members were in the civil service group and 13,464 members came under the trade group (which includes employees in health care, ambulance service, nursing homes, municipal government, education, liquor commission, and manufacturing).

Government Employees and Collective Bargaining

In Nova Scotia, provincial government employees are covered under the Civil Service Collective Bargaining Act, which was introduced in 1978, replacing the Joint Council Act. Administration of the Act rests with the Civil Service Employee Relations Board (which is comprised of three members, with provision for the appointment of alternate members). The Civil Service Employee Relations Board decides questions of 'employee' status, the status and coverage of collective agreements, whether the parties have met the duty of bargaining in good faith, and unfair labour practices. The decisions of the Board are final and binding.

A number of provisions of the Civil Service Collective Bargaining Act parallel those found in the private-sector legislation. For example, the definition of an 'employee' excludes individuals employed on a casual basis for less than 12 continuous months, appointed to temporary or summer jobs for less than six months, or working in a managerial or confidential capacity. In addition, contracts must be for a minimum of one year, the duty to bargain in good faith requires the parties to 'make every reasonable effort to conclude and sign a collective agreement', and there is a conciliation procedure if the parties are unable to reach an agreement.

However, unlike the private sector in Nova Scotia, the employer may not lock out employees and civil servants may not strike. In the event that conciliation does not result in a collective agreement, the employer or union (or both parties) must refer the issues in dispute to the Board and request that a tripartite arbitration board be established to resolve the issues in question. Note that the Act provides a schedule of issues (such as wages, work hours, vacations, holidays, etc.) that may be subject to arbitration. The award of the tripartite board is binding on both parties; however, if the parties enter into a collective agreement concerning the disputed subject matter within seven days from the rendering of the decision, the decision is determined to be of no force and effect.

The Deficit Problem in Nova Scotia

As of 31 March 1998, the net debenture debt in Nova Scotia stood at approximately $8.4 billion. Until the balanced budget in the 1996–7 fiscal year, deficits were the norm for about two decades; 1997–8 witnessed the second balanced budget in a row, and in May 1999 the Liberal government of Russell MacLellan projected a third straight balanced budget. However, on 17 June 1999, the 1 June budget introduced by the MacLellan government was defeated by a 31–19 vote. Nova Scotians went to the polls on 29 July and elected a majority Conservative government led by John Hamm.

A history of the annual budget deficit or surplus for the province is provided in Table 2.1. As the table indicates, deficits over the 1986–96 period ranged from a low of $201 million to a high of $615 million. Although the 1996–7 and 1997–8 fiscal years were not characterized by deficits, the surplus funds were relatively small ($8 million and $39 million, respectively). Similarly, the projected surplus for the 1998–9 fiscal year was $22 million.

A further indicator of the debt problem facing Nova Scotia is revealed in Table 2.1, which provides information on debt servicing charges from 1986-7 to 1997-8. During that period, debt service charges ranged from just over $550 million to more than $900 million (representing between 16.5 and 23.1 per cent of expenditures). However, there does appear to be some positive news when the projections for debt are considered as a percentage of GDP. In 1996, the provincial debt was about 44 per cent of GDP and estimates indicate that this percentage should be reduced to about 36 per cent in the year 2000 and down to 31 per cent in 2005 (Nova Scotia Department of Finance, 1997).

In terms of government expenditure, health and education, as shown in Table 2.2, remain at the top of the list when expressed as a percentage of ordinary government expenditure. Note also that the percentage of expenditures dedicated to servicing the public debt is beginning to decline. While the debt burden facing Nova Scotians is still substantial, there has been some concerted effort on the part of government to reign in spending and manage the debt problem.

Cameron's 1991 Public Sector Compensation Restraint Act

In May 1991 the Conservative government of Donald Cameron introduced the Public Sector Compensation Restraint Act. The Act defined 'public employees' very broadly to include, in addition to provincial administration, a variety of other employees and officials working in correctional services, government agencies, the courts, municipalities, education, and health care.

Table 2.1: Nova Scotia Government Surplus (Deficit) Per Year (in millions of $)

Time Period	Surplus (Deficit)	Current Expenditures	Debt Service Charges	Debt Service Charges as % of Current Expenditures
1986-7	(273.1)	2,853.2	558.2	19.6
1987-8	(226.0)	3,028.4	565.8	18.9
1988-9	(227.9)	3,246.3	560.1	17.3
1989-90	(266.3)	3,462.0	570.9	16.5
1990-1	(254.4)	3,698.9	671.7	18.2
1991-2	(402.0)	3,852.3	695.0	18.0
1992-3	(615.3)	3,981.9	803.6	20.2
1993-4	(546.9)	3,890.8	865.4	22.2
1994-5	(235.1)	3,945.6	911.6	23.1
1995-6	(201.1)	3,968.4	896.6	22.6
1996-7	8.3	4,194.2	811.1	19.3
1997-8	38.5	4,378.6	797.8	18.2

Source: Nova Scotia Department of Finance.

Table 2.2: Nova Scotia Government Expenditure Categories as a Percentage of Total Expenditure

Expenditure Item	1990–1	1993–4	1997–8
Education	22.8	22.0	21.3
Health	27.2	27.9	29.9
Social Services	10.4	4.0	12.4
Public Debt Service	17.2	22.6	19.6
Resources Development	12.6	11.9	8.3
Other	9.8	11.6	8.5

Source: Nova Scotia Department of Finance.

Any compensation plan finalized prior to 14 May 1991 had compensation rates frozen for the two-year period ending 14 May 1993—compensation changes that were to take effect in the two-year period were deferred. If a compensation plan expired prior to 14 May 1991 and a new agreement was not reached by that date, the expired plan continued in force for two more years, subject to a 5 per cent increase in compensation effective to the date the plan expired. Presumably, the 5 per cent increase was considered a fair trade because the collective agreement had expired prior to the enactment of the legislation that prohibited the parties from negotiating a wage increase. However, parties negotiating a first collective agreement were permitted to conclude their negotiations during the freeze period.

Increases in compensation during the freeze period were permitted in some circumstances (such as meritorious performance, completion of a specified work experience, successful completion of a professional or technical course, or length of time in employment) if the compensation plan contained *express* provisions for such compensation increases. Also, an increase in compensation was permitted for bona fide promotions.

Although most unwelcomed by the union movement, the Public Sector Compensation Restraint Act was not unanticipated. Federal Finance Minister Michael Wilson was encouraging provincial governments to follow the federal lead and institute wage freezes and the Newfoundland government had indicated that it was freezing wages of public employees. In March 1991, Rick Clarke, president of the Nova Scotia Federation of Labour, commented:

> We're very concerned . . . we think it is going to happen here. I think there's a clear indication that Nova Scotia is going to follow what Ottawa has done. The new premier [Donald Cameron] said he is going to reduce the deficit and I think wage freezes are where he is heading. It's not going to happen without a battle. (Tibbetts, 1991a)

Opposition leader Liberal Vince MacLean reacted strongly to the suggestion of wage restraint legislation, threatening to try to bring down the Conservative government. He encouraged the government to look elsewhere to cut costs. According to MacLean:

> If collective agreements are to be broken by legislation, I'm afraid that I can't accept that. If you're not prepared to break the contracts with others (developers, owners of the liquor warehouse, automobile leasing firms), then don't come into the legislature and say 'break contracts with people'. (Ward, 1991)

Other Liberals expressed similar views. For example, Randy Ball, a Liberal candidate in former Premier John Buchanan's old riding, noted: 'Many people are very, very upset with what's being done. The government is not listening to anyone' (Lee, 1991a). Interviews with union officials supported the position that there was no consultation with labour prior to the passing of the legislation.

Near the end of May 1991, the Nova Scotia Government Employees Union met in Sydney for its biennial convention. Included in its agenda was the matter of mounting a campaign to defeat the Cameron government. In the words of NSGEU president Greg Blanchard:

> Our members are upset but we're also pretty responsible. . . . but we will be calling on them to spend money to help defeat this government. The irritant here is that the government hasn't talked to anyone. All provincial labour groups were shut out of any consultation. When Cameron is saying his options were either to freeze wages or [institute] layoffs, he wasn't being completely honest. (MacInnis, 1991)

There was also strong response from other labour leaders outside of Nova Scotia. For instance, Canadian Labour Congress president Shirley Carr characterized the wage freeze as nothing more than a veiled attempt at union busting: 'They [the Cameron government] are not the government in this situation . . . they are the employer. And as the employer, they are nothing but union busters. I find it insidious and unacceptable and the price will be one the province won't recover from economically' (Lee, 1991b).

However, despite marches by thousands of protesters on the legislature in response to the wage freeze and strong campaigning by opposing politicians, the Cameron government had a one-seat majority in the House and the legislation was passed. While NDP leader Alexa McDonough commented that Nova Scotians would not tolerate the dictatorial approach of the government, Premier Cameron responded that public opinion polls indicated that the public was happy with the direction his government had taken (Underhill, 1991a). A public opinion poll conducted by Corporate Research Associates indicated that 41 per cent of Nova Scotians were somewhat or very satisfied with the Cameron government in the second quarter of 1991—and support for the government increased slightly during 1992.[1]

Union leaders across the province regularly commented on the impact of the legislation on labour relations. NSGEU president Greg Blanchard stated that the wage restraint law would poison government-employee relations but indicated that a strike or walkout by the union was unlikely because 'two wrongs don't make a right. We'll be the responsible ones' (Underhill, 1991b). Similarly, Nova Scotia Teachers Union (NSTU) president Russell MacDonald expressed his disgust with a 'shameful and immoral piece of legislation'. MacDonald noted that the teachers had bargained in good faith during the latest round of negotiations, only to see the government unilaterally breach the contract. According to Ron Morrison, also of the Teachers Union, 'the freeze has caused a deep rift in relations between the two groups and fostered disappointment, distrust and disgust on the part of teachers' (Underhill, 1991b).

Organized labour was also very upset by the lack of public involvement in the government's decision to freeze wages. According to Gerald Yetman, an experienced union leader who led labour's attack on the 'Michelin Bill' (presently Section 26 of the Trade Union Act) in the late 1970s, the government should have sought public input prior to introducing the legislation:

> There should be public hearings all over the province on a bill this important. This bill is the worst since Michelin and they're going to pay a price for it whenever they decide to go to the people. And they should go to the people now, before this bill is dealt with, because they have no mandate to do something like this. Freezing people on the bottom of the totem pole for three years is shameful. A contract is a contract is a contract, but only when it's with some of the government's rich friends. (Campbell, 1991)

While there was strong opposition to the wage freeze, expected to save the government $35 million in the 1991–2 fiscal year and $95 million in the following year, a major concern among several employee groups was the loss of job security flowing from the government's cap of 2 per cent on budget allocations. As stated by Nova Scotia Nurses Union president Jeanette McChesney, 'I haven't heard a lot of nurses complain about the money. I think what we're more worried about is the effects of the cutbacks' (Renouf, 1991).

In December 1991, the Nova Scotia Government Employees Union mounted an aggressive advertising campaign using the radio and print media. The thrust of the campaign was to make Nova Scotians aware of the impact of the wage freeze legislation on employees in the province. Highlighted in the advertisements were 10 employees at the Canso Causeway, who were given pink slips just 12 days before Christmas, and some of the 350 employees in the Department of Transportation, who would lose jobs with the government's program of privatizing some highway maintenance services. The campaign was part of a long-term strategy on the part of organized labour to discredit the policies of the Cameron Conservatives (Lee, 1991c).

As well, the Nova Scotia Government Employees Union joined with four other public-sector unions to have the International Labour Organization (a United Nations body in Geneva, Switzerland) investigate the wage restraint legislation that was becoming more common across the country. The Canadian Labour

Congress, which launched the complaint on behalf of the five unions, argued that wage freezes were in violation of the union's right to engage in free collective bargaining (Tibbetts, 1991b).

The 1993 Election and the 'Savage Days'

By the winter of 1992–3, public employees were looking for an end to the wage freeze and the opportunity to regain wages lost as a result of the freeze. Complicating the issue was the fact that the Conservative government of Donald Cameron was nearing the end of its term and was obligated to call an election by September 1993. Conservative Finance Minister Chuck MacNeil emphasized the need to recognize the fiscal realities of 1993 and said that the government's bargaining position would not include provisions for lost wage raises. John Savage, leader of the Liberal opposition, said that he would have to examine the province's books before indicating his position on wage increases but vowed to 'bargain in good faith' with government employees (Lee, 1993a).

In the spring of 1993, the Nova Scotia Supreme Court ruled that the wage freeze legislation enacted almost two years earlier was legal. The NSGEU and the NSTU had brought the lawsuit arguing that the wage freeze was discriminatory and in violation of the Charter of Rights. According to Judge Hilroy Nathanson, complaints about broken contracts fell into the area of contract law rather than under the Charter of Rights: 'Given the relative strength of the NSTU and the NSGEU in Nova Scotia, it is difficult to analogize their position to that of groups such as aboriginals, disabled persons, gays and lesbians and women who have sought and obtained Charter protection' (Lee, 1993b).

The Cameron government called an election in the spring of 1993 and Nova Scotians went to the polls on 25 May. Public-sector unions were heavily involved in the election campaigns, seeking to remove from office politicians who had supported the wage freeze legislation. In Newfoundland, Premier Clyde Wells, who ran on a political platform of government restraint, was returned to power shortly before the Nova Scotia election. However, in Nova Scotia, the voters elected the Liberal government of John Savage.

Shortly after coming to power, the Savage government met with the NSGEU regarding the possibility of rollbacks in the form of five unpaid leave days. The NSGEU indicated a willingness to consider the proposal in exchange for job security assurances (Fryer, 1995). Rather than negotiate with the union over the leave provisions, the government unilaterally introduced the Public Sector Unpaid Leave Act, which required public-sector employees (again, very broadly defined) earning at least $22,000 annually to take 'unpaid leave equivalent to two per cent of the employee's annual hours of work rounded to the nearest half shift or annual days of work rounded to the nearest half day' (Section 7). While the number of leave days varied, a typical full-time worker was required to take about five days off over the period from 1 November to 31 March. In Nova Scotia, the leave days became known as 'Savage days'.

Combined with the unpaid leave was a 2 per cent reduction in government payments or transfers, which government officials projected would save the province about $40 million. While union leaders and several public-sector employees expressed outright disgust with the proposal (which was similar in nature to programs in Newfoundland, Ontario, and Manitoba), some employees argued that forced leave was better than layoffs. According to one health administration employee, 'my basic concern is to keep my job and if I had to take five days' unpaid leave, I'd be happy to do it' (Tibbetts and Underhill, 1993). However, John MacDonald of the NSTU felt that all Nova Scotians should contribute to reducing the deficit:

> The province has a truly horrendous debt problem—I got sick to my stomach during his (Education Minister John MacEachern) presentation because we are in dire straits and it can't be exaggerated. Government response to it is to get money from the public service. My response was that I agreed that teachers shared in the problem as Nova Scotians, but it is a common problem, and everyone should share in finding a solution. (Nicoll, 1993a)

The deputy mayor of Halifax, Walter Fitzgerald, in a Halifax City Council meeting, said that the Savage government should be 'tarred and feathered' for extending the five-day mandatory leave program to municipal employees. Fitzgerald perceived the leave program as ill-conceived, not well thought out, and hastily put in place. He indicated that the Liberals were well aware of the state of the province's finances before they took office (Cranston, 1993).

In October 1993, protesters marched on the legislature to protest the five-day unpaid leave program and taunted Premier Savage with the line 'Johnny is a liar' (Nicoll, 1993b). Associated with the leave days was a fear of job loss. Premier Savage, in a speech to the Empire Club in Toronto, stated that there was a new ideology of cost-cutting among provincial governments regardless of the party. He made specific reference to the attempts by Bob Rae's NDP government to negotiate a cost-cutting deal with Ontario public-sector unions:

> We have to bring our finances under control, but we probably have to do it by increasing the ranks of the unemployed—that's laying off people. We must govern better by governing differently and also governing less. We have to cut out whole layers of bureaucracy. The days of guaranteed job security are gone. (*Cape Breton Post*, 3 Dec. 1993)

The Premier's comments were particularly upsetting in light of his campaign position that he would not raise taxes and that the solution to reform was not cutbacks and downsizing.

While the unpaid leave garnered all the public attention, the Savage government also initiated a number of efficiency audits to evaluate the effectiveness and efficiency of select government departments and functions. It has been argued that the Liberals were eager to embark on a new direction in public-sector management and sought to put their own stamp on the organization. Decisions concerning which departments or functions to review were made solely at the political level without input from the bureaucracy. Audits were conducted by outside consulting firms, which provided reports to both the government and the specific departments involved. It turned out that the auditors recommended massive restructuring and downsizing for several departments, including transportation, economic development, and tourism and culture (McDougall, 1993). Although aspects of the audit have been implemented in these departments, employment reductions that accompanied the changes were generally managed through attrition and transfers. Unlike other jurisdictions, Nova Scotia did not use widespread layoffs as a means of reducing labour costs. The reliance on strategies other than layoffs was acknowledged by union officials but did little to improve relations between the government and labour.

While satisfaction with the Savage government was quite high for most of 1993, it dropped dramatically with the introduction of the mandatory leave program. The Corporate Research Associates polls revealed that 63 per cent of respondents were somewhat or very satisfied with the government in the third quarter of 1993, compared with only 32 per cent for the fourth quarter.

Savage's Public Sector Compensation (1994–1997) Act

With the expiration of the Public Sector Unpaid Leave Act on 31 March 1994, the Liberal government of John Savage sought a new vehicle for controlling the wages of public employees. In the spring budget, Finance Minister Bernie Boudreau introduced the Public Sector Compensation (1994–97) Act. Similar to the wage freeze legislation of the Cameron Conservative government and the Liberal's mandatory unpaid leave law, the Act applied well beyond the civil service to include such groups as teachers, community college and university employees, judges, and health-care workers.

Section 6 of the legislation provided that all compensation plans in effect prior to 29 April 1994 were to be continued until 1 November 1997. Section 8 prohibited any increase in pay rates over this period and Section 9 established that all pay rates were reduced by 3 per cent on 1 November 1994 (with no reduction in work hours). However, no employee's pay was to be reduced to less than $25,000 a year.

While there was outrage on the part of Nova Scotia unions and public employees (and a deep sense of betrayal by the Savage government), Premier John Savage stated that the crunch on provincial finances made collective bargaining untenable. While the breaking of contracts was regrettable, the principles on which collective agreements are based were jeopardized by the fiscal situation in Nova Scotia:

> We made the decision that collective bargaining, which is important to us, is a sham
> if you have nothing to offer. We literally have nothing to offer for the next couple of
> years. The decision to go with the three per cent cut is made, and that is non-

negotiable. We are finding it difficult to get across to people that if we don't take measures to cut back public expenditures, we may have, for instance, only six hospitals in this province. . . . purely and simply, we don't have the resources to continue to provide the service we have got. (Madill, 1994)

In response to Premier Savage's comments, NDP leader Alexa McDonough replied that 'Collective bargaining rights are the very heart of the democratic system, unless your view of democracy is that it should only be at the ballot box but never at the workplace' (ibid.).

The complete lack of consultation was particularly troubling to organized labour. During one interview, a union activist told me that the union was preparing for the return to collective bargaining and had an initial meeting with government negotiators, who gave no indication that legislative intervention was imminent. A few days after the meeting, the government introduced its wage freeze and rollback bill.

In response to the legislation, Nova Scotia public-sector unions met in May to discuss a strategy to fight the government cutbacks. Options included a general strike, one-day strikes, rotating strikes, demonstrations, refusing to 'go the extra mile', and a 'whistle-blowing' campaign about government waste and mismanagement. According to Nova Scotia Teachers Union president John MacDonald:

> We are united in our resolve. We are especially concerned about the assault on the collective bargaining process and on union busting 'tactics' of the provincial government. Workers feel devalued and unappreciated. There is a feeling people are being needlessly kicked and unappreciated and there's a lot of hurt there as well as frustration. (*Mail Star*, 4 May 1994)

Unions expressed the view that the right of collective bargaining could be lost. CUPE representative Barbara Kowalski expressed concern that 'we're fast approaching a time when democracy will be gone in Nova Scotia' (MacGillivray, 1994). She said that CUPE was well aware of the financial difficulties facing the province and indicated that the union had been seeking stronger contract language relating to job security rather than significant wage gains.

Nova Scotia Government Employees Union president Greg Blanchard spoke of the discontent of government workers with the Liberal government. He noted that the NSGEU had embraced the Liberal election program for prosperity, which included no privatization, no breaking of legal contracts, no wage controls, and no tax increases. Rather, the union was anticipating increased consultation, proactive labour legislation, and a co-operative working relationship for the betterment of Nova Scotians. A few days before introducing the unpaid mandatory leave program, Finance Minister Bernie Boudreau met with the union executive, explained the need for the program in light of the deficit, apologized for the lack of consultation, and assured the union that it would not occur again. In addition, Premier Savage, Finance Minister Boudreau, and Labour Minister Jay Abbass met

with the Nova Scotia Federation of Labour and made a commitment to consultation prior to the spring budget—a commitment that was not honoured. According
to Blanchard:

> Government employees have been deceived, lied to, bullied and, most of all,
> betrayed. While preaching consultation and prosperity like a snake-oil salesman,
> the Savage government has attacked working people across the province by destroy-
> ing the collective bargaining process. Their prescription for economic renewal
> (laying off people) is a prescription that has failed over and over again in other
> provinces and countries. (Blanchard, 1994)

The NSGEU also set up a toll-free complaint hot line (1–800–970–LIES) for anyone
with a complaint against the Savage government (*Mail Star*, 16 July 1994).

Although the wage rollback was applicable to public employees earning in
excess of $25,000, news began leaking out that not everyone was being treated
equally. For instance, some firefighters allegedly were calling in sick so that colleagues could get overtime work (McLaughlin, 1994) and some senior bureaucrats were receiving increased pay as a result of being 'reclassified' to a higher
level. For example, 11 of 16 departmental human resource managers received
pay hikes due to reclassification. While NDP MLA Robert Chisholm believed that
'there tends to be evidence of pretty uneven treatment of civil servants', Human
Resources Minister Jay Abbass, formerly the Labour Minister, indicated that the
reclassification was due to the massive reorganization in government and the
additional responsibilities being assigned to managers. According to Deputy
Minister Mildred Royer, 'You don't look at this from the point of view that
nobody can get a raise—you look at it in terms of your financial targets, of fiscal restraint and downsizing. From a fiscal point of view, a substantial amount
of money is being saved' (Hays, 1995).

Not unexpectedly, public opinion was divided. Among members of the business community, there was strong support for the measures of the Savage government. According to Rob Dexter, president of the Halifax Board of Trade, 'Our
general reaction to the budget was that it was tough, gutsy, and in the right
direction. Our view of the cuts is that they are not all that bad and that it was
the only way to go' (Taylor, 1994). However, other members of the public felt
that the government should spread the fiscal pain to all Nova Scotians, not just
public employees—131 of 176 callers to a *Daily News* hotline indicated that the
government was picking on its employees to get its financial house back in order
(*Daily News*, 9 May 1994). Support for the Savage government dropped markedly with the introduction of the wage rollback legislation. In the second quarter
of 1994, only 24 per cent of survey respondents were somewhat satisfied with
the performance of the government and a mere 1 per cent were very satisfied.
Throughout the Savage years, public support remained fairly low.

In the fall of 1994, the Canadian Labour Congress submitted a complaint
against the provincial government on behalf of the National Union of Public and

General Employees and the NSGEU. The International Labour Organization, in a decision released in the summer of 1995, concluded that freezing and cutting wages of employees directly or indirectly working for the government constitutes a severe restriction on the right of collective bargaining. The ILO did not accept the government's argument that the fiscal situation of the province demanded legislative intervention into the collective bargaining process:

> The committee [of the ILO] deplores that the government did not give priority to collective bargaining as a means of determining wages of workers in the public sector, but that it felt compelled to adopt these legislative measures. The committee insists that the government refrain from taking such measures in the future. (ILO, 1995)

The ILO considered the government's argument that economic stabilization justified its legislative actions and noted that legislative intervention may be compatible with the ILO Convention if it leaves a *substantial* role for collective bargaining and allows workers and their unions to participate fully and meaningfully in designing the overall bargaining framework:

> The Committee notes that general public consultation meetings were held by the Government but is concerned that there appears to have been a very limited number of specific meetings between government representatives and public employees' organizations. The Committee insists that the Government allow a full return to normal collective bargaining in the public sector and to keep it informed in this regard. (ILO, 1995)

While the ILO pronouncement was a moral victory for the union movement, Premier John Savage said that the province was still in a dire financial position. As the Premier noted, 'we anticipated the ruling and it will not give us any change' (Shaw, 1995).

The End of Cutback Legislation

On 1 November 1997 the wage rollback legislation ended, paving the way for the return of collective bargaining between the government and its unions. In its policy statement on the upcoming negotiations, the NSGEU stated that the resumption of collective bargaining should be an emerging priority of Russell MacLellan's Liberal government.[2] NSGEU president Dave Peters also highlighted the challenges the union had confronted including the mandatory leave program, wage freezes and rollbacks, and the massive restructuring of the public sector, including the establishment of the Queen Elizabeth II Health Sciences Centre, the new community college system, the new amalgamated school boards, the new regional municipalities, and the new regional health boards—all of which were introduced without consultation with the relevant union or the affected organizations (Peters, 1997). It should be emphasized that the restraint programs of the Cameron and Savage governments were not targeted only at public-sector unions but, rather, reflected major policy shifts in the way government should function.

The drop in civil service membership from 9,289 in December 1995 to 5,772 in April 1997 represented a decrease of about 40 per cent. However, it would be misleading to think that all of the former employees lost their jobs; downsizing and privatization moved a significant proportion of employees from the civil service to the private sector and under the Trade Union Act (*NSGEU Newsletter*, 1997).

On 28 October 1997 the NSGEU and the Department of Human Resources made opening statements and in mid-November the parties faced off against each other at the bargaining table. The negotiations represented the first time the parties had engaged in collective bargaining since 1989. As noted by Human Resources Minister Allister Surette, 'what's important to me as employer of the civil service is that we do have a process laid out whereby we are at the bargaining table for true collective bargaining' (Nicoll, 1997a). Surette explained that in addition to monetary issues, other important matters revolved around technological change, growing computerization, the major alterations in how the government delivers programs and services, and the substantial restructuring within government.

From the union perspective, major issues included salaries, pension benefits, job security, and privatization of the public service. According to the NSGEU's Peters:

> Some of us are starting to think the work we do has no value. That perception has to change. If the government goes on like it is, we will not recognize the public service in four years time. Those of us that have jobs at all will be working for private companies, with reduced wages and benefits. Decisions (relating to the delivery of services) are being made for a variety of reasons, not all of which are in the best interests of Nova Scotia taxpayers. The NSGEU is not trying to fight change, but let's make sure that it's done right, and in everyone's best interests. (DeCoste, 1997)

The union was seeking an 18 per cent wage increase over a two-year period. Peters stated that the government could afford such a raise, citing a number of recent spending announcements on the part of Russell MacLellan's Liberal government and the willingness of the government to let money leave the province in the form of payments to private investors (for example, the privatization of Nova Scotia Power and the province's first toll road).

Surette's position was that the province's financial situation was still fragile and the law requires the government to ensure balanced budgets:[3] 'On one hand, yes we do recognize the sacrifice made by the public servants over the last number of years. On the other hand, we're trying to restore financial stability' (Power, 1997). In the April 1997 budget, no clear item indicated how much the government had set aside for wage increases of government employees (although the budget contained one line item of $31.5 million for restructuring costs, including early retirement incentives, severance packages, and labour negotiations). According to Finance Minister Bill Gillis, 'I doubt the union is going to negotiate for a decrease, so we've put a little money in there. But we're not going to quantify it; that's for the bargaining table' (Nicoll, 1997b).

Although the government was able to reach a deal with the Nova Scotia Teachers Union in late 1997 (which provided for the elimination of the 3 per cent rollback, a 1.9 per cent wage increase in August 1998, and an additional 1.9 per cent raise in April 1999), the winter of 1998 was characterized by considerable labour unrest and dissatisfaction with the pace of negotiations. Bargaining was particularly difficult because of the massive restructuring in government, major amalgamations in health care, education, and municipal government, and the number of contracts coming up for negotiation with the expiration of the wage freeze and rollback legislation.

By late February, union officials were becoming frustrated with the slow progress on the negotiation front. Further complicating the picture was the announcement by Premier Russell MacLellan that Nova Scotians would be going to the polls on 24 March. NSGEU president Peters argued that the Liberal government should not be calling an election with so many contracts outstanding, since Premier MacLellan stated that the government's goal was to achieve solid collective bargaining and to see the process through to the end:

> It has been totally irresponsible of this government to go to the electorate without resolving the public sector contracts. They took our contracts away from us and they have not restored them. They're clearly trying to provoke some kind of strike action. They've thrown the gauntlet down to the public employees. We're here to serve the public, but when is enough? We've been treated so terribly that if we don't take some action, even the public won't have quality service at the end of the day. (Sherwood and Smith, 1998)

The March election returned to power Russell MacLellan's Liberal government. However, the election was extremely close, with both the Liberals and New Democrats winning 19 seats and the Conservatives taking 14 seats. Given the minority government, organized labour was expected to have more influence on policy. In the words of Rick Clarke, president of the Nova Scotia Federation of Labour:

> When I look at the election results, I think workers have a little bit more of an ally in that there's going to be a way and means to keep the pressure on. Now that the election is over, government still has some wrongs to right. They legislated these problems that have gone on for so long, and now they have to take a look at it. (Sherwood, 1998)

Early April brought an end to negotiations between the government and the bulk of civil service employees, represented by the NSGEU. The ratification of a 29-month contract provided for the repeal of the 3 per cent rollback as of

1 December 1997, a 1.9 per cent increase on 1 November 1998, and a 2.2 per cent increase on 1 April 1999. The agreement also provided for increased job security, a $750 lump sum for employees not affected by the 3 per cent wage roll-back imposed by the Savage government in 1994 (employees earning $25,000 or less), and due to a pension surplus, employees received their pension contribution from April 1997 to March 1998 in a lump sum in mid-June of 1998.[4] In some ways, the agreement was patterned on the settlement reached with the NSTU a few months earlier.

With high expectations for a substantial settlement, there was considerable unrest among civil servants, who grudgingly ratified the agreement—only 3,608 of the union's 5,639 members participated in the ratification vote, with 66 per cent of voters supporting the contract (Brooks, 1998). Their dissatisfaction with the current agreement was also evidenced in interviews with union officials.

It should be noted that the most recent set of negotiations resulted in a *Master Agreement* for eight of the nine employee groups represented by the NSGEU. Prior to this agreement, each of the nine groups negotiated separate contracts with the government. The only group not involved in the negotiation, the Education Component, had not reached an agreement as of March 1999.[5]

The Queen Elizabeth II Health Sciences Centre Decision

Further complicating the return to collective bargaining was the issue of whether the 3 per cent rollback imposed by the Savage government in 1994 would end with the expiration of the cutback legislation on 31 October 1997 or whether that increase was lost for good. While the union position was that the old collective agreements with the pre-rollback salary levels would come into effect upon the expiration of the legislation, the Nova Scotia government argued that the 3 per cent cut remained in effect and the wage bargaining would start from there. In early December 1997, arbitrator Eric Sloane, in the case of the Queen Elizabeth II Health Sciences Centre, supported the union position and ruled that the health complex had to restore the 3 per cent taken away from employees as a result of the wage rollback.[6] Human Resources Minister Surette stated that the decision could potentially extend to all 'public' employees and cost the government as much as $30 million (Nicoll, 1997c).

The Queen Elizabeth II Health Sciences Centre appealed Sloane's ruling and in January 1998, Nova Scotia Supreme Court Justice Walter Goodfellow quashed the arbitration award.[7] He found in favour of the employer, who had argued that the intention of the government was not to restore the 3 per cent rollback of wages upon expiration of the legislation (Rodenhiser, 1998). The decision was devastating to employee morale—as one shop steward put it, 'the arbitrator's ruling was like a glimmer that at least I'm going to get paid what I had' (*Mail Star*, 12 Jan. 1998).

The NSGEU, which represented about 5,400 employees at the QEII complex, appealed the decision of Justice Goodfellow to the Nova Scotia Court of Appeal. In April 1998, the Court of Appeal reversed the decision and held that wages should have been restored to their previous levels as soon as the wage rollback legislation expired.[8] According to the Court, the harsh nature of the 3 per cent rollback was to combat the deficit problem but was not intended to have a lingering effect. While the decision applied to the employees at the QEII Health Sciences Centre, Human Resources Minister Wayne Gaudet stated that the government was going to implement the decision for all affected employees (MacKinlay, 1998).

Examining the Impact of Government Restructuring

What has been the impact of government restructuring on public-sector labour relations in Nova Scotia? What significant changes have resulted? What is the current industrial relations climate? These are the questions that will be addressed in this section.

Establishing the Department of Human Resources

In 1993, as part of the restructuring within the provincial government, a new Department of Human Resources was established to provide leadership in the development and implementation of human resource policies and practices applicable to the civil service. The department also provides advisory services to government and is responsible for the negotiation of collective agreements with the civil service. Prior to 1993, contract negotiations with the NSGEU were handled by what was known as the Civil Service Commission (Department of Human Resources, 1998).

The department is divided into three divisions—business services, client services, and corporate services—and its goal is to 'develop, in partnership with management, a productive and skilled workforce in a healthy and safe work environment'. There is a movement towards greater attention on policy and strategic management and increased policy research and analysis. Over the past few years, the department has established a strategic plan and begun monitoring outcomes relating to government employment and working conditions. For example, recent department estimates suggest that about 1.6 per cent of payroll is spent on training. In addition, the percentage of civil servants participating in training programs has increased from 20 per cent in 1994–5 to 41 per cent in 1997–8.

A major problem is the rate of absenteeism among government workers. Between 1994 and 1997, civil servants were absent from work about 11 days a year. Absenteeism levels are being monitored by Human Resources and a number of recent policies (Attendance Management, Occupational Health and Safety, Employee Assistance Program, and Disability Management) have helped to reduce the rate of absenteeism by almost 10 per cent.

The government's revised affirmative action policy was implemented on a pilot basis in 1998-9, and since 1993 more than 60 per cent of civil service employees have completed the Diversity and Employment Equity Awareness Program. An Occupational Health and Safety (OHS) policy was developed in 1996-7 after consultation with government departments and organized labour. Its key features include leadership with the NSGEU as co-chair of the Joint OHS Master Committee, establishment of a communications plan promoting employee and public awareness of safety, educational workshops provided in conjunction with organized labour, and greater monitoring and analysis of safety issues. A Workforce Adjustment Strategy was also implemented, and 139 civil service employees voluntarily resigned from the government over the November 1996–March 1998 period, thus reducing the need for involuntary layoffs.

Deficit Reduction and Employment Trends

As noted earlier, Nova Scotia entered the 1990s with a growing provincial debt and a succession of budget deficits. Although extremely unpopular with public sector employees and unions, the wage restraint and rollback measures (and decreases in government transfers or payments to departments and public agencies) did reduce costs, and in the 1996-7 fiscal year the province recorded its first budget surplus in several years. Although this was followed by a budget surplus the following year, the lifting of restraint legislation and the desire to reward Nova Scotians for their resolve in fighting the deficit brought into doubt the likelihood of a third straight budget surplus. The first-quarter report of the Department of Finance projected an $81 million deficit, due at least in part to a devalued Canadian dollar and overspending by the departments of Economic Development and Health (*Globe and Mail*, 16 Oct. 1998). Members of the business community greeted the news with alarm. According to Peter O'Brien, Atlantic vice-president of the Canadian Federation of Independent Business, 'The "be happy, don't worry" attitude of the premier (MacLellan) was not an encouraging sign for business or anyone concerned about our financial well-being. The Economic Development department is already nearly one-third over budget for the year and there is little to show for the expenditure' (O'Brien, 1998).

Tables 2.3 through 2.5 provide estimates of the change in employment in the Nova Scotia government sector. Depending on the definition of civil service employment and the accounting for part-time and casual workers, the results vary somewhat, as these tables indicate. In addition, while the former Civil Service Commission provided an annual report of its activities, the new Department of Human Resources does not follow this practice but instead makes information available as it relates to the goals and objectives of the department. Finally, the data provided by the NSGEU obviously relate only to members of the union.

What do the data tell us? During the three decades beginning in 1960, the Nova Scotia Civil Service experienced considerable growth in employment.

Table 2.3: Changes to Civil Service, 1962–3 to 1989–90

Time Period	Number of Employees
1962–3	4,243
1967–8	6,396
1972–3	7,927
1977–8	9,135
1982–3	9,648
1983–4	10,032
1984–5	10,126
1985–6	10,189
1986–7	10,123
1987–8	10,468
1988–9	11,440
1989–90	11,892

Source: Civil Service Commission Annual Reports.

Accompanying the wage restraint legislation of the 1990s was a slow decline in government employment, with a dramatic drop in the number of government workers in 1996–7 (see Tables 2.4 and 2.5). While one might assume that there was a massive downsizing of the public service, the reality is that changes in legislation moved a large number of workers (particularly in health care) out of the civil service to employers coming under the jurisdiction of the Trade Union Act (rather than the Civil Service Collective Bargaining Act applicable to public ser-

Table 2.4: Nova Scotia Government Appointment Head Count, 1990–1 to 1997–8

Time Period	Civil Service Employees	Casual Employees	Contract Employees	Total Number of Employees*
1990–1	11,994	1,078	79	19,197
1991–2	11,556	1,280	98	18,439
1992–3	11,661	1,318	89	18,477
1993–4	11,544	961	94	17,970
1994–5	10,840	1,437	115	17,070
1995–6	10,892	1,413	136	17,229
1996–7	7,799	1,031	148	11,801
1997–8	7,325	1,125	144	11,309

*Includes civil servants, contract, Order-in-Council appointments, statutory appointments, relief, boards, foremen (M/F), tradespersons, and fees. The dramatic drop in employment in the 1996–7 period was due largely to the movement of a number of employees out of the civil service to employers coming under the Trade Union Act.
Source: Nova Scotia Department of Human Resources, 1998.

Table 2.5: Nova Scotia Government Employees Union Membership, 1962–1998

Time Period	Number of Civil Service Members	Total Number of Members	Civil Service Membership as % of Total Membership
1962	2,526	2,526	100.0
1967	4,760	4,760	100.0
1973	6,876	6,876	100.0
1977	7,514	7,850	95.7
1982	8,037	8,739	92.0
1983	n.a.*	9,549	n.a.
1984	n.a.	9,994	n.a.
1985	n.a.	10,116	n.a.
1986	8,447	10,822	78.1
1987	n.a.	n.a.	n.a.
1988	8,719	10,828	80.5
1989	9,411	11,711	80.4
1990	9,999	12,760	78.4
1991	10,041	12,933	77.6
1992	9,744	12,986	75.0
1993	9,851	13,083	75.3
1994**	9,595	14,782	64.9
1995	9,318	14,467	64.4
1996	9,300	14,522	64.0
1997	6,539	16,350	40.0
1998	5,715	17,825	32.1

*n.a. = data not available.
**From 1991 to 1998 the data refer to the month of January, with the exception of 1994, where the data refer to June.
Source: Nova Scotia Government Employees Union.

vants). For example, while the civil service membership of the NSGEU plummeted from 9,300 members in 1996 to 5,715 in 1998, the number of members in the trade section of the union rose from 5,222 to 12,110 over the same period.[9] As shown in Table 2.5, civil service membership as a percentage of the overall membership of the NSGEU dropped from 78.4 per cent in 1990 to 32.1 per cent in 1998.

What motivated the government to move employees from the public service to the private sector? Discussions with union and government officials suggested that the province wanted to get out of the business of being a direct health-care provider (which it was with respect to former employees of the Victoria General Hospital). As a result of the Queen Elizabeth II Act, four health-care facilities in Halifax (including the Victoria General Hospital) were amalgamated. In addition, the province established four regional health boards. Although the Queen Elizabeth II Centre is grappling with a considerable deficit, the government perceived that these changes would improve the quality of health care in the province and reduce costs (for instance, by avoiding duplication of services).

With the Queen Elizabeth II amalgamation, existing collective agreements remained in force until the freeze on collective bargaining was lifted on 1 November 1997. The NSGEU became the representative for the four major bargaining units[10] within the complex and new collective agreements were negotiated over 1997–8.

Two other points about the downsizing and restructuring of government deserve mention. First, while we have seen some reduction of government employees, the Nova Scotia experience was not characterized by the involuntary layoff of large numbers of government employees. While there were some layoffs, the shedding of employees was carried out by attrition, instituting a hiring freeze, transferring employees to other departments,[11] and providing early retirement and voluntary severance packages. As one union official put it, 'members of the public, when asked about restructuring in government, often think that changes were brought about by mass layoffs. This is not really the case.' However, there appears to be a growing use of casual and contract employees in the past few years. For example, between the 1996 and 1997 fiscal years, the number of casual employees increased about 10 per cent, from 1,031 to 1,125 (see Table 2.4).

Second, the wage freeze and rollback legislation did cut into the real wages of Nova Scotians in the broader public sector, which had a devastating impact on employee morale. This came out both in my survey of union officials (described later in the chapter) and in discussions with union officials. However, it would be wrong to conclude that employees' salaries or wages remained fixed from 1991 to 1994, then were cut by 3 per cent and stayed there until late 1997: many workers saw some increase in pay as a result of re-classification, promotion, progression through the ranks, and/or merit adjustments.

Labour Relations

In 1994 and 1997, I conducted surveys of Nova Scotia union officials. Although the surveys were not designed with this particular project in mind, some of the findings increase our understanding of what has happened in the province.[12] To preserve the anonymity of respondents, I include in the sub-sample the findings from the broadly defined provincial public sector (including government and health care).[13] The results provided in this part of the report are based on 24 responses from union officials in 1994 and 18 responses in 1997. Obviously, considerable care should be taken in the interpretation of these results since the sample is quite small.

When considering employee relations, one section of the survey asked about the use of 'progressive decision-making ideology' (Goll, 1991). Each of the statements was measured using a six-point scale (1 = strongly disagree; 6 = strongly agree). Union officials generally disagreed that the employer used participative decision-making (the average score was 2.35 in 1994 and 2.33 in 1997). Results were slightly more positive with reference to the employer's explanation of proposed changes to those affected (average score of 2.48 in 1994 and 2.61 in

1997) and the presence of open channels of communication (average score of 2.61 in 1994 and 2.89 in 1997), with modest increases over the 1994-7 period.

Also contained in the survey were measures of labour climate (Dastmalchian, Blyton, and Adamson, 1991).[14] Based on the same six-point scale, union perceptions of labour climate were somewhat negative, and changed only slightly over the period (from an overall average score of 2.98 in 1994 to 3.15 in 1997). In 1994, 45 per cent of respondents reported that their union made concessions relating to job assignments and 57 per cent indicated concessions addressing job classifications—these numbers dropped dramatically in 1997, with 24 per cent reporting job assignment concessions and 18 per cent indicating job classification concessions. In 1994, 83 per cent of respondents indicated that there had been a permanent reduction of bargaining unit employees, compared with 41 per cent in 1997.

A series of questions addressed employer performance issues. Participants were asked to indicate their response to each item using a six-point scale (1 = very low; 6 = very high). The average scores for productivity were 3.86 (1994) and 3.73 (1997), while the results for service quality were 4.38 (1994) and 4.50 (1997), indicating fairly high levels on both measures. These results are generally consistent with the comments obtained in interviews. For example, one union official indicated that the quality of service is quite good but that *access* to service has declined. A common concern was 'the need to do more with less', and there was also concern about the 'downloading' of responsibilities to both government workers and agencies outside the civil service.

The results addressing employee satisfaction painted a picture of a civil service characterized by low levels of job satisfaction and employee morale (the job satisfaction scores were 3.04 in 1994 and 3.00 in 1997; the employee morale scores were even worse—2.39 in 1994 and 2.35 in 1997). While these results are perceptual measures of the opinions of union officials, the findings were generally confirmed in the interviews. One participant, when asked about morale, had a one-word answer—'terrible'. These findings are not surprising considering the massive restructuring of government services, the wage restraint and rollback programs, and the high level of job insecurity (several employees expressed a strong 'fear' of losing their jobs). Moreover, the results are consistent with past academic work reporting the negative consequences associated with downsizing (Cascio, 1993; Cameron, 1994; Mone, 1994).

A number of other issues affecting labour relations emerged from the interviews. For instance, while examples of contracting out of government services were mentioned, this issue was not receiving nearly as much attention over the past year.[15] This may be due to a change in government philosophy and language in the recent collective agreement, which requires consultation with the union on the possibility of contracting out.

Both labour and government acknowledged the absenteeism problem in the public sector. Absenteeism rates are among the highest in the country and the collective agreement provides workers with substantial protection, including 18 general 'sick days' a year and generous short-term illness leave benefits.

Lastly, a frequent issue for discussion was the 'casualization' of government—the trend to hiring new employees on fixed-term contracts. Such employees typically do not receive benefits and are not members of the bargaining unit. Union officials cited examples where an employee would be hired on a series of short-term contracts but would not attain a full-time position in the civil service, and Table 2.4 indicates that while the number of civil service employees has been reduced substantially over the past few years, there has been some increase in the use of casual and contract employees. Recent changes in the current collective agreement, which substantially tightened the requirements for job posting, are aimed at addressing this issue.

How are the relations between labour and the government? Although a number of employees were not satisfied with the wage gains in the current contract, the return to collective bargaining was viewed as a positive step. There was a substantial increase in communication between the parties, and Russell MacLellan's Liberal government made a commitment to the collective bargaining process. A number of joint committees with employer and union representation were established and there was a greater sense of the parties 'working together' on issues such as technological change and workplace safety.

While the current collective agreement took almost six months to negotiate (and more than 40 days of bargaining), this was to be expected, given the duration of the suspension of collective bargaining rights, the considerable government restructuring, and the massive changes in how government services are provided. My overall impression of the current relationship was summarized in one interview with an NSGEU official, who spoke of 'relatively good labour relations with a genuine effort on the part of both parties to resolve workplace issues'.

Conclusion

Although some observers argue that the adversarial bargaining stance and increased government intervention into the bargaining process may be spelling the end of collective bargaining in the public sector, Fryer (1995) maintains that collective bargaining will probably survive, but in an altered form. Fryer calls for change on the part of both management and labour. He believes that government must empower the workforce to develop new and efficient methods of service delivery and be willing to share decision-making with the employees. In Nova Scotia, we have witnessed the return to collective bargaining after a long period of government intervention, major changes in the delivery of government services, and greater joint efforts between workers and the employer. Although the union has not been co-opted by management, there appears to be a desire to open up the channels of communication and work together to solve common problems.

Fryer also asserts that unions must move away from the adversarial approach to labour relations with government because the 'adversarial model has limited usefulness at the government level' (Fryer, 1995: 365). He sees the need for both labour and management to redefine the bargaining agenda by altering the focus on monetary and compensation issues and placing increased emphasis on the work environment. In addition, the parties must play an active role in reforming government. Again, we are observing this trend in Nova Scotia with a growing focus on employee rights and quality of life at the workplace.

It would be misleading to suggest that the relationship is one of true co-operation—the negotiations between the NSGEU and the government involved tough bargaining and there are several issues where the parties differ dramatically (such as the privatization of the public service). However, the parties appear to have a mutual respect for one another and there is a 'relief' that the wage restraint programs have finally ended and collective bargaining has been reinstated.[16] In addition, the MacLellan government seemed to have moved away from the 'slash-and-burn' strategy (Belman, Gunderson, and Hyatt, 1996) to a more 'value-added' approach that sees workers as assets capable of playing an important role in improving government services (Verma and Cutcher-Gershenfeld, 1996). While it remains to be seen how the recently elected Conservative government of John Hamm will manage the civil service, there is considerable unrest among members of the civil service. The Hamm government stated that the budget surpluses reported by the Liberal government were a sham because several high-cost items, such as health and school board deficits, were left off the balance sheet. The Hamm government has ordered an internal review of all government programs with the aim of identifying areas in which costs can be cut and services privatized (*Mail Star*, 15 Oct. 1999). Government employees are very concerned about the possibility of wage freeze or rollbacks, job cuts, and the move to a four-day workweek (with a resulting cut in pay).

Previous research demonstrates that organizations engaging in downsizing and restructuring tend to focus on cutting employment while ignoring the critical aspects of redesigning the organization and implementation of cultural change. While almost all organizations stress the first component (workforce reduction), only about half make some attempt at work redesign and less than a third implement a systematic change strategy (Cameron, 1994). The Nova Scotia governments' restructuring efforts were typical, being focused on cost control with little attention to the more long-term (but exceedingly more difficult) strategies of work redesign and systematic change. The restraint programs introduced by the Cameron and Savage governments involved virtually no consultation with the union or employees and provided insufficient attention to the survivors of restructuring, which led many employees to become defensive and try to protect their turf and jobs. Overall, there was little evidence of a proactive, well-planned strategy on the part of government.[17]

While there has been a trend towards greater co-operation between labour and management in the most recent past, co-operative programs are very fragile and rarely survive in a climate of downsizing and restructuring. Although it could be argued that the restraint programs of the Cameron and Savage governments did play a role in achieving balanced budgets, the pain and hardship associated with the government's actions must also be acknowledged and documented.

Notes

I would like to thank the Nova Scotia Government Employees Union, the Nova Scotia Department of Labour, and the Nova Scotia Department of Human Resources for their co-operation in completing this project. Information on public opinion trends was generously provided by Corporate Research Associates (Halifax), and Tasha McGann and Darryl Williams provided invaluable research assistance.

1. For the past several years, Corporate Research Associates (Halifax) has been polling Nova Scotians concerning satisfaction with the provincial government. The specific question asked was: How satisfied are you with the overall performance of the provincial government led by Premier _____? Response categories included: very satisfied, somewhat satisfied, somewhat dissatisfied, very dissatisfied, neutral or no opinion.

2. In March 1997, Premier John Savage indicated that he was resigning as leader of the Liberal Party. Russell MacLellan became Premier after he won the Liberal leadership race in July 1997.

3. See, for example, the Appropriations Act of 1998 and the Financial Measures Act.

4. For more detail on changes in the broader public sector, see National Union of Public and General Employees (1998).

5. For more details on the terms of the agreement, see the *Master Agreement between the Province of Nova Scotia (represented by the Department of Human Resources) and the Nova Scotia Government Employees Union*.

6. Sloane's ruling of 5 December 1997 is available from the Nova Scotia Department of Labour.

7. Justice Goodfellow's decision is reported in (1998) 165 *Nova Scotia Reports* (2d) 193.

8. The Court of Appeal's decision is reported in (1998) 166 *Nova Scotia Reports* (2d) 194.

9. Not all of the growth in NSGEU membership was due simply to having members transferred out of the civil service. The union was also successful in organizing workers coming under the Trade Union Act.

10. In cases where another union (such as the Nova Scotia Nurses Union or Canadian Auto Workers) sought to represent the unit, run-off elections were held.

11. A number of civil service employees related to me that while there were cutbacks within their departments, they were able to obtain other positions within the government.

12. Surveys were addressed to local union officials and addresses were obtained from *Labour Organizations in Nova Scotia*, available from the Department of Labour. Response rates to the 1994 and 1997 surveys were 52 per cent and 41 per cent, respectively.

13. Note that respondents from municipal government and the education sector were not included in the analysis.

14. Items included: grievances are normally settled promptly; the parties make sincere efforts to solve common problems; the parties exchange information freely; and the parties have respect for each other's goals.

15. The NSGEU has expressed strong concern over the PPP (public-private partnering) program and has developed a five-point protection plan to address the privatization issue (NSGEU, 1998).

16. While the decision on the part of the government to apply the *Queen Elizabeth II Health Sciences Centre* ruling to the civil service meant the elimination of the 3 per cent rollback imposed by the Savage government, there was considerable dissatisfaction within the civil service concerning the current collective agreement. Consequently, the degree to which civil servants bought into the initiatives of the MacLellan government is open to considerable debate.

17. Many downsizing efforts have failed to meet organizational objectives. See, for instance, the December 1998 issue of the *Canadian Journal of Administrative Sciences*, which is devoted to the topic of downsizing and restructuring.

References

Belman, D., M. Gunderson, and D. Hyatt. 1996. 'Public Sector Employment Relations in Transition', in Belman, Gunderson, and Hyatt, *Public Sector Employment in a Time of Transition* (Madison, Wis.: IRRA), 1–20.

Blanchard, G. 1994. 'Now is the Time to Bargain', *Halifax Mail Star*, 25 May.

Brooks, P. 1998. 'Civil Servants Ratify Deal', *Halifax Chronicle-Herald*, 9 Apr.

Cameron, K. 1994. 'Strategies for Successful Organizational Downsizing', *Human Resource Management* 33: 189–211.

———, S. Freeman, and A. Mishra. 1991. 'Best Practices in White Collar Downsizing: Managing Contradictions', *Academy of Management Executive* 5: 57–73.

Campbell, J. 1991. 'Labor Leader Demanding Hearings on Wage Freeze', *Cape Breton Post*, 6 July.

Cascio, W. 1993. 'Downsizing? What Do We Know? What Have We Learned?', *Academy of Management Executive* 7: 95–104.

Civil Service Collective Bargaining Act, 1978, c. 3.

Cranston, M. 1993. 'Halifax Council Vents Anger at Forced Unpaid Leave', *Halifax Daily News*, 15 Oct.

Dastmalchian, A., P. Blyton, and R. Adamson. 1991. *The Climate of Workplace Relations*. London: Routledge.

DeCoste, J. 1997. 'Wage Demands Must Be Put in Proper Context: Peters', *Kentville Advertiser*, 25 Nov.

Fryer, J. 1995. 'Provincial Public Service Labour Relations', in G. Swimmer and M. Thompson, eds, *Public Sector Collective Bargaining in Canada* (Kingston, Ont.: IRC Press), 341–67.

Goll, I. 1991. 'Environment, Corporate Ideology, and Involvement Programs', *Industrial Relations* 30: 138–49.

Hays, P. 1995. 'No Salary Freeze for Some', *Halifax Daily News*, 14 Dec.

International Labour Office. 1995. *Case No. 1802—Complaint Against the Government of Canada (Nova Scotia)*.

Lee, C. 1992. 'After the Cuts', *Training* 29: 17–23.

Lee, P. 1991a. 'Labour Focuses on Tory Defeat', *Halifax Mail Star*, 13 June.

——. 1991b. 'N.S. Wage Cap "Union Busting"', *Halifax Mail Star*, 8 June.

——. 1991c. 'Union Ads Use Pain to Drive Home Point', *Halifax Mail Star*, 28 Dec.

——. 1993a. 'Government Workers Eye Catch-up Raises', *Halifax Mail Star*, 24 Feb.

——. 1993b. 'Provincial Pay Freeze Legal, Court Rules', *Halifax Mail Star*, 16 Apr.

McDougall, T. 1993. 'Grits Will Scrap Unpaid Leave in '94, Says Gillis', *Halifax Chronicle-Herald*, 31 Dec.

MacGillivray, D. 1994. 'End of Democracy Near, Says CUPE's Kowalski', *Cape Breton Post*, 5 May.

MacInnis, S. 1991. 'Campaign to Defeat Cameron to Be Weighed at Convention', *Cape Breton Post*, 29 May.

MacKinlay, S. 1998. 'Decision's Cost May Be More Than 2.2 m.', *Halifax Daily News*, 9 Apr.

McLaughlin, P. 1994. 'Pay Cut "Backfiring," Aldermen Fear', *Halifax Daily News*, 29 May.

Madill, J. 1994. 'Cash Crunch Makes Bargaining a Sham', *Halifax Mail Star*, 7 May.

Mone, M. 1994. 'Relationships Between Self-Concepts, Aspirations, Emotional Responses, and Intent to Leave a Downsizing Organization', *Human Resource Management* 33: 281–98.

National Union of Provincial Government Employees. 1997. 'Collective Bargaining and Restructuring in the Public Sector', mimeo, Dec.

Nicoll, C. 1993a. 'Unions Balk at Province's Days-for-Debt Talk', *Halifax Daily News*, 27 Aug.

——. 1993b. 'Angry Rally Rejects Grit Cutbacks', *Halifax Daily News*, 9 Oct.

——. 1997a. 'NSGEU, Province Start Bargaining', *Halifax Daily News*, 19 Nov.

——. 1997b. 'Unions Want Rollback Rolled Back', *Halifax Daily News*, 3 Oct.

——. 1997c. '30m Wage Price Tag Feared', *Halifax Daily News*, 10 Dec.

Nova Scotia Department of Finance. 1995. *Nova Scotia Statistical Review*. Halifax: Department of Finance.

Nova Scotia Government Employees Union. 1994. *History Aspects of the NSGEU*. Halifax: NSGEU.

——. 1997. *NSGEU Newsletter*: 6–7.

——. 1998. *NSGEU Newsletter*: 4–8.

——. 1998. *The Union Stand*, Oct.

O'Brien, P. 1998. 'Province's Overspending is Real Cause for Alarm', *Cape Breton Post*, 17 Oct.

Peters, D. 1997. 'Notes for a Statement on the Union's Approach to Upcoming Negotiations and Its Challenge to the Premier and Other Party Leaders', NSGEU, 21 July.

Power, B. 1997. 'Unions Want Big Pay Raise', *Halifax Mail Star*, 8 Oct.

Public Sector Compensation Restraint Act, 1991, c. 5.

Public Sector Compensation (1994–97) Act, 1994, c. 11.

Public Sector Unpaid Leave Act, 1993, c. 10.

Renouf, M. 1991. 'Unions Renew Promise to Battle Government', *Halifax Daily News*, 10 July.

Rodenhiser, D. 1998. 'Talks to Start at Zero—Surette', *Halifax Daily News*, 9 Jan.

Shaw, C. 1995. 'UN Sides with Labor on Wage Rollbacks', *Halifax Mail Star*, 6 July.

Sherwood, J. 1998. 'Unions Seek Political Ally', *Halifax Chronicle-Herald*, 6 Apr.

—— and A. Smith. 1998. 'Strike Possible, NSGEU Warns', *Halifax Chronicle-Herald*, 18 Feb.

Taylor, R. 1994. 'Businessmen Love Budget', *Halifax Mail Star*, 30 Apr.

Thomson, A. 1983. 'The Nova Scotia Civil Service Association, 1956–1967', *Acadiensis* 12: 81–105.

———. 1989. 'From Civil Servants to Government Employees: The Nova Scotia Government Employees Association, 1967–1973', in M. Earle, ed., *Workers and the State in Twentieth Century Nova Scotia* (Fredericton, NB: Gorsebrook Research Institute).

Tibbetts, J. 1991a. 'Labour Expects N.S. to Freeze Civil Service Wages', *Halifax Mail Star*, 9 Mar.

———. 1991b. 'NSGEU Among Unions Taking Wage Freeze Complaint to UN', *Halifax Mail Star*, 6 Nov.

——— and B. Underhill. 1993. 'Civil Service Urged to Take Unpaid Leave', *Halifax Chronicle-Herald*, 27 Aug.

Underhill, B. 1991a. 'Wage Freeze Battle Not Over—MacLean', *Halifax Chronicle-Herald*, 22 June.

———. 1991b. 'Labour Leaders Vow to Fight Wage Freeze Bill', *Halifax Mail Star*, 26 June.

Verma, A., and J. Cutcher-Gershenfeld. 1996. 'Workplace Innovations and Systems Change', in D. Belman, M. Gunderson, and D. Hyatt, eds, *Public Sector Employment in a Time of Transition* (Madison, Wis.: IRRA), 201–41.

Ward, B. 1991. 'MacLean Warns Against Pay Freeze', *Halifax Chronicle-Herald*, 9 May.

———. 1994. 'Expect a Strike—Unions', *Halifax Mail Star*, 12 May.

Chapter 3

From Softball to Hardball: The Transition in Labour-Management Relations in the Ontario Public Service

Joseph B. Rose

From 1942 to 1985, the political landscape in Ontario was stable and dominated by Progressive Conservative governments. During their tenure, the Tories pursued a balanced approach to economic and social policies. They developed economic investment strategies to satisfy business interests and introduced moderate social reforms to accommodate labour interests. The Tories also developed close ties with union leaders based on their belief that stable labour relations were essential to attracting business investment. Accordingly, labour reforms followed a gradualist path and reflected pragmatism and political opportunism, e.g., when a minority government existed or the New Democratic Party (NDP) was the official opposition. The pursuit of 'centrist' economic and social policies continued under the Liberals in the late 1980s but unravelled in the 1990s. This coincided with marked political shifts, first to the left and then to the right, and a major economic recession.

The 1990s represent the most turbulent period in the history of labour-management relations in the Ontario public service (OPS). This period can be divided into two stages. The first was marked by the election of the NDP in 1990, which set out to establish a new era in labour-management relations based on a partnership with the Ontario Public Service Employees Union (OPSEU). This move was motivated by a desire on the part of the NDP to replace adversarialism with consensus-building and to develop a better appreciation of the limited resources available to government. This 'softball' approach was embodied in the 1992–3 OPS collective agreement and represented a 'restraint for security' package. Specifically, it provided modest wage increases in exchange for job guarantees. The same approach was reflected in the NDP's rationale for the Social Contract, namely, government assurances of job security in exchange for substantial expenditure reductions from public-sector partners. Unfortunately, the crippling effect of the recession and the growing restlessness with budget deficits cast a long shadow over efforts to sustain a new partnership.

The failure to reach consensus on the Social Contract represented the onset of what I call the 'hardball' approach to labour relations. This approach refers to confrontational bargaining and encompasses both the process and outcomes of bargaining (Voos, 1994), including legislative infringements on collective bargaining. The hardball period began with the Social Contract Act. It effectively coerced employers and unions throughout the public sector to meet the government's expenditure targets and imposed penalties if they failed to do so. Following the election of Mike Harris's Tory government in 1995, confrontational bargaining escalated. The Tories adopted a low-cost strategy based on massive downsizing of the OPS, removal of legal protections it saw as impeding its restructuring agenda, and demands for major changes in the OPS collective agreement. This resulted in the first strike in Crown employee bargaining history. The strike, which involved nearly 1.1 million person-days lost, was the fifth largest strike in Ontario in the post-World War II period (Workplace Information Directorate, 1996).

This chapter provides a review and analysis of labour-management relations in the Ontario public service in the 1990s. The primary focus is on collective bargaining developments, the restructuring of the OPS, and the effect of these changes on other human resource management initiatives. The chapter begins with an overview of how collective bargaining developed in the sector. This is followed by an extensive treatment of the following four issues: (1) the political changes prior to and during the 1990s; (2) the economic conditions in the province and the political response to them; (3) an analysis of the three major bargaining rounds in the 1990s, including legal enactments restricting and expanding collective bargaining rights; and (4) an analysis of the nexus between collective bargaining and restructuring initiatives. The chapter concludes with a discussion of the results and a prognosis for future labour-management relations.

The Evolution of Collective Bargaining in the OPS

The collective bargaining system has evolved through four stages. Between 1947 and 1962 it was characterized by informal consultation through the Joint Advisory Council comprised of three representatives of the government, three representatives of the Civil Service Association of Ontario, and one member of the Civil Service Commission, acting as the chairperson (Arthurs, 1971). This body was similar to other 'association-consultation' models found at the federal and provincial levels. Consistent with the trend elsewhere in Canada, as disillusionment with association-consultation spread (e.g., it was advisory, narrow in scope, and failed to provide a method of dispute resolution), pressures mounted to establish collective bargaining rights for Crown employees (Ponak, 1982). The second stage was marked by the emergence of a formal model of negotiations (1962–72) under the Public Service Act of 1962 and subsequent amendments. This model included 'direct negotiations, mediation and compulsory arbitration of interest disputes', but did not contemplate 'the execution of collective agreements of the private sector style' (Arthurs, 1971: 105, 124). Instead, agreements became effective through Orders-in-Council, amendments to Ontario regulations, and other government directives.

With the spread of new public-sector collective bargaining laws in Canada, the province initiated a review of the OPS system by Judge Walter Little (Little, 1969). The third stage of development was marked by the passage of the Crown Employees Collective Bargaining Act (CECBA) in 1972. It created a formal collective bargaining model based on a service-wide bargaining unit and the designation of Management Board of cabinet as the employer bargaining representative and the Ontario Public Service Employees Union (OPSEU) as the union bargaining agent—OPSEU was the new name given to the Civil Service Association of Ontario and the name change signified 'the shift away from an association beholden to a civil service identity' (Roberts, 1994: 170). By 1977, a system of two-tiered bargaining evolved that 'maintained uniformity in respect of benefits and other conditions of employment while establishing eight categories or bargaining groups, each of which negotiates separately in respect of salary scales' (Adams, 1981: 162). Under the CECBA, the scope of bargaining was circumscribed by the requirement that every collective agreement recognize the employer's exclusive right to manage in areas such as the organization of the public service. This had two practical effects. First, the statutory management rights clause could only be modified by legislation. Second, certain issues—the merit system, training and development, appraisal, and pensions—could not be the subject of collective bargaining and were outside the jurisdiction of an arbitration board (Hebdon, 1995). The CECBA also prohibited the right to strike, established compulsory arbitration of interest disputes, and created the Grievance Settlement Board (GSB) to arbitrate grievances.

The fourth stage of development resulted from significant amendments to the CECBA introduced by the NDP government in 1993. There were five major changes.

1. Crown employees were granted the right to strike.
2. The parties were required to negotiate essential service agreements in the event of a work stoppage.
3. The scope of bargaining was expanded by repealing the requirement that every collective agreement contain a deemed management rights clause.
4. Six bargaining units were created within the OPS.
5. Collective bargaining rights were extended to 4,000 formerly excluded employees (e.g., managerial, administrative, and professional staff). These employees comprise a seventh bargaining unit.

Acquiring the legal right to strike was recognized by many within OPSEU as a challenge to the traditional role of the union's leadership and its members. As described by Frank Rooney, an OPSEU communications officer:

> OPSEU both reflects and reacts to the reality of bargaining under CECBA. Its lobbying, brief-writing and legal strengths are matched by a corresponding weakness: It lacks the experience in developing a strategic approach based on the ability to strike. Under CECBA, OPSEU rarely had to take responsibility for its bargaining stance. Put

bluntly, no union activist in the public service ever had to convince a member to give up wages on a picket line in order to achieve a bargaining objective. Staff, activists and members most often did not have to make hard choices. The final decisions were left to arbitrators. (Roberts, 1994: ix)

As described in greater detail below, the union was to be put to the test in the 1996 OPS strike.

The Fall of the Tories: 1985–1990

The political landscape in Ontario changed dramatically in 1985 when 42 years of Conservative rule came to an end in the provincial election of that year. Based on a political accord with the NDP, the Liberals under David Peterson formed a minority government from 1985 to 1987. During this period, a number of social and labour reforms were introduced, including one of North America's most generous pay equity laws and first-contract arbitration for newly certified unions (Dyck, 1997; Walkom, 1994). The Liberals formed a majority government in 1987 and entered their mandate on good terms with organized labour.

Following the recession of the early 1980s, the province's economy experienced robust growth and allowed the Liberals to increase social spending significantly. Real GDP in Ontario grew dramatically between 1983 and 1990, outpacing the rate of growth for most of the G-7 countries (including Canada) (Ontario Ministry of Finance, 1996a). During the Liberal reign, government revenues soared, increasing from $25.8 billion to $41.2 billion between 1985-6 and 1989-90 (see Table 3.1). Although total spending also increased under the Liberals (from about $28.4 to $41.1 billion), government expenditures as a percentage of GDP were relatively stable (averaging just over 15 per cent). This period began with a relatively small deficit ($2.6 billion in 1985-6) that gradually declined before a surplus was achieved in 1989-90 ($90 million). As a result, there was only a modest increase in the provincial debt in this period (from $32.9 to $39.3 billion). The debt as a percentage of GDP decreased from 17.9 per cent in 1985-6 to 14.1 per cent in 1989-90 and, as a result, interest on the debt as a percentage of annual revenue fell from 10.8 per cent in 1985-6 to 9.3 per cent in 1989-90 (and 8.8 per cent the following year) (Ontario Ministry of Finance, 1994, 1996b).

Whereas the economy was booming, relations with organized labour soured during the late 1980s. OPSEU was upset over several issues, including the government's failure to deliver on political rights for public servants (eventually awarded by the Supreme Court of Canada) and its attempt to increase OPSEU member contributions to the pension plan. As well, there was a major pension dispute with teachers and continuing discord with the Ontario Medical Association (OMA) in the wake of the physicians' unsuccessful strike over extra-billing. When Premier Peterson called an early election, labour mobilized to

Table 3.1: Ontario Economic Indicators, 1985–1997 ($ millions)

Year	Total Revenue	Total Expenditure	Annual Deficit	Total Debt	GDP at Market Prices	Total Expenses as % of GDP	Total Debt as % of GDP	Public Debt Interest as % of Revenue
1985–6	25,785	28,399	2,614	32,904	183,732	15.5%	17.9%	10.8%
1986–7	29,215	31,849	2,634	35,103	202,710	15.7%	17.3%	11.0%
1987–8	32,158	34,647	2,489	36,981	223,862	15.5%	16.5%	10.8%
1988–9	36,991	38,470	1,479	39,014	252,946	15.2%	15.5%	10.2%
1989–90	41,225	41,135	(90)	39,256	278,724	14.8%	14.1%	9.3%
1990–1	42,892	45,921	3,029	42,257	280,172	16.4%	15.1%	8.8%
1991–2	40,753	51,683	10,930	53,083	281,136	18.4%	18.9%	10.3%
1992–3	41,807	54,235	12,428	68,607	286,389	18.9%	24.0%	12.7%
1993–4	43,674	54,974	11,300	79,439	293,148	18.7%	27.1%	16.3%
1994–5	46,039	56,316	10,277	88,580	307,379	18.3%	28.8%	17.0%
1995–6	49,473	58,273	8,800	101,396	324,846	17.9%	31.2%	17.1%
1996–7	49,450	56,355	6,905	101,511	333,068	16.9%	30.5%	17.4%
1997–8	52,110	57,313	5,203	105,048	350,400	16.4%	30.0%	16.7%

Source: Ontario Ministry of Finance (1994: 118–19; 1996b: 70–1; 1996c: 18; 1998: 56–7).

unseat the Liberals. The first co-ordinated election campaign sponsored by labour and other groups began when OPSEU, the OMA, and the Ontario Teachers' Federation held a joint news conference to attack the Peterson government for its failure to provide an open, consultative government and to deliver improvements in health, education, and car insurance costs. OPSEU spent $1 million on its anti-Liberal campaign (Gagnon and Rath, 1991). The strong opposition of organized labour contributed to the Liberal defeat and the stunning upset victory of the NDP.

On the collective bargaining front, Management Board and OPSEU concluded an OPS collective agreement in May 1990 covering working conditions and benefits. The new contract, which took 18 months to negotiate and covered the period 1 January 1989 to 31 December 1991, resulted in three notable changes. First, government employees won the right to five months' advance notice where a reorganization, a closure of a facility, divestment, relocation, or contracting out of a government operation results in 20 or more employees being declared surplus. (The previous collective agreement provided three months' notice.) Second, the government was required to create permanent positions for jobs performed by casual employees for two or more years. Third, the contract incorporated the anti-discrimination provisions of the Human Rights Code (Galt, 1990; Lancaster Labour Law Reports, 1990). Wage bargaining, which was negotiated separately by occupational categories, resulted in an average base wage settlement increase of 6.83 per cent for 1990 (Ontario Ministry of Labour, 1992).

The NDP Years: 1990–1995

The NDP came to power just as the provincial economy plunged into a recession. Initially, the government embraced Keynesian policies and, like their Liberal predecessors, exhibited a penchant for major spending initiatives. Although 1991 average annual wage settlements with occupational categories in the OPS fell to 5.8 per cent, they were generally regarded as generous. Having initially chosen 'not to participate' in the recession, the NDP government subsequently came to the realization it was sitting on an economic powder keg. The Liberal's appetite for spending had produced an $8 billion structural deficit when the full impact of declining revenues became apparent in the spring of 1991.

Bargaining for a new OPS collective agreement commenced in October 1991. In this bargaining round, the NDP government wanted to create a unique partnership with OPSEU. A first step in that direction was the voluntary settlement reached between Management Board and OPSEU in January 1992 (the shortest round of negotiations in the history of OPS bargaining). Despite what appeared to be public ambivalence towards the recession, the government bargaining objective was to achieve a moderate settlement. The settlement, which covered the period 1 January 1992 to 31 December 1993, provided a wage increase of 1 per cent in the first year and 2 per cent in the second year. This represented the lowest pay increase since formal collective bargaining began in 1972. It also provided for flexible work arrangements, including variable workdays and work-weeks and job-sharing. The government hailed the agreement as a model for restraint for the public sector generally (Lancaster Labour Law Reports, 1992). The settlement also provided for the introduction of a COLA (cost-of-living allowance) in the second year (although it never became operational). COLA protection had been a long-standing union bargaining goal.

The quid pro quo for wage restraint and improved flexibility was a comprehensive job security package that went far beyond the advance notice requirements established in the 1989–91 OPS collective agreement. The centrepiece of the new job security improvements was the guaranteed job offer set out in articles 24.6.1 and 24.17.1 of the collective agreement (Collective Agreement, 1992–3: 39, 45).

Redeployment

24.6.1 Where an employee is identified as surplus he shall be assigned on the basis of his seniority to a vacancy in his ministry within a forty (40) kilometre radius of his headquarters provided he is qualified to perform the work and the vacancy is:

- in the same class or position as the employee's class or position;
- in a class or position in which the employee has served during his current term of continuous service; or
- another vacancy.

24.17.1 Effective January 1, 1992, employees whose jobs become surplus as a result of contracting out; divestment or comparable transfer from the Ontario Public Service to a Crown agency, broader public sector, non-profit organization, or the private sector; or relocation of an operation will be guaranteed a job offer in accordance with this Article.

Other significant improvements in job security included: (1) six months' notice of layoff or pay in lieu thereof; (2) a separation allowance and an education allowance for employees who resign; (3) a provision for six months' employment-related training for surplus employees; (4) recall rights within the employee's ministry for up to 18 months; and (5) establishment of a redeployment committee with equal representation from the union and management to oversee retraining programs related to redeployment and the resolution of employer-employee disputes respecting the training needs of redeployment candidates.

Negotiating improvements in job security protection became a necessity to OPSEU as the economic situation deteriorated. The severity of the recession in Ontario was reflected in most economic indicators. In 1990 and 1991, real GDP declined by 2.4 per cent and 3.2 per cent. The decline for Canada as a whole in these years was more modest (0.2 and 1.8 per cent) confirming that Ontario was hit much harder by the recession than the rest of country (Ontario Ministry of

Finance, 1997). As shown in Table 3.1, the recession led to a decline of more than $2 billion in government revenues between 1990–1 and 1991–2. Partial evidence of the NDP's belief it could spend its way out of the recession can be found in expenditure statistics. Between 1990–1 and 1992–3, government spending rose by over 18 per cent and government expenditure as a percentage of GDP climbed from 16.4 per cent to 18.9 per cent. With spending outpacing revenues, the budget deficit skyrocketed from $3 billion in 1990–1 to $10.9 billion the following year. It peaked at $12.4 billion in 1992–3 and deficits exceeding $10 billion continued through 1994–5. As a result the provincial debt more than doubled, from about $42.2 billion in 1990–1 to $88.6 billion in 1994–5. As well, the debt as a percentage of GDP more than doubled, from 15.1 per cent in 1990–1 to 31.2 per cent in 1995–6, and interest as a percentage of annual revenue reached 17.4 per cent (twice the 1990–1 rate) (Ontario Ministry of Finance, 1994, 1996b, 1996c).

By early 1993, the effects of the recession on the deficit could no longer be ignored. Persuaded it had hit the debt wall (with a projected deficit of $17 billion in the next fiscal year), Premier Bob Rae entered what he called the 'social contract tunnel of doom' (Rae, 1996: 208). Eschewing legislated wage restraints and hard bargaining approaches, the Premier opted to enlist the support of public-sector partners to enter into negotiations aimed at achieving a comprehensive economic agreement. In April, he proposed a Social Contract that would provide job security in exchange for cuts in public expenditures. When this failed, the government forced the issue by introducing the Social Contract Act (SCA). This represented a shift from a search for consensus to a strategy based on coercion. The SCA required negotiations in eight subsectors, including the OPS, to achieve targeted savings of $6 billion for the period 1 April 1993 to 31 March 1996. Each of the eight was given until 1 August to achieve a sectoral framework agreement. Local parties were given until 10 August to negotiate and ratify their agreements within the sectoral framework agreement. Failure to achieve an agreement by the imposed deadline would result in the imposition of the 'fail-safe' provision of the SCA, i.e., a three-year compensation freeze. If the compensation freeze failed to meet the savings target, employees would be required to take up to 12 unpaid days annually for three years (known as 'Rae days') (Fryer, 1995).

The sectoral framework agreement for the OPS was reached by the 1 August deadline. Among other things, it provided a virtual guarantee of no layoffs for permanent staff and prohibited merit increases or progress through the ranks for three years (and precluded counting service during the Social Contract period towards merit increases or grid movement following expiry of the Act). The sectoral agreement was implemented by a local appendix that specified a savings target of $132.8 million per fiscal year and identified various means of achieving savings, including unpaid days.

The day after these agreements were ratified, the government announced a shutdown of operations for 20 and 27 August and 3 September, and indicated these would constitute unpaid days. In response, OPSEU alleged this constituted a violation of the sectoral and local agreements. After the union failed to get a court injunction to block the shutdowns, the matter was submitted to expedited arbitration. In a decision issued on 1 September, the arbitrator found that the government's right to schedule shutdown days was subject to the requirement that it 'first consider other sources of savings before it acts on that right' *(Re Ontario Public Service Employees Union and Her Majesty The Queen in Right of Ontario,* 1993 [Shime]: 14). Having determined that other sources of savings had not been considered, he directed that the third government shutdown be postponed until a review of other cost savings was made. Subsequently, a mediated settlement reduced the number of unpaid days in the first year of the Social Contract from 8.5 to 6.5 days (and total unpaid days from 18.5 to 16.5 days over the three-year period).

Despite improvements in the economy beginning in 1993, the Social Contract was an albatross around the neck of the NDP government. In the end, the Social Contract was perceived as an attack on free collective bargaining and the sanctity of collective agreements. It alienated organized labour, including many of the NDP's strongest supporters among public- and private-sector unions, and precipitated a 'crisis of the left' (McBride, 1996). It led to the resignation of CAW president Buzz Hargrove from 'the prestigious Premier's Council on Economic Renewal and the Premier's advisory committee on labour-management relations' (Galt, 1993: A2), the resignation of Julie Davis, secretary-treasurer of the OFL, from the presidency of the Ontario NDP, and loss of financial contributions from organized labour (Galt and Mittelstaedt, 1993). The loss of political and financial support contributed to the downfall of the NDP in the 1995 election.

The Harris Years: 1995–1998

The Harris election campaign was based on what was described by the Tories as 'the Common Sense Revolution'. It was a plan to spur economic growth, investment, and job creation by stressing fundamental changes in the role of government, scaling back social services, and recognizing the need for fiscal responsibility (Ontario Progressive Conservative Party, 1994). The plan to restore consumer confidence and economic health can be seen as part of an international trend involving a transformation of the role of government. As described by Yergin and Stanislaw (1998: 13), 'the scope of government, the range of duties it takes on in the economy, is decidedly receding. The world over, governments have come to plan less, to own less, and to regulate less, allowing instead the market to expand.'

The Common Sense Revolution also represented a fundamental shift from the paternalism and pragmatism that characterized Tory rule for more than 40 years to a neo-liberal agenda similar to that of the Klein government in Alberta. In marked contrast to the Tory tradition in the province and the Rae government's failed attempt to involve unions in the negotiation of a Social Contract, there was no interest in accommodating labour's interests. On the contrary, because organized labour was perceived as a vested interest group and an impediment to economic renewal, the Harris government adopted a confrontational strategy (Hebdon and Warrian, 1999).

There were five pillars to the Common Sense Revolution. First, provincial income taxes would be cut by 30 per cent ($4 billion) over three years to spur consumer spending, investment, and job creation. Second, 'non-priority' government spending would be reduced 20 per cent over three years. This included initiatives such as downsizing the provincial government workforce by 15 per cent (13,000 jobs) and welfare reform. Third, government barriers to job creation, investment, and economic growth would be removed, e.g., by cutting high payroll taxes. With respect to labour law reform, the document promised to repeal the NDP's Bill 40 (which it described as 'a proven job killer') and to adopt a 'balanced labour law package that will restore balance between labour and management' (Ontario Progressive Conservative Party, 1994: 15).[1] Fourth, the size of government would be scaled back to do better with less, e.g., through the introduction of performance standards for government services, elimination of waste, operating government like a business, and selling assets such as the Liquor Commission. Fifth, a balanced budget would be adopted within the first mandate.

The new direction charted by Tories was influenced by developments elsewhere in Canada. Pointing to the policies adopted by Premier McKenna in New Brunswick and Premier Klein in Alberta, Harris observed: 'I believe the blueprint is there' (Blizzard, 1995: 96). That said, the Harris action plan was not a carbon copy of Klein's approach. Notwithstanding the similarities between Ontario's deficit and spending problems and those of the pre-Klein period, the Harris government, given the substantially higher tax rates in Ontario, stressed the need for tax relief and reducing government bureaucracy. Further, rather than adopting Klein's approach of across-the-board spending cuts, Harris 'vowed to cut the fat and leave health care and schools untouched' (ibid.).

Since winning the June 1995 election, the government has instituted its $4 billion tax cuts, reduced welfare benefits, introduced workfare, eliminated employment equity, and cut over 14,000 public service jobs. It has also introduced new labour laws and repealed or amended others (e.g., including repeal of most features of Bill 40). The substance and tone of these labour policy changes, coupled with shifts in social policies and budget cuts, have politicized labour relations and produced major confrontations between organized labour and the government. These confrontations have included: one-day, city-wide, rotating 'Days of Protest' spearheaded by the Ontario Federation of Labour; massive opposition by public-sector unions, including police and firefighters, over the way Bill 136 proposed to alter collective bargaining in the wake of amalgamations among municipalities, hospitals, and school boards (for non-teaching staff); and a two-week walkout by the province's five teacher unions over the introduction of Bill 160 (which, among other things, imposed increases in teacher workloads and removed issues such as class size from the scope of bargainable issues).

There has also been a significant improvement in the economy. When the Harris government assumed power, there were signs of an economic recovery. In 1997, there was robust growth with real GDP rising by 4.8 per cent. With tax cuts, rising personal income, increases in real consumer spending, and low interest rates, real economic growth in the province is projected to outpace all the G-7 major industrial countries between 1998 and 2000. The increase in government revenues, coupled with large spending cuts, improved the province's fiscal situation (see Table 3.1). Spending as a percentage of GDP fell to 16.4 per cent in 1997-8 (from 17.9 per cent in 1995-6), the deficit as a percentage of GDP fell to 1.5 per cent in 1997-8 (from 2.7 per cent in 1995-6), and the provincial debt as a percentage of GDP has stabilized around 30 per cent over the past three years. In dollar terms, the deficit fell to $3.2 billion in 1998-9 (less than half the 1995-6 deficit). The strength of the economy, along with a continuation of spending restraints, has led to projections of a balanced budget in 2000-1, with debt as a percentage of GDP falling to 28.5 per cent (Ontario Ministry of Finance, 1994, 1996b, 1996c, 1998).

The 1995–1996 Bargaining Round

In 1995, talks aimed at renewing the current collective agreement actually commenced while the NDP was still in power. Under the Social Contract Act, collective bargaining was permitted as long as any collective agreement did not conflict with the Act, i.e., provide for improvements in compensation. Although OPSEU sought an early settlement, the talks initially involved protracted negotiations to establish essential service agreements. By the time the parties turned to substantive issues, the NDP government was reluctant to enter into an agreement given the impending election and concerns about possibly binding a new government with its deal.

The approach of the Harris government represented a dramatic shift in bargaining strategy. This bargaining round was marked by a hybrid strategy based on legislative intervention and hard bargaining. There were two legislative initiatives. First, the government amended CECBA in 1995 by removing the successor rights provisions. This change would allow the government to privatize Crown agencies and services without requiring the transfer of the union's bargaining rights and the terms of the collective agreement to the new employer. It will be recalled that the 1992-3 collective agreement provided ironclad job security for permanent employees. The government's objective was to remove restrictions on its ability to privatize and downsize the OPS. As well, there appears to have been pressure on the provincial government to institute this change from sectors likely to be affected by privatization and devolution, i.e., hospitals and municipalities.

The second legislative change that concerned public servants involved threats to their pension rights. Specifically, Bill 26, the Savings and Restructuring Act,

1996, would exempt 'the government from the plan wind-up provision of the *Pension Benefits Act* in the case of a mass layoff' (Lancaster's Collective Agreement Reporter, 1996: 1). Given the government's intention to cut 13,000 jobs, the new law would limit employee benefit entitlements:

> under s. 69 of the province's *Pension Benefits Act (PBA)*, the Superintendent of Pensions for Ontario has the power to order a wind-up of a pension plan . . . [including] situations where a significant number of plan members cease being employed by the employer, or where a significant portion of the employer's business is discontinued. (Ibid.).

The practical effect of the legal change is that the Superintendent is precluded from directing the government to top up benefits of members in the event the pension plan is wound up. Bill 26 vests this power exclusively in cabinet.[2] Legislative intervention respecting pensions and successor rights, combined with the government's retrenchment plans, galvanized support for strike action by OPSEU members.

It is noteworthy, as well, that the government never seriously considered removing Crown employees' right to strike and restoring compulsory arbitration. The government felt that a strike-based system was the best way of controlling labour costs in the long run. As well, the newly elected government considered the OPS talks as an early opportunity to affirm its mandate and beat back any challenge from labour. Just as the NDP government had concluded that the OPS agreement was too expensive (e.g., job guarantees, redeployment language, and COLA), the Harris government seemed determined to tackle these issues firmly and aggressively.

The government seemed quite confident it could successfully implement a hard bargaining strategy. This appears to have been based on several factors. First, the union had never directed an OPS strike and there was considerable doubt it could muster support for a strike. This perspective was not shaken by what was regarded as a 'soft' strike mandate (about 66 per cent of the 71 per cent participating in the vote rejected the government's final offer). Second, there was strong public support for the government's mandate for change. Given OPSEU's poor public image, the union would be unable to garner public support for its position. Third, the government appeared indignant over OPSEU's apparent lack of respect for its mandate and the union's decision to challenge directly its agenda. For the government, the talks represented a test of its resolve to implement the Common Sense Revolution. The government was determined to achieve a successful outcome that would set the tone for the rest of the public sector.

The OPSEU objective was to gain enhanced job security by enshrining successor rights in the collective agreement. Failing that, the union would seek employment stability requiring job guarantees for privatized workers without reductions in pay, benefits, and accrued seniority. It was also seeking improvements in bumping rights and severance and pension packages. Considering their respective positions, the parties were on a collision course. Of the 67,000 members in the OPS unit, about 55,000 were eligible to strike (the remainder were designated as essential). On 26 February 1996, approximately half of the employees eligible to strike commenced picketing. Two days later, the remainder joined the strike. The staggered approach to the strike was an attempt to pressure the government to negotiate and to avoid losing public sympathy by withdrawing all services immediately (Mittelstaedt, 1996a).

Initially, the massive picketing across the province was disruptive. In and around Queen's Park, it took awhile to adjust to the picket lines at government offices. In the early stages of the strike, there was no progress in the talks. Indeed, during the first two weeks of the strike, the parties spent much of their time arguing about the adequacy of essential service agreements and little attention was directed at resolving key contract issues (Rusk, 1996d). In the third week of the dispute, a mediator, John Mather, entered the talks. Following the tabling of a new offer to kick-start negotiations by Dave Johnson, the Management Board chairman, and a mediator-imposed news blackout, the talks intensified and progress was made (Rusk, 1996e). However, the talks hit a snag over the issue of bumping rights.

As in most high-profile public-sector strikes, both sides engaged in extensive media campaigns before and during the dispute to sway public opinion. Prior to the strike, the government ran newspaper and radio advertisements describing its contract offer as fair and reasonable. In addition to seeking public support, the campaign appeared to be aimed at persuading moderate OPSEU members to accept the government's proposal. For its part, OPSEU adopted a $600,000 radio and television campaign highlighting its proposals to reduce government expenditures (Rusk, 1996b). Over the course of the dispute, the parties frequently skirmished over the costs associated with their respective contract proposals.

The chief spokespersons for the parties acquitted themselves well in the public limelight. Leah Casselman, the recently elected president of OPSEU, stated the Tories were out to crush the union and set the tone for bargaining elsewhere in the public sector. She made it clear the union was prepared to fight the bully tactics of the Harris government. The OPSEU media campaign stressed that the strike was not about money but the fair treatment of public servants, that is, the need to cushion the effect of displacement for long-time employees and to maintain the rights of employees whose jobs are privatized. She also portrayed the dispute in broader terms by arguing that the Tories' deficit-slashing agenda represented a threat to the quality of public services such as health and education. This perspective was bolstered early in the strike when the government cut $400 million in education spending and school boards issued thousands of layoff notices (Mittelstaedt, 1996b). Throughout the dispute, Casselman demonstrated strong leadership in her dealings with the media and this no doubt contributed to maintaining solidarity on the picket lines. Notwithstanding their inexperience with strikes, the financial burden involved, and the severity of picketing in winter, the overwhelming majority of OPSEU members looked to Casselman for guidance. Although the government attempted to weaken rank-and-file support for the strike by announcing the number of strikers crossing picket lines was rising, it appears that only about 10 per cent of strikers did so. There can be no doubt the union effectively managed the strike.

For its part, the government tried to capitalize on the public's antipathy towards 'big labour' by portraying OPSEU as an interest group opposed to the newly elected government's reform program. Johnson appeared to have a clear vision of what he wanted to achieve. He stressed the need for a settlement that would maintain the government's ability to restructure, that would fall within his projected cost of a collective agreement, and that would be in the interests of taxpayers. Perceiving OPSEU to be a weak union, the government appeared to have as its objective an agreement on its terms without a strike. Failing an agreement, however, there did not appear to be a downside risk to waiting the union out. On the one hand, a strike by Crown employees would not attract the degree of public attention as would a strike involving garbage collection or teachers (especially where essential services were protected). Further, there would be cost savings accruing as the strike dragged on. (It is estimated the salary savings amounted to $200 million.)

The first-ever strike by Crown employees lasted five weeks. Several factors contributed to its length. At the outset, there appeared to be a miscalculation about the likelihood of a strike. Although negotiators for Management Board felt a strike was inevitable, the government doubted OPSEU would get a strike mandate, let alone initiate strike action. Contrary to both Management Board and government expectations that a strike might, at best, last up to two weeks, OPSEU succeeded in maintaining membership support for five weeks. The show of solidarity appears to have been aided by the media coverage the union received and its efforts to keep members informed on a daily basis. Efforts by the government to undermine the strike with daily tallies of the number of strikebreakers were not successful.

Most importantly, the government's demeanour reassured many OPSEU members they were doing the right thing. The strike was largely defensive in nature. The government was seen as the protagonist, having resorted to legislative fiat to strip union members of successor rights and pension benefits, and remained steadfast in its determination to slash the size of the OPS. The threat to job and income security angered Crown employees and enabled union leaders to mobilize support for strike action based on restoring their rights and achieving a fair settlement. Crown employees recognized their jobs were on the line and developed a shared vision that a strong united front was the only means of achieving their bargaining objectives. Consistent with Wheeler's (1985) theory of industrial conflict, all the 'hot house' facilitating factors for aggressive collective action against the employer were present—a common cause, a shared perception of the likelihood of success, and a belief that collective action was required to be successful. In addition, the labour movement, still bristling over the repeal of Bill 40, eagerly provided moral and financial support to prevent the government from steamrolling over OPSEU.

The length of the strike can also be attributed to some marked differences between these negotiations and previous OPS bargaining rounds. For one thing, the Harris government is more ideologically driven than previous governments in terms of its view of unions and its overall political agenda. While this was well known, OPSEU may have underestimated the government's commitment to its position or its steadfastness. In addition, unlike prior OPS bargaining rounds, negotiators for Management Board did not have the customary broad mandate and autonomy to make decisions at the bargaining table. This tended to slow down the bargaining process.

At the same time, there was little public pressure to settle. Outside of some problems maintaining essential services, e.g., psychiatric hospitals and corrections, the parties appear to have adjusted to the effects of the strike after two weeks. On the whole, the strike did not have a significant and negative impact on the public. The government never seriously considered abandoning its tough bargaining strategy in favour of back-to-work legislation. Indeed, the government was prepared to let the strike run its course to achieve a settlement consistent with its bargaining objectives. Given the absence of strong political pressure for a settlement and the savings achieved in wages and salaries, the strike had a salutary effect on the net cost of the final settlement for the government.

A noteworthy and parallel development to the OPSEU strike was the first contract negotiations between Management Board and the Association of Management, Administrative and Professional Crown Employees of Ontario (AMAPCEO), which had been voluntarily recognized by the government as the bargaining agent for the previously excluded employees under the CECBA. The voluntary recognition agreement provided for first contract arbitration of outstanding contract issues. The timing of the settlement is significant for two reasons. First, an interim job security agreement, which was reached on 6 March about one week after the OPSEU strike began, contained 'reasonable effort' language with respect to privatization. Thus, AMAPCEO achieved contract language that OPSEU was out on strike to achieve. The government announced the settlement publicly to demonstrate its ability to bargain constructively. Second, it appears the government attempted to use the AMAPCEO agreement as a lever in the OPSEU talks, i.e., to isolate OPSEU. However, the agreement did not hasten an early settlement of the OPSEU strike. Nor did it hasten a collective agreement for AMAPCEO. Even though the interim job security agreement was to be dovetailed into a collective agreement at a later date, AMAPCEO remained without a collective agreement until May 1998 despite having the option of first-contract arbitration.[3]

The final OPS settlement, which covered the period 1 January 1994 to 31 December 1998, reveals job security provisions were weakened through the elimination of the guaranteed job offer provision. However, OPSEU secured 'some protection against privatization, improved bumping rights for employees receiving notice of layoff, and increased benefits for those employees who eventually lose their jobs through downsizing' (Lancaster's Collective Agreement Reporter, 1996: 1). The collective agreement also established a job registry 'to make redeployment to available vacancies a viable option for surplus employees' by creating a 'system for tracking vacancies throughout the Ontario Public Service' (ibid., 2). The registry is the responsibility of the Central Employee Relations Committee (a joint committee dealing with matters of mutual concern for the entire OPS). In light of the historic importance of the strike, it is useful to consider the key job security issues in greater detail.

Successor Rights

To fill the void left by the legal removal of successor rights, the collective agreement contains a provision requiring the government to make a 'reasonable effort' to ensure employees are offered jobs under similar terms of employment by the new employer. If the new employer is not prepared to offer 85 per cent of the employee's salary or to recognize the employee's seniority and service, the employee can exercise rights pursuant to the redundancy provisions of the collective agreement. At the time of the settlement, there was some uncertainty about how much protection this would give employees and how much effort would be required for the government to comply with the provision. This provision has turned out to be a serious problem for the government. In a series of arbitration awards, the Grievance Settlement Board found the government was shirking its responsibility to employees by failing to make reasonable efforts when attempting to privatize operations (e.g., highway maintenance, collection services, and mail distribution at Queen's Park). Specifically, the GSB held that 'reasonable effort' requires extensive discussion between the government and OPSEU, as well as effective negotiations by the government to secure employment for employees whose jobs are being privatized.

The two leading cases were decided by arbitrator William Kaplan and dealt with the transfer and closure of facilities providing residential and other services to developmentally handicapped adults and the awarding of highway maintenance contracts for provincial highways in the southwestern part of the province.[4] In the awards, the employer was directed to adhere to the following principles in satisfying its obligation to make reasonable efforts.[5] First, reasonable effort obligations must commence as soon as the decision to divest has been made. Second, OPSEU must be involved in discussions with the relevant ministry about how the ministry proposes to meet its obligation to make a reasonable effort. Such discussions must commence immediately following the decision to divest. Third, in negotiated transfer situations, the government must do more than simply inquire into whether the new employer is interested in hiring a public servant. The government must engage in meaningful negotiations with the new employer. Fourth, the government must revise its Human Resource Factor (HRF) to take into account differences in bids for government services and to ensure that it is consistent with its obligation to make reasonable efforts to help find jobs for public servants. In assessing overall bids, the HRF is a measure designed to assess the elements of the employment offers to be made to public servants. Fifth, in tendering situations, the government is to negotiate with the successful bidder in an attempt to help public servants find jobs and/or improve the terms and conditions of jobs offered. Sixth, the government should be prepared to use savings from severance payments that would no longer be required to offer financial incentives to new employers to hire public servants. Seventh, the government must keep careful records of its reasonable efforts and all surplus activity arising out of disposition.

As a result of the GSB rulings, numerous privatization initiatives were put on hold and a freeze was placed on issuing surplus notices to employees. Whereas these decisions indicate that OPSEU members have substantial job security protection under their collective agreement, the problem remains that the government has shown an unwillingness to take these steps unless ordered to do so. By the same token, the 'reasonable effort' criterion has been viewed as such an impediment to privatization that the government has considered legislation to override the requirement (Mackie, 1998a).

Bumping

Another contentious matter in negotiations was the scope of bumping rights and the number of permissible bumps. At issue was how to achieve job security protection without creating administrative chaos in light of impending job cuts. Under the 1992–3 collective agreement, chain bumping was permitted, but the exercise of bumping rights was restricted to the same or a lower job classification in the ministry 'an employee works in and to jobs within 40 kilometres of the current place of work' (Rusk, 1996f: A4). OPSEU sought to retain an unlimited chain bumping clause in the collective agreement, establish bumping rights within a reasonable commuting distance (often beyond 40 km), and expand the scope of the provision to allow surplus employees to bump into other ministries. Management Board, on the other hand, wanted to limit the number of bumps following the issuance of layoff notices. In its final offer prior to the strike, the employer proposed a two-bump limit. Considering the prospect of large-scale downsizing, OPSEU was seeking to expand job security for senior members while Management Board was seeking administrative flexibility (Rusk, 1996a, 1996c). In the end, the number of bumps was limited at two and the scope of bumping was expanded across ministries and beyond the 40-kilometre radius of the employee's headquarters in specified circumstances.

Severance

Severance pay also figured prominently in negotiations. In a bid to avert a strike, the government's final offer included a provision of double severance pay for Crown employees who are laid off. The offer provided two weeks' severance pay for each year of service to a maximum of 52 weeks' pay (the initial offer was for one week for each year of service to a maximum of 26 weeks' pay). OPSEU favoured incentive packages based on early departure and early retirement incentives, e.g., packages similar to those offered to Ontario Hydro employees and federal public servants. In each of these instances, the maximum buyout approached two years' pay. Generally, buyout incentives are more generous than severance plans. The government opposed the union's approach because it was too costly and would restrict its ability to manage downsizing. The government wanted to avoid situations 'with job vacancies in ongoing programs and surplus employees who would still have to be laid off' (Rusk, 1996b: A6). The final settlement reflected the government's final offer on severance pay. In addition, the settlement provided for pension improvements, including expanded pension bridging options and a reopener under the Factor 80 program (based on age plus years of service) to assist employees subject to layoff to take early retirement.

In the final analysis, it is difficult to conclude that the strike produced a winner and a loser. The union gave up provisions such as the guaranteed job provision, the COLA, and joint determination of job classifications. Although OPSEU was unsuccessful in enshrining successor rights in the collective agreement, the GSB awards indicate that the 'reasonable effort' provision provides significant job protection against privatization and, in some respects, may even enhance employee rights (i.e., reasonable effort may provide greater recognition of employees' seniority and service than successor rights). For its part, even though the government appeared to miscalculate OPSEU's determination and ability to mount an effective strike, the final result appeared to be a cost-effective settlement (Mittelstaedt, 1996c). It also gave the government greater flexibility to manage the downsizing of the OPS, save the 'reasonable effort' clause.

To the extent that the strike might be regarded as a stalemate reflects the inability of either side to garner decisive public sympathy. The strike did not significantly inconvenience the public and consequently there was not a pronounced public outcry. One public opinion poll reported that 87 per cent of the 500 respondents were not personally affected by the strike (Poling, 1996). A Decima Research poll found that 38 per cent of the respondents felt the union was 'being the most reasonable and fair-minded' in the dispute whereas 36 per cent expressed a similar view with respect to the government (Mittelstaedt and Abbate, 1996: A6).

The effect of the strike on the union as an institution was mostly positive. It had the effect of invigorating an organization that for decades had been traumatized by writing briefs and making submissions to interest arbitration. When the membership was confronted by threats to job security and a strong-willed government, legitimate questions were asked about the union's ability to mobilize rank-and-file members. In the end, the union demonstrated remarkable solidarity on the picket lines and achieved a settlement that was endorsed by 95 per cent of the membership. By the same token, there was divisiveness respecting strikers who crossed picket lines. However, given that the proportion who did so was relatively modest, this did not loom large in the overall picture.

Perhaps an even more unsettling and indeed embarrassing situation for OPSEU was the bargaining dispute with its staff employees' union, the Ontario Public Service Staff Union (OPSSU). Shortly after the OPS strike was settled, OPSEU announced plans to cut 51 staff positions (a 20 per cent reduction) and insisted on compensation concessions in response to its budgetary woes. Citing a current debt of $6 million, an outstanding debt related to the OPS strike ($25 million), and a projected drop in revenue from OPS downsizing, OPSEU's Casselman argued that the union needed to reduce spending by up to 25 per cent in its fight for survival (Girard, 1996c). The irony was not lost on OPSEU staff, who had worked hard in support of the OPS strike. The OPSSU denounced Casselman for adopting the same ruthless, cost-cutting tactics the Harris government employed during the OPS strike (Girard, 1996b). After months of fruitless negotiations, 97 per cent of OPSSU members voted in July to strike (Girard, 1996a). Following a three-week strike in September 1996, disappointed staff members, with 61.5 per cent voting in favour, ratified a settlement containing major concessions. To save the jobs of the 51 staff members slated for layoff, OPSSU agreed to 'the loss of employer pension contributions, the loss of a statutory holiday, three unpaid days off this Christmas and five next Christmas, the loss of vacation bonuses and other benefit reductions' (Girard, 1996d: A9).

Restructuring the OPS

The Harris government made good on its pledge to downsize government by eliminating over 14,000 jobs, or about 20 per cent of the OPS, between June 1995 and the end of 1997 (Brennan, 1998). In the process, the OPS has been consolidated over the past five years 'from 28 operating ministries and central agencies down to 16 ministries and three central agencies' (Government of Ontario, 1997: 1). In addition, in response to the recommendations of the Task Force on Agencies, Boards and Commissions (known as the Wood Reports), numerous government bodies have been eliminated, amalgamated, or transformed to achieve cost savings (Government Task Force, 1996, 1997a, 1997b).

In June 1995, steps were taken to transform the OPS based on the following vision of a public service organization (Government of Ontario, 1997: 1):

1. focused core business;
2. ensuring quality service to the public;
3. smaller and more flexible;
4. integrated and cohesive; and
5. accountable.

To achieve these goals, the government has been pursuing a business planning process, exploring alternative service delivery, introducing the latest technologies, re-engineering administrative processes, and developing performance measures. These developments are based on the notion of 'reinventing government' (Osborne and Gaebler, 1992) or what Warrian (1996) refers to as the 'new managerialism'.

In 1996, Management Board developed a framework for alternate service delivery based on a more businesslike, results-based approach to program delivery (Management Board Secretariat, 1996). The intent was to increase private-sector involvement through privatization, partnerships, and licensing/franchising arrangements. Accordingly, individual ministries began formulating business plans in which they identified the programs and activities comprising their core businesses and developed strategies for alternative service delivery. The alternative systems include the purchase of services from the private sector (e.g., translation services) and enhanced partnerships with the broader public sector (e.g., 400 staff from the Ministry of Agriculture and Rural Affairs were relocated at the University of Guelph to spur increased private-sector funding for agri-food research) (Government of Ontario, 1997). There have also been numerous private-sector partnerships. Examples of such initiatives include the Integrated Justice Program establishing electronic linkages among components of the justice system (i.e., police, Crown attorneys, courts, corrections, parole, and the private bar), a partnership with Teranet Land Information Inc. for electronic filing of real property registration,[6] and the Telecommunications Access Partnership (TAP) projects to increase Internet access in rural and remote communities by upgrading telecommunications (Government of Ontario, 1998).

In line with these initiatives, a 'Privatization Review Framework' was developed to assess government businesses on a case-by-case basis (Office of Privatization, 1997). One of the first candidates considered for privatization, the Metro Toronto Convention Centre, was rejected in 1998. Further, the key operations initially targeted for privatization by the Harris government—the Liquor Commission, TVO, and Ontario Hydro—have been sidestepped. With the exception of the $3.1 billion sale of the world's only electronic toll highway (Highway 407), privatization has been benign (Mackie, 1998b). It appears that both political considerations and the rulings of the GSB have inhibited a major privatization thrust.

In the wake of the 1999 provincial election, downsizing of the OPS will likely continue, albeit at a slower rate and with more emphasis on the devolution of services.[7] The downloading of services is also based on business plans for alternate service delivery developed by individual ministries. The initial announcements of government transfers affected thousands of OPS employees (Mackie, 1997: A7).

> The Community and Social Services Ministry will lose 1,524 of its 8,224 employees mainly through the transfer of social assistance workers delivering family benefits to the control of the municipalities, according to government projections.
>
> The Finance Ministry will lose 2,235 of its 5,100 employees, primarily through the shifting of responsibility for property assessment to the municipalities.
>
> The Health Ministry, with 10,428 employees, will move 4,500 off its payroll, mainly those working in psychiatric hospitals or other health-care agencies operating directly under the ministry, including ambulance services.

A number of other initiatives are in the planning stages. The province transferred to municipalities the title to water and sewage treatment facilities that were held by the Ontario Clean Water Agency, a Crown corporation. As well, the Ministry of Transportation will transfer control and funding of local transportation services to the municipalities (Government of Ontario, 1998). Since much of this activity involves offloading of services to other parts of the broader public sector, it is unlikely that layoffs will figure prominently in the transfers.

For the most part, the restructuring of the OPS has been based on a cost-reduction strategy rather than a comprehensive human resource strategy, i.e., an approach emphasizing that labour is 'not so much a cost to be cut but rather a resource to be effectively utilized and involved in the process of where and how to reduce costs' (Belman, Gunderson, and Hyatt, 1996: 6). The political imperative has been to cut the size of the OPS and to maximize cost savings quickly. Large-scale downsizing does, of course, have implications for human resource management, notably in the areas of skills training and development. A human resource strategy for OPS renewal will include a Human Resources Plan (HRP) for the Senior Management Group. Development of the HRP began in 1998 and is expected to receive approval before the end of the year. The transformation to a leaner and more integrated OPS, with a greater emphasis on alternative service delivery, has heightened the need to develop new skills. Accordingly, training for service managers will concentrate on areas such as 'program design, policy development . . . contract management . . . setting performance measures and tracking results' (Government of Ontario, 1997: 11).

Another major human resource management initiative is the overhaul of the job classification system in the OPS (known as the Bargaining Unit Overhaul Project or BUO). The system of job classifications—706 job classifications with 40,000 position specifications—was overhauled through six new job evaluation systems, one for each bargaining unit. This task was completed by the 31 May 1998 deadline and resulted in just under 8,000 new job classifications.

The BUO, which began in 1990 when the Rae government provided funding for it, was largely a response to the age of the system rather than a response to restructuring *per se*. Indicative of the obsolescence of the system were the thousands of outstanding classification grievances. Over the years, arbitration awards resulted in many new classifications being created (at higher wage rates) to deal with inconsistencies in the system. These inconsistencies often resulted because various ministries were permitted to interpret job categories since there was no central control over the evaluation system. From the government standpoint, there was a need to create consistent and defensible job descriptions across the OPS and improve compensation cost control. Both parties acknowledged the overhaul was needed because the job classification system was outdated for pay equity purposes.

It is noteworthy that the union's involvement in the overhaul of job classifications diminished as a result of changes in the 1994–8 collective agreement. Under the terms of the 1992–3 collective agreement, the parties agreed to a classification system overhaul with a target completion date of 31 December 1993. Appendix 13 of the collective agreement recognized the need 'for a long term solution based on a jointly developed overhaul of the bargaining unit job evaluation system' and stated that 'the parties will meet as soon as possible to agree on the joint process for undertaking the overhaul' (Collective Agreement, 1992–3: 142). It also established a moratorium on the referral of classification grievances to the GSB (the moratorium was extended to 1998). OPSEU assumed a joint role in the process for several years preceding the settlement of the OPS strike in March 1996.

The Harris government felt this approach was too slow and cumbersome. In an attempt to speed up the reform of the classification system, the joint process was rolled back in the 1994–8 collective agreement. This gave the government responsibility for developing the new job classification system and entitled the union to be consulted on an ongoing basis. As described in Appendix 7 (Collective Agreement, 1994–8: 156):

1. The parties agree as follows:
(b) The Employer shall continue and complete the development of the new classification system, including the six (6) new classification plans and as much as possible of the factor models and related work already jointly completed.
(c) The Employer will consult with the Union at each stage of the project and will attempt to reach consensus before moving on to the next stage. The Employer will provide to the Union an outline of the stages of the project and target date for completion.

The consultation process involved establishment of the Joint System Subcommittee (JSSC) of the Central Employee Relations Committee. Consultation with OPSEU included regular meetings and the exchange of information. As no consensus has been reached on the new system, OPSEU has retained its right to challenge it at a later date.

In September 1998 information sessions were held with employees and the new job descriptions were distributed. At that time, establishing wage rates for the new system was regarded as a major challenge for the upcoming negotiations.[8] In addition, pressure has arguably built up in recent years because of the moratorium on the arbitration of classification grievances until the new system is in place. As a result, some employees may feel they are currently misclassified. Under Appendix 7 of the 1994–8 collective agreement, employees can make complaints about being improperly classified. However, there is no effective dispute resolution mechanism for such complaints because the JSSC reviewing these disputes is comprised of an equal number of representatives from the government and OPSEU, and failing a majority vote, the complaint will not be successful.

Other Effects of Government Cost-Reduction Strategies

The adoption of cost-reduction strategies by recent governments has reflected top-down political decisions without meaningful union participation or input. The magnitude and manner in which downsizing has been implemented has had a spillover effect on other aspects of labour-management relations.

To begin with, government-OPSEU relations have become more adversarial. A turn for the worse began with the Social Contract and deteriorated further in the 1996 bargaining round when the government adopted a legislative/hard-bargaining strategy to maintain its flexibility to restructure the OPS. At the political level, there is virtually no relationship to speak of between the Premier and the president of OPSEU. Whereas former premiers, such as Bill Davis (1971–85), never appeared to covet close ties with OPSEU and relations were often strained, there nevertheless was a willingness to consult on matters of mutual interest.[9] In contrast, the Harris government has shown an antipathy towards OPSEU (and unions generally) and no willingness to consult on economic and social policy issues. It has steadfastly maintained its commitment to implement the Common Sense Revolution. Indeed, it has shown disdain for labour and other organizations opposed to its policies and programs.

At other levels, the effects of bargaining and restructuring have also been felt. Although a businesslike relationship has been maintained between negotiators for OPSEU and Management Board, the union's overall role in joint governance has diminished. Joint committees, such as the Central Employee Relations Committee and the ministry employee relations committees, continue to consult at the central and ministerial level on matters of mutual interest, including issues arising from the administration of the collective agreement. Further, similar committee structures have been established for the AMAPCEO bargaining unit. That said, the capacity of these committees to fulfil their mandate, i.e., to foster constructive and harmonious relations, has been eroded by the cost-reduction strategies initiated by the last two governments. The reliance on legislative fiat and hard bargaining to facilitate restructuring, coupled with the unilateral decision to downsize the OPS, has created a climate of mistrust, apprehension, and insecurity among union officials and Crown employees. The arbitration rulings documenting the government's failure to make reasonable efforts when embarking on privatization initiatives have reinforced these concerns.

In other respects, there is generally less union involvement in human resource management initiatives. Whereas the flexible work provisions (compressed workweek and job-sharing arrangements) embodied in the 1992–3 collective agreement have been retained, in areas such as labour adjustment and the overhaul of the job classification system OPSEU's role has declined as a result of changes made in the 1994–8 collective agreement. Fiscal constraints, downsizing, and the reconceptualization of the role of government have also had a significant impact on the perceptions and morale of individual Crown employees. The traditional perception of government employment as long-term, stable, and with opportunities for career advancement has given way to one based on employment insecurity, layoffs, and an increase in contingent employment arrangements. This change, which occurred in a relatively short time span and was accompanied by increasingly hostile labour-management relations, left many civil servants feeling betrayed and unappreciated.

Another indicator of a possible spillover effect of bargaining and restructuring on labour relations is whether grievance and arbitration activity has increased. Unfortunately, there are two broad difficulties associated with conducting such an analysis. First, we have been unable to elicit data from the GSB. Second, although Management Board has compiled grievance statistics from the individual ministries, these data do not lend themselves to analysis of trends in grievance activity.[10] Notwithstanding these difficulties, it is possible to make some general observations from these data and other sources.

Table 3.2 summarizes total grievance activity by year and reveals three identifiable characteristics. First, the number of grievances fell during the period coinciding with the Social Contract (1993–4 to 1995–6). This pattern appears to be linked to the restrictions placed on compensation increases under the SCA and the moratorium on job classification grievances. Second, there was a dramatic rise in grievances in 1996, the year of the OPS strike. It is difficult to attribute this increase to strike-related grievances as they comprised a relatively modest share of total grievance activity (119 strike-related grievances or 2.2 per cent of the total).[11] A more likely explanation for the increase appears to be growing concern about job security. Even though precise figures are not available for the earlier years, there is general agreement that grievances over job security and management rights have increased. These issues accounted for nearly 30 per cent of all grievances in 1996 and 1997. This is hardly surprising given the magnitude of the downsizing of the OPS and the union's success in challenging management decisions in high-profile cases, e.g., the Shime and Kaplan awards. Third, there was a major decline in grievances in 1997. As this was a non-bargaining-round year, grievance activity was broadly similar to the levels recorded in the early 1990s. There also seems to have been a drop in grievances related to discrimination/harassment and health and safety in recent years. This may reflect the parties greater familiarity with these issues and their ability to use joint committees to prevent and resolve such disputes.

Table 3.2: Annual Grievance Activity

Year	No. of Grievances	% Change
1990–1	3,171	–
1991–2	3,136	– 1.1%
1992–3	3,848	+ 22.7%
1993–4	2,672	– 30.6%
1994–5	2,669	– 0.1%
1995–6*	2,168	– 18.8%
1996	5,437	+150.8%
1997	3,239	– 40.4%

* Annualized estimate for fiscal year is based on data for nine months (i.e., 1,626 grievances between 1 April and 31 December 1995).

Summary and Prognosis

The 1990s witnessed a severe economic recession, a substantial rise in budget deficits, and significant political swings, beginning with the NDP election victory in 1990 and followed by the Conservative triumph in 1995. These developments contributed to the upheaval in labour relations. Collective bargaining experienced two major shocks—the Social Contract and the first Ontario Public Service strike in history. The OPS strike was fought over job security issues related to the government's decision to embark on massive downsizing. Whereas the NDP government initially sought to enlist OPSEU (and other unions) in a new partnership based on information disclosure and assurances of job security, the Harris government has substantially reduced the size of the OPS and eschewed a conciliatory tone in favour of confrontational bargaining.

There have also been significant changes to OPSEU. Although the effects of restructuring have altered the size and composition of the union, the OPS strike transformed it into a more vibrant organization. Under the system of compulsory interest arbitration, the membership was passive, the leadership was not required to make hard choices, and dissatisfaction with bargaining outcomes was attributed to arbitrators. After gaining the right to strike, the membership became more active and the leadership had to develop sophisticated bargaining and strike strategies. The 1996 OPS strike demonstrated the increased militancy of Crown employees and the union leadership's ability to mobilize members and manage an effective strike. For Crown employees, the transformation of the OPS has led to stronger union commitment and weaker employer commitment.

Conclusion

The Harris government's determination to stay the course and the renewal of OPSEU appeared to put the parties on a collision course in efforts to achieve a new collective agreement in early 1999. In March 1999, however, the parties reached a three-year agreement. The final settlement involved significant compromises by both sides and reflected their desire to avoid another work stoppage. It appears the government did not want to risk a strike in advance of an election call and union members were apprehensive about the prospect of another lengthy walkout. The settlement included the first wage increase for Crown employees in six years (1 per cent, 1.35 per cent, and 1.95 per cent in successive years and pay adjustments for some classifications affecting about 5,400 employees). The wage settlement was achieved after OPSEU scaled back its demands and the government increased its offer at the last minute and dropped its proposal to establish merit pay (i.e., 'pay for performance'). Job security provisions were not significantly altered. There was an extension of the early retirement plan for employees declared surplus through 31 March 2002. In addition, OPSEU retained bumping rights, but did not improve protection for temporary or contract employees. With respect to grievance resolution, the parties agreed to a new mediation/arbitration process to alleviate grievance backlogs, but did not modify the procedure for classification grievances in any significant way (Mackie, 1999; OPSEU, 1999).

Since the 1999 settlement took place in an election year, it would not be prudent to consider it a harbinger of a new direction in labour-management relations. As in the recent past, labour-management relations in the OPS will continue to be shaped by economic and political forces. The province's economy and fiscal situation have improved considerably in recent years. As a result, policy-makers have shifted their attention to balanced budgets and whether budget surpluses should be allocated to debt reduction or spending increases. In all likelihood, spending increases will be targeted at high-priority areas to reap political dividends. This was illustrated by the major cash infusion for health care in advance of the 1999 provincial election. With the re-election of the Tories, there will be continued fiscal vigilance and support for redefining the role of government. Compared to its first term in office, the Harris government may adopt a modified retrenchment strategy in response to improvements in the province's fiscal situation. Under this scenario, expenditure reductions and restructuring would continue at a slower pace, the size of the OPS would contract further, and job security and labour adjustment would remain dominant collective bargaining areas.

The major collective bargaining challenge faced by the parties will be their willingness and ability to accommodate change in a newly restructured OPS. Improvements in the province's economy should increase the opportunities for accommodation. However, absent major policy changes and a more conciliatory tone from the Harris government, there is little likelihood that relations with OPSEU will improve. The Tory election platform and the rhetoric directed at unions generally suggest that the prospects for more conciliatory government-OPSEU relations are slim. It is reasonable to expect that collective bargaining will remain tense and difficult. A downturn in the economy would compound these difficulties.

Notes

The author wishes to acknowledge the valuable research assistance provided by Barbara Markham and Brad Ridge. As well, a debt of gratitude is extended to management and union officials who participated in interviews and co-operated with requests for information.

1. For an alternative and balanced assessment of the possible effect of Bill 40 or, more precisely, strike replacement legislation on investment, see Jain and Singh (1997).
2. By way of background, the legislation came after the union staged a successful court challenge of the government's right to achieve the same end by cabinet order.
3. A tentative agreement was reached on all but five issues. The terms of the settlement were approved by 96 per cent of AMAPCEO members participating in

the ratification vote and the agreement was implemented following ratification. The outstanding issues that have been submitted to arbitration include: (1) salary/wages, including merit; (2) hours of work; (3) compressed workweek, flexible hours, and job-sharing; (4) reclassification to another bargaining unit; and (5) compensation option credit, including conversion to cash value.

4. *Re The Crown in right of Ontario (Ministry of Community and Social Services) and Ontario Public Service Employees Union* (1997), 64 L.A.C. (4th) 22 (Kaplan); *Re The Crown in the right of Ontario (Ministry of Transportation) and Ontario Public Service Employees Union* (1997), 64 L.A.C. (4th) 38 (Kaplan).

5. The government submitted the GSB decision in *Re Ministry of Transportation, supra,* for judicial review. The Divisional Court dismissed the case in November 1997.

6. Although Teranet is the most heralded public-private partnership, it came into being prior to the Harris government. The establishment of this strategic alliance began in 1987 and Teranet was incorporated in 1991.

7. Devolution has always been part of the government's reorganization plan to identify core businesses and develop alternative delivery systems (Government of Ontario, 1997). More recently it has involved downloading of services to municipalities in exchange for centralized control over education.

8. In the renewal collective agreement, the parties agreed to defer implementation of the new system.

9. Premier Davis never respected OPSEU or its officials in the same way as he respected other labour leaders. As a result, OPSEU was not perceived as a major player from a labour relations perspective (Roberts, 1994).

10. There are four data limitations. First, some grievance statistics have been collected by fiscal year (1990–1 to 1994–5) and others by calendar year (e.g., 1996 and 1997). Second, there is a small gap in the time series, i.e., grievance statistics are not available for either fiscal year 1995–6 or calendar year 1995. The only figures available corresponding to this period are figures for May 1994–31 March 1995 and 1 April 1995–31 December 1995. An estimate for fiscal year 1995–6 has been made by prorating the number of grievances between April and December 1995. Third, the type of grievance is not available for all years and the classification of grievances is not standardized. Fourth, there is no assurance that the reporting procedures of individual ministries were standardized.

11. These grievances deal with numerous issues, including premium payments, discipline, retaliation/harassment, and alteration of work schedules.

References

Adams, George W. 1981. 'The Ontario Experience with Interest Arbitration: Problems in Detecting Policy', in Joseph M. Weiler, ed., *Interest Arbitration* (Toronto: Carswell), 135–74.

Arthurs, H.W. 1971. *Collective Bargaining by Public Employees in Canada: Five Models.* Ann Arbor: Institute of Labor and Industrial Relations, University of Michigan—Wayne State University.

Belman, Dale, Morley Gunderson, and Douglas Hyatt. 1996. 'Public Sector Employment Relations in Transition', in Belman, Gunderson, and Hyatt, eds, *Public Sector Employment* (Madison, Wis.: Industrial Relations Research Association), 1–20.

Blizzard, Christina. 1995. *Right Turn: How the Tories Took Ontario*. Toronto: Dundurn Press.

Brennan, Richard. 1998. 'Harris Axe Hits 14,330 and He's Not Done', *Hamilton Spectator*, 22 Jan., E7.

Collective Agreement. 1992–3. Management Board of Cabinet and Ontario Public Service Employees Union.

———. 1994–8. Management Board of Cabinet and Ontario Public Service Employees Union.

Dyck, Rand. 1997. 'The Socio-Economic Setting of Ontario Politics', in Graham White, ed., *The Government and Politics of Ontario*, 5th edn (Scarborough, Ont.: Nelson Canada), 19–48.

Fryer, John. 1995. 'Provincial Public Sector Labour Relations', in Gene Swimmer and Mark Thompson, eds, *Public Sector Collective Bargaining in Canada* (Kingston: IRC Press), 341–67.

Gagnon, Georgette, and Dan Rath. 1991. *Not Without Cause: David Peterson's Fall from Grace*. Toronto: HarperCollins.

Galt, Virginia. 1990, 'Provincial Employees Win Right to 5 Months Notice of Job Changes', *Globe and Mail*, 26 May, A14.

———. 1993. 'CAW Cuts Support to NDP', *Globe and Mail*, 21 Aug., A1, A2.

——— and Martin Mittelstaedt. 1993. 'Ontario NDP President Quits Over Labour's Painful Divorce', *Globe and Mail*, 23 Nov., A1, A7.

Girard, Daniel. 1996a. 'OPSEU Staff Back Strike Over Layoffs, Benefit Cuts', *Toronto Star*, 23 June, A12.

———. 1996b. 'OPSEU in New Strike—By its Own Employees', *Toronto Star*, 3 Sept., A6.

———. 1996c. 'OPSEU Employees to Vote on Tentative Agreement', *Toronto Star*, 24 Sept., A8.

———. 1996d. 'OPSEU Staff Vote in Favor of Deal to End Three-Week Strike', *Toronto Star*, 25 Sept., A9.

Government of Ontario. 1997. *Building the Ontario Public Service for the Future*. Toronto: OPS Restructuring Secretariat.

———. 1998. *Ontario Government Business Plans 1998–1999*. Toronto: Management Board of Cabinet.

Government Task Force on Agencies, Boards and Commissions. 1996. *Backgrounder*. Toronto: Government of Ontario, May.

———. 1997a. *Report on Operational Agencies*. Toronto: Government of Ontario, Jan.

———. 1997b. *Report on Restructuring Regulatory & Adjudicative Agencies*. Toronto: Government of Ontario, Feb.

Hebdon, R. 1995. 'The Freezing Effect of Public Sector Bargaining: The Case of Crown Employees', *Journal of Collective Negotiations in the Public Sector* 24, 3: 233–54.

——— and Peter Warrian. 1999. 'Coercive Bargaining: Public Sector Restructuring Under the Ontario Social Contract, 1993–1996', *Industrial and Labor Relations Review* 52, 2 (Jan.): 196–212.

Jain, Harish C., and Parbudyal Singh. 1997. 'Strike Replacement Laws in Canada, Mexico and the United States: Policies and Issues', *Canadian Employment and Labour Law Journal* 5, 3: 287–320.

Lancaster Labour Law Reports. 1990. 'Provincial Government Employees Win Five Months' Notice of Closures, Relocations, Contracting Out', *Contract Clauses* 14, 6 (June): 1–2.

——. 1992. *Contract Clauses* 16, 1 (Jan.): 2.

Lancaster's Collective Agreement Reporter. 1996. 'OPSEU and Harris Government Settle Contract After First-Ever Provincial Government Employees' Strike in Ontario', 20, 3–4 (Mar.-Apr.): 1–4.

Lancaster's Pension and Benefit Law Reporter. 1996. 'Dust-up Over Wind-up: OPSEU Battles Harris Government Over Move to Exempt Pension Plan from Wind-up Provisions', 13, 12 (Jan.-Feb.): 1–3.

Little, Walter. 1969. *Report on Collective Bargaining in the Ontario Government Service*. Toronto: Queen's Printer.

McBride, Stephen. 1996. 'The Continuing Crisis of Social Democracy: Ontario's Social Contract in Perspective', *Studies in Political Economy* 50 (Summer): 65–93.

Mackie, Richard. 1997. 'Ontario to Shed 6,000 Workers', *Globe and Mail*, 10 July, A1, A7.

——. 1998a. 'Job Protection in Peril, OPSEU Head Warns', *Globe and Mail*, 19 Mar., A8.

——. 1998b. 'Unloading Key Assets Not Harris Priority', *Globe and Mail*, 27 May, A5.

Management Board Secretariat. 1996. *Alternative Service Delivery Framework*. Toronto: Government of Ontario.

Mittelstaedt, Martin. 1996a. 'OPSEU Plans Selective Strikes', *Globe and Mail*, 23 Feb., A1

——. 1996b. 'Quick Resolution of Ontario Strike Remains Remote', *Globe and Mail*, 11 Mar., A2.

——. 1996c. 'OPSEU Members Vote to End Strike', *Globe and Mail*, 1 Apr., A3.

—— and Gay Abbate. 1996. 'Ontario Fears Unrest in Jails', *Globe and Mail*, 1 Mar., A6.

Office of Privatization. 1997. *The Ontario Privatization Review Framework*. Toronto: Government of Ontario.

Ontario Ministry of Finance. 1994. *1994 Ontario Budget*.

——. 1996a. *1996 Ontario Economic Outlook and Fiscal Review*.

——. 1996b. *1996 Ontario Budget*.

——. 1996c. *Province of Ontario Annual Report*.

——. 1997. *1997 Ontario Economic Outlook and Fiscal Review*.

——. 1998. *1998 Ontario Budget*.

Ontario Ministry of Labour. 1992. *Ontario Collective Bargaining Review*. Toronto: Office of Collective Bargaining Information.

Ontario Progressive Conservative Party. 1994. *The Common Sense Revolution*. Toronto: Progressive Conservative Party of Ontario.

Osborne, David, and Ted Gaebler. 1992. *Reinventing Government: How the Entrepreneurial Spirit is Transforming the Public Sector*. New York: Addison-Wesley.

Poling, Jim. 1996. 'Prisons at Point of Turning Violent', *Calgary Herald*, 29 Feb., A3.

Ponak, Allen. 1982. 'Public-Sector Collective Bargaining', in John Anderson and Morley Gunderson, eds, *Union-Management Relations in Canada* (Don Mills, Ont.: Addison-Wesley), 343–78.

Rae, Bob. 1996. *From Protest to Power: Personal Reflections on a Life in Politics*. Toronto: Penguin.

Re Ontario Public Service Employees Union and Her Majesty The Queen in Right of Ontario, 1 Sept. 1993, unreported (Shime).

Re The Crown in right of Ontario (Ministry of Community and Social Services) and Ontario Public Service Employees Union (1997), 64 L.A.C. (4th) 22 (Kaplan).

Re The Crown in the right of Ontario (Ministry of Transportation) and Ontario Public Service Employees Union (1997), 64 L.A.C. (4th) 38 (Kaplan).

Roberts, Wayne. 1994. *Don't Call Me Servant*. North York, Ont.: Ontario Public Service Employees Union.

Rusk, James. 1996a. 'Ontario Sweetens Severance Offer to Workers', *Globe and Mail*, 7 Feb., A6.

——. 1996b. 'Contract Dispute Turns into an Ad Duel', *Globe and Mail*, 13 Feb., A10.

——. 1996c. 'Job Security at Heart of OPSEU Walkout', *Globe and Mail*, 27 Feb., A1, A5.

——. 1996d. 'Impatience Shows as OPSEU Strike Continues', *Globe and Mail*, 6 Mar., A8.

——. 1996e. 'OPSEU Strike Talks on Track', 18 Mar., A3.

——. 1996f. 'OPSEU Talks Falter on Bumping Rights', *Globe and Mail*, 25 Mar., A4.

Voos, Paula. 1994. 'An Economic Perspective on Contemporary Trends in Collective Bargaining', in Voos, ed., *Contemporary Collective Bargaining in the Private Sector* (Madison, Wis.: Industrial Relations Research Association), 1–23.

Walkom, Thomas. 1994. *Rae Days: The Rise and Follies of the NDP*. Toronto: Key Porter Books.

Warrian, Peter. 1996. *Hard Bargain*. Toronto: McGilligan Books.

Wheeler, Hoyt. 1985. *Industrial Conflict: An Integrative Theory*. Columbia: University of South Carolina Press.

Workplace Information Directorate. 1996. Human Resources Development Canada, special data request.

Yergin, Daniel, and Joseph Stanislaw. 1998. *The Commanding Heights*. New York: Simon & Schuster.

Chapter 4

Fiscal Restraint, Legislated Concessions, and Labour Relations in the Manitoba Civil Service, 1988–1997

Paul Phillips and Carolina Stecher

Introduction

In 1996, Manitoba recorded the third highest loss in working days due to industrial disputes in the province's history. Disputes in the public sector were a major component of the sharp increase in strike activity in 1996, though most did not directly involve civil servants. Godard (1998: 15) concludes that the government's policies and actions contributed directly and indirectly, by the creation of 'a climate which made the labour movement increasingly insecure and employers increasingly emboldened . . . motivated by a belief that they would help facilitate public sector cutbacks.'

The first major question this assessment raises is the extent to which these cutbacks were motivated by an increasingly neo-liberal political agenda as opposed to a perception of fiscal crisis engendered by the debt and deficit debate.[1] This debate became increasingly prominent as the 1980s progressed and was accompanied by major cutbacks in federal expenditures and transfers to the provinces.

A second issue addressed is the extent to which the government's policies contributed to a deterioration in the climate of industrial relations between the provincial government and its employees—and if any such deterioration was temporary or may be expected to persist.

Industrial relations do not take place in a historical, political, legal, and economic vacuum. This is particularly true in regard to government's relations with its own employees since the government wears 'three hats' at the bargaining table—the employer who must tax to raise the revenue to pay its employees, the economic policy-maker responsible for fiscal and economic stability, and the rule-maker and adjudicator of industrial relations not only in respect to its own employees, but also with all organized workers and employers in the province. Therefore, this chapter begins with a survey of the historical, legal, and political context of industrial relations in Manitoba in the decade or so preceding the election of the Filmon Conservative government. This is followed by an analysis of the fiscal and economic situation that faced the Conservatives and their programs and policies after 1988, with particular emphasis on labour legislation and relations with government employees. The third section deals with the response of the Manitoba Government Employees' Union (MGEU); the final three sections focus on the outcomes of the decade in terms of government employment, incomes, the province's fiscal position, and the labour relations climate within the Manitoba public service.

The Historical, Political, and Legal Context to 1988

Many of the foundations of later developments in government-civil service relations were established in earlier decades. Two dates are relevant in this regard: 1969, with the election of a New Democratic Party government under Edward Schreyer, which was accompanied by a new approach to organized labour and union legal rights; and 1988, with the election of the Conservative government under Gary Filmon, which altered not only the relations between the government and organized labour generally, but also the fiscal context within which the provincial civil service operated.

The earliest manifestation of union organization within the Manitoba civil service—the Manitoba Civil Service Association—dates back to 1919, although it was not registered as a trade union at that time but as a charitable and patriotic organization.[2] In 1950 the organization changed its name to the Manitoba Government Employees' Association (MGEA) to reflect its representation of not only civil servants but also the growing number of employees of Crown corporations and other agencies.

When the government announced in 1957 that Crown corporation employees were governed by the Labour Relations Act, the MGEA[3] was forced to seek certification from the labour board for the affected groups of employees and became a union with respect to the non-civil servant component of its membership. It was almost another decade before the MGEA was officially recognized by the province as the sole bargaining agent for the civil service, under the provisions of the Civil Service Act (which did not include the right to strike).

In 1969 the province's first NDP government was elected. Almost immediately the new government extended to the MGEA the right to interest arbitration, a right it had been seeking for some time. Three years later, when the NDP overhauled labour legislation in the province and announced that civil servants would be given the right to strike, the MGEA lobbied the government hard against extending the strike right. The government conceded to the Association's wishes and withdrew the proposal.[4] Two years later an arbitration award gave the civil servants *less* than the government's final offer, promoting discontent among the ranks, but opposition to the right to strike continued among the majority of the civil service. The gradual conversion of the MGEA, or at least of its leadership, to the use of the strike, however, did not occur until the mid-1990s in response to the continuing suppression of meaningful collective bargaining under the Filmon Conservative government's fiscal restraint program. The question of whether or not the MGEA has the right to strike even now is not clear. There is no mention of it in the Civil Service Act and the legal advice obtained by the union and the government is contradictory.

In 1977, a newly elected Conservative government under Sterling Lyon adopted a hard-right, anti-labour, anti-public sector stance, promising 'acute protracted fiscal restraint'. However, according to Gary Doer, former president of the MGEA, Lyon's 'bark was worse than the bite' and relations with the MGEA were not seriously compromised as layoffs were primarily restricted to contract employees and substantial wage increases, ranging from 9.5 to 13 per cent, were negotiated between 1978 and 1981 (Doer, 1998).

In 1981, when the New Democrats were returned to power under Howard Pawley, the MGEA had little expectation of being able to continue to get the high wage settlements of the late Lyon years but rather began to direct its strategy at broader objectives, 'rights not money' (Doer, 1998). Nevertheless, just before the 1981–3 recession, the union negotiated a two-year deal that raised salaries by approximately 13 per cent in the first year and provided for a cost-of-living increase plus 1.5 per cent in the second. With the onset of the deep economic recession and the spectre of repressive public-sector labour legislation in other provinces, the MGEA agreed to reopen the contract with the cabinet. By delaying the scheduled 1983 wage increase for three months, the employees saved the government $10 million, which it used to establish a jointly managed job creation fund. In exchange, the MGEA obtained a no-layoff agreement and a long-run disability clause (Smith, 1993: 235).[5]

Perhaps one indication of the cosy relationship between the governing party and the MGEA was that its president, Gary Doer, resigned in 1985 to run as an NDP candidate in the upcoming provincial election.[6] The NDP's relationship with the electorate, on the other hand, was less cordial. In the 1986 election, the NDP was narrowly returned to office but subsequently lost its majority in the legislature, prompting the election of 1988. Under its new leader, Doer, the NDP went down to inglorious defeat, being reduced to third-party status, though the Conservatives under their new leader, Gary Filmon, were not able to form a majority government. The Liberals, led by Sharon Carstairs, became the official opposition.[7] The NDP era, which stretched back to 1969 (with the brief Lyon interlude), had come to an end. Consequently, the social democratic approach to both labour and social legislation was over.[8]

The Provincial Fiscal Context and Public Employment Policy, 1988–1997

Filmon's first minority government came at a relatively good time in fiscal and economic terms—the national and provincial economies were nearing their cyclical peak; provincial government deficits, which had ballooned during the recession in the early 1980s, were on their way towards balancing as a result of both the improving economy and the major tax increases implemented by the previous NDP administration (and a major contributor the NDP's electoral defeat). In fact, the Tories inherited an operating budget that was in a strong surplus position.

On the other hand, federal deficits continued to mount as a consequence of the Bank of Canada's restrictive monetary policies and tax cuts to business and those with higher incomes (Statistics Canada, 1991). In response, the federal government sought to cut transfers to the provinces to pay for social programs. Further, the Bank of Canada's monetary policies also served to produce an overvalued Canadian dollar,[9] resulting in unemployment rates that never fell below 7 per cent in either Canada or Manitoba during the period under study.

The deficit and debt, however, began to take on a political life of their own, unrelated to their relative size, at least in Manitoba. One reason was the 'fiscal crisis of the state' argument, which states that with the collapse in productivity growth in the 1970s the welfare state programs could no longer be financed from the 'growth dividend' (O'Connor, 1973). This meant that taxes had to be increased, deficits incurred, or social programs reduced. Though taxes were increased, particularly on the middle class, there were offsetting pressures to decrease taxes, at least on business and the wealthy, as a consequence of the increasing globalization of business and the international mobility of capital.

The fiscal crisis of the state contributed to an ideological shift to the right among many Western nations, embodied by Margaret Thatcher in Britain, Ronald Reagan in the United States, and Brian Mulroney in Canada. These three governments were founded on the neo-liberal ideology of reducing the absolute size and scope of government activities, which dictated the range of policy options—reducing the welfare state or privatizing it where reduction was not feasible. The fiscal crisis of the state was supportive of the neo-liberal agenda, providing a plausible economic rationale for dismantling social services—'there is no alternative'—if fiscal collapse is to be averted. The neo-liberals had the support of financial capital through the bond-rating agencies, which played a powerful role in dramatizing the fiscal crisis and in dictating how it would be resolved.

This was the ideological, fiscal, and economic context within which the Conservative government rode to victory in 1988. Based on the fiscal results summarized in Table 4.1,[10] the following observations can be made. Provincial revenues increased steadily throughout the 1980s, with a particularly large jump in the 1987–8 period reflecting NDP tax increases. Between 1989 and 1993, revenues from own (provincial) sources stagnated, in part due to the economic recession, in part due to declines in corporate income tax revenues, which bottomed out in 1991.[11] Steady increases in personal income and sales taxes throughout most of the period kept own revenues from falling more significantly. Federal transfers, which increased steadily until 1992, also buoyed total revenues throughout the period. In percentage terms, federal transfers actually increased in importance during the depth of the recession, representing an average of 34.3 per cent of provincial revenues from 1988 through 1990, 35.6 per cent from 1991 through

Table 4.1: Fiscal Reference Table, Manitoba, 1981–1996

Year	Total Revenues (million $)	Federal Transfers (% of Revenues)	Total Expenditures (million $)	Debt Charges (% of Expenditures)	Net Debt (million $)
1980–1	1,968	42.4	2,058	3.8	1,064
1981–2	2,181	38.4	2,432	4.7	1,436
1982–3	2,409	38.1	2,844	5.7	1,857
1983–4	2,797	37.1	3,226	7.4	2,512
1984–5	2,925	37.5	3,407	7.2	3,144
1985–6	3,117	35.5	3,645	8.6	3,861
1986–7	3,387	34.3	3,946	10.4	4,621
1987–8	4,039	32.5	4,338	11.3	5,162
1988–9	4,543	34.5	4,484	9.8	5,249
1989–90	4,606	36.0	4,748	10.3	4,856
1990–1	4,678	35.4	5,037	9.9	5,248
1991–2	4,967	36.7	5,271	9.0	5,295
1992–3	4,698	37.2	5,464	10.8	6,179
1993–4	4,876	33.4	5,336	10.9	6,834
1994–5	5,205	36.4	5,401	11.1	7,364
1995–6	5,517	33.9	5,505	10.8	6,814

Source: Canada, Department of Finance (1997: Table 23).

1994, and 35.2 per cent in 1995–6. Total revenues, however, only really began to pick up again after 1994. The net effect was that the main fiscal crunch from the revenue side persisted from approximately 1990 to 1994.

Total expenditures, on the other hand, expanded steadily until 1992–3, declined dramatically the next year, and did not exceed the 1992–3 level until 1995–6. Table 4.2 reports total expenditures and the percentages of the total represented by health, education, and family services, debt servicing, and all other government programs.[12] It is startlingly clear that the major social services dominate. To the extent that these areas are politically sensitive and therefore not easily altered (particularly if expenditures are mandated to some extent by conditions of federal transfers) and debt payments are determined exogenously by national and international interest rates, the provincial government has limited discretion, with most pressures falling on other program expenditures or on the deficit. In the earlier years of the Conservatives mandates, the provincial government spent an average of 60 per cent of its total expenditures on social services, just under 30 per cent on other program spending. After the 1990–4 recession and fiscal restraint, social spending rose to about two-thirds of total expenditures, while other program spending fell below 25 per cent. Debt expenditures remained relatively constant. The 'balance wheel' was the deficit, which peaked during the recession at $652 million in 1992–3. Obviously, the brunt of fiscal cutbacks was taken by 'other program spending' though spending on social services did fall absolutely in fiscal year 1993–4.

Federal-Provincial Transfers

As noted previously, federal-provincial transfers ranged between just under a third to just over two-fifths of provincial revenues during the 1980s and 1990s. The popular perception that there have been deep cuts in these transfers in the last decade is not supported by the facts (see Table 4.3). The only period where federal transfers fell significantly, thus affecting provincial revenues, was 1992–4,[13] due to a decline in equalization payments (reflecting the impact of the recession in the 'have' provinces) and in the health and higher education transfers, particularly after 1992–3.

Provincial Employee Compensation

Given the relative stagnation in provincial revenues from the 1990–1 to 1993–4 and the rise in the provincial deficit to over $650 million in 1992–3, there was strong pressure within the government not only to increase revenues but, even more, to reduce expenditures. Although social programs consume the largest

Table 4.2: Expenditures by Program Area and Deficits, Manitoba, 1987–1997

Year	Total Expenditures (million $)	Expenditures on Health, Education, and Family Services (% of total expenditures)	Debt Charges (% of total expenditures)	Other Program Spending (% of total expenditures)	Deficit or (Surplus)* (million $)
1986–7*	4,014	59.6	10.3	30.1	627
1987–8	4,695	61.0	11.3	27.7	324
1988–9	4,876	59.8	9.9	30.3	(28)
1989–90	5,095	61.7	10.3	28.0	119
1990–1	5,369	62.2	9.9	27.9	339
1991–2	5,521	64.1	8.6	27.3	300
1992–3	5,732	65.2	8.8	26.0	652
1993–4	5,614	66.2	10.3	23.5	414
1994–5	5,708	65.7	10.3	24.0	192
1995–6	6,124	66.0	10.0	24.0	(83)
1996–7	6,141	66.9	9.1	24.0	(35)

*Excludes extraordinary items and increases in equity in government enterprises.
Fiscal years ending 31 March.
Source: Manitoba, Report of the Provincial Auditor (1987–97).

Table 4.3: Federal Transfers: Total Value and Distribution, 1987–1997

Year	Transfers (million $)	Equalization (million $)	Health and Higher Education (million $)	Shared Cost and Other (million $)
1986–7	1,161	509	418	235
1987–8	1,346	621	433	292
1988–9	1,604	863	420	314
1989–90	1,699	911	432	358
1990–1	1,749	971	406	373
1991–2	1,829	1,046	443	340
1992–3	1,757	898	499	353
1993–4	1,636	821	438	376
1994–5	1,904	1,074	463	369
1995–6	1,960	1,064	435	459

Note: The data include fiscal stabilization claims under federal transfers from 1993 to 1995, though these are minor.
Source: Manitoba, *Report of the Provincial Auditor* (1987–97).

portion of government spending, these services are politically difficult to cut. One alternative is to reduce provincial employee compensation, but these wages and salaries make up less than 15 per cent of total provincial expenditures (see Table 4.4). A downward trend in salaries as a proportion of provincial expenditures actually began in the mid-1980s, with a more rapid decline beginning in 1990. There was a strong upward trend in the total salary bill until 1990–1, after which it tended to level out or fall slowly. Nominal average salaries actually declined in three years between 1990 and 1996 (1991–2, 1993–4 and 1995–6), with the result that salaries increased by only approximately 3.3 per cent over the period—a considerable drop in real terms.

Table 4.5 indicates that the major reductions in civil service compensation were mainly achieved by cutting employment, particularly of unionized employees covered by the Civil Service Commission, beginning in the fiscal year 1991–2. The cut was particularly severe in 1993–4. Overall, the drop in the total number of employees between the fiscal years ending in 1991 and 1997 was 22 per cent, the biggest decline (2,029 or almost 12 per cent) coming in 1993–4.[14] Moreover, most of the cuts were from the ranks of the MGEU, which accounted for over 89 per cent of total government employees at the beginning of the period, falling to around 86 per cent by 1996. Contract, casual, and sessional employment peaked in 1987–8 but did not show a significant downward trend until 1993–4 before stabilizing at 14–15 per cent of provincial employment.

With these salaries amounting to a small proportion of government expenditures, cutbacks in the civil service made a relatively modest contribution to the campaign to balance the budget. This was no doubt why the government attempted to reduce wages and employment in the health and education sectors, where there were greater potential savings. However, the political sensitivity to cutting health and education services translated into a larger impact on employment, though not on wages, in the civil service than the broader public sector.

The Government Fiscal Restraint Program, 1988–1997

Given its precarious minority position after the 1988 election[15] the new Conservative government moved very cautiously and Premier Filmon did honour the no-layoff clause in the MGEA contract despite promising a 'leaner government' (Smith, 1993: 260). Generally speaking, relations between the government and its major union, with a couple of exceptions, remained fairly good during the years of the minority government.[16]

The most significant dispute between the parties resulted from the government's plan to begin the decentralization of civil service employment. Approximately 600 civil service jobs and 100 Crown corporation jobs were to be moved to over 60 rural communities. The MGEA and the government had been negotiating a voluntary transfer scheme when the government unilaterally made its announcement pre-empting a negotiated solution. The MGEA (and the opposition parties) believed that the government's move was designed merely to solidify the rural vote that was the backbone of the Conservatives' electoral support, particularly with the expectation of an early election given the govern-

Table 4. 4: Civil Service Salaries as a Percentage of Total Government Expenditures, Manitoba, 1981–1996

Fiscal Year	Total Salaries (000s $)	Salaries: % of Prov. Expenditures	Average Salary ($)
1981–2	362,493	14.91	21,951
1982–3	423,077	14.88	23,452
1983–3	461,875	14.32	23,379
1984–5	503,293	14.77	26,072
1985–6	535,619	14.69	26,349
1986–7	536,682	13.60	26,132
1987–8	590,708	13.62	28,173
1988–9	609,367	13.59	28,796
1989–90	655,724	13.81	30,775
1990–1	692,141	13.74	32,329
1991–2	680,668	12.91	32,101
1992–3	695,038	12.72	32,863
1993–4	677,945	12.71	32,810
1994–5	679,062	12.57	33,543
1995–6	681,688	12.38	33,334

Source: Fiscal Reference Tables, Oct. 1997; CANSIM Data Series.

Table 4.5: Provincial Government Employment

End of Fiscal Year (March)	Total	Unionized*	Regular (all shift, hourly, and term)	Other** (contract, casual, and sessional)
1987	17,803	16,101	14,997	2,826
1988	18,400	16,213	15,392	3,008
1989	18,092	15,464	15,269	2,823
1990	18,397	16,725	15,674	2,723
1991	18,435	15,906	15,519	2,936
1992	17,630	15,738	14,851	2,779
1993	17,239	15,220	14,605	2,634
1994	15,210	13,605	13,053	2,157
1995	15,081	13,371	12,834	2,247
1996	14,495	12,766	12,368	2,127
1997	14,373	n.a.	12,271	2,102

*The vast majority (99 per cent in 1987, 98 per cent in 1996) of these are MGEU members. Other 'unions' are professional associations of lawyers, Crown attorneys, doctors, and other professions.
**'Comparative employment for other employees paid on a time worked basis. This includes departmental, casual, sessional and as, if, when employees'—Civil Service Commission definition. These may or may not be union members: political appointments are not; nor are seconded employees or casual or part-time employees with less than two months or 336 hours continuous employment.
Source: Data supplied by the Manitoba Civil Service Commission.

ment's minority position. Another effect would be to further scatter provincial employees around the province, thereby reducing the cohesiveness of the union. The MGEA fought the government through the media since there was no redress under the collective agreement. It also enrolled the aid of Winnipeg's mayor and city council, but with little success.[17]

In September 1990 Filmon called an election to seek a majority mandate and the Conservatives were elected, but with only a one-seat majority. The main beneficiary of the election was the NDP, which become the official opposition.[18]

Despite the moderate image projected by Filmon during his minority government and the election campaign, once elected with a majority the party's more neo-liberal agenda began to emerge in its employee relations. In June 1991 the government introduced Bill 70, The Public Sector Compensation Management Act, which froze all wages and benefits of the civil service and other provincial employees (approximately 48,000 in all) retroactive to 1 September 1990 by extending the previous agreements by one year.[19] (The last MGEA contract had expired 21 September 1990 and a new contract had not been negotiated until the spring of 1991.)

According to the Minister of Finance, Clayton Manness, this measure was required because of the economic recession and the need to 'find a balance between continuing to provide needed services and jobs while at the same time living within the means of our limited tax dollars' (Manitoba, 1991: 3). He had already announced over 950 job cuts, including vacant positions and term employees, and threatened to lay off 4,000 because of the 'outrageous' demands of the union. The MGEA's protests to both the job cuts and the wage rollback were ignored, and since staffing was a managerial right under the collective agreement there was little it could do. Further, local newspapers and opinion polls indicated that the public supported the government's position and agreed with the contention that all civil servants were underworked and overpaid.

What did happen was an enormous jump in the number of grievances filled with the Civil Service Commission, from 408 in 1990 to over 900 in 1991, mainly associated with layoffs and the continuing decentralization program. The union took 10 cases to arbitration and won on the issue of 'bumping' rights, but this proved to be a pyrrhic victory since the arbitrator also upheld the 'competitive test', which was defined so narrowly that the union lost all of its bumping cases.[20]

The new three-year collective agreement negotiated between the government and the MGEA covering the period September 1991 to September 1994, which called for annual salary increases of 3 per cent, 3 per cent, and COLA, was superseded by the new government legislation. In April 1993, Bill 22 allowed the provincial government, Crown corporations, and other public-sector employers to require their employees to take up to a maximum of 15 days leave without pay (which became known as 'Filmon Fridays') in two consecutive 12-month periods. Like Bill 70, it was introduced without notice or consultation with the unions to combat the 'debt crisis' by again suspending the collective agreement. The unpaid days effectively 'clawed back' pay increases in the collective agreement as they amounted to a wage reduction of 3.8 per cent. The bill allowed for a 30-day consultation period with the unions on the unpaid leave days, after which the employer could unilaterally impose the number and timing of the days off.[21]

Once again, the MGEA was left with no legal recourse other than to voice its opposition during committee hearings on the legislation. It did lodge an official complaint with the International Labour Office (ILO) for the province's contravention of the international convention on the right to collective bargaining, and though the ILO condemned the province it only has the power of moral suasion. The province, on its part, was not persuaded.

The government's position was based on its desire to take $15 million out of the total government salaries budget[22] by reducing employment (which did continue and was particularly drastic in the 1993–4 fiscal year, when employment fell by 12 per cent) or by instituting compulsory days off. Despite the union's vociferous opposition, the Civil Service Commission and the government argued that employees preferred the reduced workweek to greater layoffs, even suggesting that the workers wanted the summer four-day workweek to continue indefinitely, though there was never any evidence presented to support this contention.[23]

In the next three years two shorter-term agreements were signed between the MGEU and the province (1 October 1994–29 March 1996; 30 March 1996–28 March, 1997).[24] According to the union and other observers, one can hardly use the term 'negotiated' to describe the proceedings. The government announced its plans, in one case to the media before even talking to the union, and basically refused to entertain any significant counter-proposals. The Civil Service Commission, which handled the bargaining for the government, had virtually no 'wiggle room' in the negotiations. Monetary limits were established by the Finance Minister in the budget and departmental allocations. At the same time, the cabinet was quite adamant in resisting any encroachment on the management rights clauses in the contract. As a result, wages were frozen at the September 1994 levels and the 10 unpaid days off were continued, though now included for the first time in the contracts covering the fiscal years 1995–6 and 1996–7.

The Conservative government's bargaining position with its employees in 1996 was greatly strengthened by the results of the provincial election in April 1995. Though the NDP again picked up seats, so did the Conservatives—both at the expense of the Liberals. The Conservatives finally gained a solid working majority in the legislature, taking advantage of the undeniable popularity of the Premier (often referred to in the media as 'the Teflon man'). There was little public support for the MGEU, which had carried out a $70,000 campaign during the election, attacking the government for its public-sector cutbacks.

With its new majority, the government now began arguing that restraint was made necessary by reduced federal government transfers. In March 1996 the province cut 150 positions, one-third from education, and served notice to the MGEU that it intended to contract out cleaning and maintenance positions throughout Manitoba just as the 1996–7 negotiations were reaching an impasse. This led the MGEU to call for its first-ever strike vote in April. Although the members voted 57 per cent against striking with a 75 per cent turnout, the results were taken as indicative of a rising militancy within the ranks of the public service.[25]

It is difficult to determine whether the increased fiscal stringency after 1992–3 was a response to falling revenues and the rising deficit caused by the recession and by decreases in federal transfers, or if these factors merely gave the government the excuse and rationale to cut back the public sector and provincial health and education programs. During the 1990 election, Filmon denied there was a right-wing agenda, but in its internal correspondence the party spoke of the need for a majority government because of its difficult program 'to restore a much needed pro-business environment in Manitoba' (Smith, 1993: 267–8).[26] Furthermore, there is ample evidence from the government's own pronouncements that it wanted to establish a pro-business, low-tax, low-wage environment, which it believed was necessary to attract international business investment, particularly in the new 'free trade' era.[27] This, in turn, meant weakening labour standards and unions that, the government claimed, had been favoured by the previous NDP administration. Though the major attack on organized labour would not come until 1996, the government believed it could take the lead in its relations with its own employees in both the civil service and the quasi-public health and education sectors.

Outside of the civil service proper, union militancy was considerably higher. Professors at the University of Manitoba struck for three weeks in the fall of 1995 to protect academic freedom from cutbacks initiated by the provincial government. The following spring and summer home-care workers, Manitoba Lotteries employees, and provincial nursing-home workers went out on strike, while Liquor Control Commission employees and prison guards were negotiating and threatening job action. It was probably the strike by the home-care and nursing-home workers, combined with the continuing health and education program cuts, that caused a change in public opinion. As the government was claiming credit for having finally tamed the debt/deficit dragon, there were growing accusations by the unions, the opposition, and social action groups that the government was more concerned with attacking social programs and downsizing the public sector than it was with fiscal responsibility.

As the 1996–7 contract was due to expire, it seemed that the climate had changed somewhat. Negotiations began with the usual announcement that the government wanted to maintain Filmon Fridays, but the Minister of Labour responsible for the civil service also admitted that the 'government could loosen its purse strings'. In November, after five years of wage freezes and unpaid days off that cost MGEU members an estimated $100 million in lost wages,[28] the parties reached a three-year agreement that included small wage increases and the phasing out of Filmon Fridays. The terms of the settlement were:

Year one (29 March 1997 to 28 March 1998): 1 per cent wage increase plus 1.5 per cent signing bonus; 10 unpaid days.
Year two (29 March 1998 to 27 March 1999): 1 per cent wage increase; 5 unpaid days.
Year three (28 March 1999 to 24 March 2000): 2 per cent wage increase; 0 unpaid days.

The contract also called for the implementation of a vision care plan in 1998.

The negotiators for the MGEU noticed a 'different climate of negotiations' with 'some meaningful dialogue' (Olfert and Comstock, 1998). Nevertheless, there was little movement until the MGEU applied for arbitration, after which the government returned to the bargaining table and sufficient concessions were made to achieve the agreement.[29]

The bargaining relationship had returned to something akin to what prevailed prior to the period of acute fiscal restraint introduced by the Conservatives after their election in 1990. Representatives of both the Civil Service Commission and the MGEU maintained in interviews that, despite the strains of the 1990–7 period, relations between the government and its employee unions remained 'professional' and untainted by personal and ideological antagonisms.[30] Conflicts and relations between the union and the commission did not become politicized or personal. The union obviously felt that its battle was with the government and its fiscal policies, not with the Civil Service Commission and its human resource management practices.

Provincial Fiscal Policy, Public Employment, and Compensation: An Evaluation

There have been three phases in fiscal policy since the election of the Conservatives in 1988. The first, beginning with the minority administration of 1988–90, could be characterized as relatively easy. The second, beginning at the depth of the recession in 1992 and continuing through the slow recovery to around 1996–7, was one of protracted restraint. The third, beginning with the 1997 MGEU contract and the 1998 budget, indicates a slightly more expansive phase following the modest recovery from the recession and the elimination of provincial budgetary deficits (see Tables 4.1 and 4.2).

The question that arises is whether the protracted restraint followed from the province's deteriorating fiscal position or from the legislature's changing political composition after the 1990 election. The decline in provincial expenditures, both total and program, did not begin in earnest until after the disastrous drop in revenues and the ballooning deficit in 1992–3, though in some previous years the increase in budget expenditures did not keep pace with inflation so that real expenditures fell. The drop in revenues was the result of both a decrease in tax yields and a major decrease in federal transfers. Though corporate and personal income taxes were not increased, the broadening of the sales tax base, the reduction in tax credits, the imposition of or increase in many user fees, and growing revenues from government-sponsored gambling had the effect of rapidly increasing tax (own-source) revenues after 1992–3 while federal transfers also jumped after 1993–4. Although any reductions in the province's credit rating were seized upon by the government to defend its fiscal stance, as Table 4.6 demonstrates there was very little change in the province's credit rating over the period. Only the Canadian Bond Rating Service (CBRS) marginally downgraded Manitoba's credit rating at the depth of the recession in 1993–4. Furthermore, although total debt rose significantly between 1992 and 1994, due primarily to stagnant or falling revenues (see Table 4.1), the ratio of debt to gross domestic product (GDP), the true measure of the 'debt burden', rose only slightly before falling again after 1995. By 1995–6 the debt-to-GDP ratio was only marginally greater than it had been when the Conservatives took office in 1988, while the percentage of public expenditures spent on servicing the debt fluctuated generally between 10 and 11 per cent throughout the period. These facts fail to justify the government's argument that restrictive fiscal policies were required to prevent the provincial debt from getting out of control.

The progress of the general fiscal policy stance of the government can also be seen through a review of the provincial budgets over the period. In the first few budgets of the new Conservative administration there was little indication of a concern with fiscal restraint; rather, reducing taxes on business while moderately increasing public spending on social programs appeared to be the policy thrust. Revenues were buoyant due to the tax increases introduced by the NDP just prior to its defeat and economic growth that 'was stronger than expected and brought exceptional revenue to the Province by way of federal transfers' (*Manitoba Budget Highlights*, 1989). As a result, the government created the Fiscal Stabilization Fund (the 'rainy-day fund') 'to pay for vital programs in future years when revenue flows are low'. However, in the following year, federal transfers were less than anticipated and the province withdrew $100 million from the fund, which nevertheless continued to grow, in part due to funds from the sale of Crown corporations. At the same time expenditures for health, education, and family services continued to grow and there were a number of smaller tax cuts for Manitoba firms.

The 1991 budget marked the beginning of the transition to fiscal conservatism and more intense economic neo-liberalism. While Finance Minister Clayton Manness criticized the federal government for reducing transfer payments and off-loading program responsibilities, his budget did the same thing to local government in the province, cutting municipal funding by 13.6 per cent. Total expenditures increased less than the inflation rate, a cut of almost 1,000 public-sector jobs was announced, and, soon after, Bill 70 was introduced, rolling back and freezing public-sector wages.

The 1992 budget froze major taxes, while there were some expenditure increases in education, health, family services, day care, and job creation, financed by a $201 million withdrawal from the 'rainy day' fund (leaving its projected balance at only $25 million). The 1993 budget reverted to a much tighter fiscal posture: gasoline taxes increased, the retail sales tax base expanded significantly, and tax credits were reduced substantially. Simultaneously, there were tax cuts to businesses in the form of increased exemptions from payroll taxes and lower fuel taxes for railways and airlines. The Conservatives also began to reduce significantly funding for universities and allocations for government administration. Though the deficit peaked it would have been considerably greater if not for the growth of lotteries and video lottery terminals (VLTs), which contributed $367 million in revenue that year. This pattern continued in the 1994 budget. Health-care spending was cut by $4 million, funding for universities by

Table 4.6: Manitoba Bond Ratings

Year	Standard and Poors	Moody's	Dominion Bond Rating Service	Canadian Bond Rating Service
1986	A+	A1	not rated	AA–
1987			A	
1988			A (low)	
1989			A	
1993				A+
1994				A
1997	A+ (Positive)			A+ (Stable)

Source: Department of Finance, Government of Manitoba.

2.7 per cent. Income taxes, consumption taxes, and payroll taxes remained unchanged, but there was a series of tax cuts to business and the mining industry. The projected deficit, while less than the previous year, was still substantial and a factor in the reduction in the province's bond rating by the CBRS.

The 1995 budget projected a small surplus to be achieved by transferring $145 million in lottery revenues. Expenditures were slated to increase by 1.9 per cent, which meant a small decline in the level of real expenditures. The budget speech also announced the government's intention to bring in balanced budget legislation.

Fiscal austerity continued in 1996 despite the improvement in the provincial economy and a projected small budgetary surplus. Major taxes were again frozen, but effective taxes were increased on many individuals by cuts in property tax credits. The Health Department, hospitals, family services, agriculture, the public schools, and the universities all suffered major funding reductions, while the budget also announced a further cut of 350 government jobs.

The first sign of any relaxation in the government's attack on the public sector came in the 1997 budget. There were modest funding increases for day care, public schools, and home care as well as funding for new Aboriginal health and child poverty programs and for capital spending on provincial hospitals and old-age homes. A balanced budget was projected with a small repayment on the provincial debt, achieved by a $100 million transfer from the 'rainy-day fund', which the Minister of Finance said was necessary to offset lower federal transfers (*Winnipeg Free Press*, 15 Mar. 1997).

Budget intentions corroborate the pattern of actual expenditures and revenues, with the period of protracted restraint beginning around 1991 and intensifying from 1993 to 1996 before exhibiting some slight relaxation beginning in 1997. In 1995, Manitoba became the fourth province to pass 'balanced budget' legislation, but in many ways its legislation was the most extreme. Annual budgets must be at least balanced, or in surplus, and debt must be paid down by at least 1 per cent per year (Loxley, 1995: 19). Deficits could only be sanctioned in the case of natural disasters, war, or economic depression resulting in a fall in revenues of more than 5 per cent; and these would have to be made up the following year. Revenue shortfalls of less than 5 per cent must be financed from a fiscal stabilization fund to be created by required government savings until the fund reaches 5 per cent of annual expenditures. All of these provisions were designed to prevent this or future governments from taking a proactive, Keynesian policy stance.[31] Furthermore, increases in personal or corporate income taxes, sales taxes, or employment levies can only be implemented after a positive referendum, to ensure that budget shortfalls and required surpluses are financed by cutbacks in government expenditures rather than by raising these taxes.[32]

The provisions and goals of the balanced budget legislation strongly suggest that policy was driven by an ideological commitment to what (prior to Keynes) was known as 'sound finance'. Debt and deficits were just symptoms of 'unsound finance'. Given this ideological commitment, the problem that faced the Conservatives was how to cut expenditures. The largest component of public service expenditures (about 80 per cent) is wages. However, as we have already noted, most of this expenditure was outside the civil service in the health, education, and family service sectors. Civil service salaries amounted to less than 14 per cent of total government expenditures and six years of major staff cuts and wage restraints only managed to reduce this percentage by just over 1 per cent (see Table 4.4). Balancing the budget at the height of the recession by civil service cuts would have meant reducing staff or their salaries by an average of two-thirds. This was the rationale for extending the coverage of Bill 22 to virtually all public employees, reducing health, education, and social services spending, and off-loading expenditures onto local governments.

As the MGEU was wont to point out, cutting government payrolls was a double-edged sword. Every cut in payroll expenditure also entailed a cut in government revenues. To make its point, the union conducted its own study of the net effect of Bill 22 in 1993. Once the costs of maintaining essential services, revenue loss due to reduction in tax receipts, increased welfare cost, and employment multiplier effects are taken into account, the MGEU estimated that actual government savings were $11.4 million, only 10 per cent of the Conservative government's claim and less than 3 per cent of the deficit in the year Bill 22 was implemented (MGEU, 1993: 1). While some of the assumptions made in the study may be questioned, it is clear that the net savings from Bill 22 were much lower than the government figure.

In the final evaluation, therefore, it is easy to conclude that cuts to the provincial civil service through staff reductions or wage rollbacks in whatever form did not play a major *direct* part in curbing the deficit. However, these cuts and rollbacks were a necessary component of the government's overall fiscal policy after 1992. The downsizing of the civil service also had an important 'demonstration effect' for other public and private-sector employers.[33] It constituted a part of what was widely believed by labour, the opposition, the media, and social action groups to be the province's 'business-friendly, low-wage' policy for attracting economic development.

The Union Response

The response of the MGEU, which represented almost all civil service employees, was muted for a number of reasons. First, the union could not legally challenge either the staff cuts or the two bills that rolled back compensation, Bills 70 and 22, because staffing and related matters are management rights under the Civil Service Act. The union did exercise its contractual rights of notice of large-scale layoffs, of bumping, and of seniority, which caused the huge increase in grievances following the 1991 decentralization of the civil service. Grievance numbers have remained high since then, but a number of factors have made the grievance procedure relatively ineffectual. The government, in most cases, ceased the practice of mass layoffs, resorting to frequent layoffs of small numbers of employees where notice is not required. In addition, the civil service initiated a 'vacancy management' program (described below) that obviated the need for a continuation of large-scale layoffs.

The union's muted response can also be attributed to public opinion. Polls, encouraged by editorial opinion and the government's own propaganda, continually reported that public-sector workers were considered well-paid, if not overpaid, and that there was a great deal of 'fat' (overstaffing) in the system. It was not until the medicare crises in 1997–8 caused by hospital understaffing that the public began to understand that cuts in public employment have a real cost in terms of services. This occurred well after the major period of provincial civil service reductions. Furthermore, the union faced the problem of having many members located in rural areas where it was difficult, given the relatively low rural wages, to convince local communities of the importance of reasonably paid public servants.

The third and perhaps most important reason why the union was slow to respond in a more militant manner was the entrenched ideology of the civil servant, the same ideology that had opposed the organization obtaining union status and the right to strike for most of its history.[34] The MGEU only adopted the appellation 'Union' at the end of 1992 and it was 1997 before it held its first strike vote. The MGEU faces a number of difficulties in developing a cohesive, collective face. Its membership tends to be scattered, not only geographically but also by department and function. Traditionally, its most militant units have been those where members work closely together in institutions, such as corrections and hospitals, and/or are composed of more homogeneous groups, such as the non-civil service units in lotteries and the Liquor Control Commission.[35]

The extended period of fiscal restraint served to politicize the MGEU, making the union more active in educating both the public at large and its own membership, as well as in forging more links with organized labour and other community groups to lobby governmental and business organizations.[36] Civil servants obtained the right to be politically active in 1974 from a previous NDP government, over the opposition of the MGEA executive. However, the union itself has always avoided any institutional or endorsement ties to any political party, including the NDP. Throughout this period, of course, the NDP has been headed by the former president of the MGEU, Gary Doer, so that the opposition party had obvious informal links to the union and, in Doer's words, they have maintained a 'co-operative relationship' with particular emphasis on protecting job security.

The intensification of union action against the government's labour policies was also restrained by the need for the MGEA to work with the Civil Service Commission to ameliorate the effects of the downsizing on its members. It did claim some success in combating the 'privatization' of the community colleges, the transfer of government activities to new agencies, and contracting out by retaining successor bargaining rights for the affected workers. It did spend heavily in the 1995 election, not in support of the NDP but in opposition to the continuing cuts in the civil service and the quasi-public sector represented by the MGEU. In the run-up to the 1996 strike vote, the union ran a campaign to get a positive vote—the 'Yes! We Can!' campaign—that, despite falling short of a strike mandate by 7 per cent, did, in the opinion of the union leaders, raise awareness and militancy among the membership (Olfert and Comstock, 1998). The union also lobbied with local governments to gain support for its opposition to layoffs of workers providing services to the local citizenry. However, direct pressure on the government through briefs and presentations to the legislative committees considering the contentious labour legislation, such as Bill 22, by and large met with a brick wall.[37] As a final resort the MGEU appealed the legislation to the International Labour Office, which condemned the province. However, as previously noted, the Manitoba government ignored it.

According to MGEU officials, the overall impact of the various actions was hard to gauge. 'The problem has been the almost overwhelming number of issues . . . . The MGEU has had to run so many campaigns' (Olfert and Comstock, 1998).

The union may have been more successful in getting the government to lessen the impact of layoffs and downsizing on individual members. At the simplest level, this included opposition to the government practice of meeting people to be laid off or terminated with security guards to oversee the cleaning out of their desks, collecting their keys, and then escorting them to the door. The disruptions and grievances that resulted proved counterproductive, leading management to attempt to settle such issues through other means. Now, laid-off or dismissed workers are treated more humanely. Similarly, by introducing a 'pre-bumping' process aimed at finding new positions for potential layoffs, the parties sought to settle some disputes in advance. According to MGEU officials, after a period of sparring, management developed a 'new attitude'.[38]

Under pressure from the union, the Civil Service Commission developed and implemented the Vacancy Management Program and the Voluntary Separation Incentive Program (VSIP) to reduce the trauma associated with layoffs and terminations.[39] As early as 1991, the MGEA joined with the government in an adjustment committee to find employment for laid-off court reporters within the civil service, though many preferred to take a severance package instead. A similar committee was established to retrain workers whose careers were eliminated by the cancellation of the children's dental program. In 1992 a joint Workforce Adjustment Committee was established (composed of four government and three MGEA representatives, plus one laid-off worker) to help find work, initially within the civil service, for those being laid off. When positions within government dried up, the committee turned its sights on the outside labour market. Establishing the committee also made the laid-off workers eligible for up to two years of retraining financed by Unemployment Insurance.

These forms of adjustment within the civil service were institutionalized in the Vacancy Management Program and the VSIP. Under the VSIP, workers were given the opportunity during limited periods (February 1993, 1994, and 1996) to choose early retirement with enhanced severance pay equal to 30 weeks' pay, 15 weeks more than what was provided by the collective agreement. The Civil Service Commission officials explicitly rejected the 'golden handshake' (retirement buyout) approach, which had become quite common in the private sector and was used by the City of Winnipeg, as too expensive and disruptive of industrial relations. Although the severance enhancement was not as generous as retirement incentives in other sectors, 50–60 per cent of those eligible accepted. The scheme was sufficiently successful that there is now doubt whether it will be offered again (Irving and Pruden, 1998).

The purpose of the VSIP was either to substitute a retirement for a layoff or to create a vacancy that could be filled by someone facing a layoff. The general principle was that as vacancies became available either through early retirement or normal attrition, they would be allocated in the first instance to people who were targeted for future layoff or, second, to laid-off workers on the re-employment (recall) list, a list that in recent years has consistently contained between 50–100 names. One variant of this program was the 'buddy system' that allowed a redundant employee to 'trade' his or her position with someone who wanted early retirement but whose position was not targeted to be abolished. These matches were allowed both within and between departments. Another and even more widely used variant was the 'business case' system, where a vacancy occurred within a department through normal attrition but the department involved agreed not to fill it for a year. The vacancy was equated to a layoff, and if it had to be filled after the one-year period, workers were hired from the re-employment list where possible.

There is little doubt that these labour management programs reduced the pain of government downsizing, but despite their best efforts hundreds of employees were still involuntarily dismissed or laid off. Furthermore, the pain was also felt by the remaining employees who had to maintain their own workloads plus absorb the work of terminated workers. This was compounded by the days off without pay. Government employees were expected to complete an expanded workload in fewer working hours, which often translated into a considerable amount of unpaid overtime.

Given the MGEU's non-militant and non-partisan tradition, plus the legal limits placed on its ability to oppose the government's agenda, the union was more or less limited to trying to pressure the government through publicity and education campaigns, demonstrations, legislative presentations, and lobbying. In addition, it worked with the Civil Service Commission to make the downsizing process more humane, both reducing the number of layoffs and helping displaced workers find alternative employment. This was a significant achievement. One by-product of the campaigns was to increase the political awareness of the union's membership and consequently to increase the militancy, albeit perhaps only marginally, within the ranks of the civil service. How lasting this result will prove to be, however, only the future will reveal.

Economic and Industrial Relations Outcomes: The Later 1990s

The Current Fiscal Situation

In terms of the stated goal simply of balancing the budget the government has claimed success. The provincial budget went into small surplus in fiscal year 1995–6 and has remained in surplus since that time. However, two qualifications should be made—these balanced budgets have only been achieved either by dipping into the rainy-day fund or by the transfer of burgeoning revenues from the Lotteries Corporation.[40]

The problems with dependence on gambling revenues for financing regular government programs are well known: the social costs of addiction, the regressive nature of gambling 'taxes', and the diversion of expenditure from other, more productive, economic activities. Whether the backlash that has developed will result in any actual decline in VLT and lottery revenue is uncertain, but it does mean that it is unlikely that gambling will be the provincial revenue growth industry it has been in recent years. In terms of the fiscal stabilization fund, to the extent that the fund has been financed by the sale of Crown corporations, the transfers to offset program spending merely represent the dissolution of capital assets, a process limited by the amount of saleable assets.

Provincial Government Employment

Total employment in the provincial government sector declined after 1991 back to levels of the mid-eighties. The brunt of the cuts to provincial employment came in the civil service, which averaged employment of about 18,300 between 1988 and 1991 before declining by over 20 per cent to 14,373 in 1997. Over 80 per cent of these cuts were from the regular civil service, almost all of the rest from the 'other' category ('departmental casual, sessional, and as, if, when employees'). Table 4.7 gives the percentage of total employment accounted for by regular full-time employees and their distribution by sex. Although there is little evidence of a government strategy to increase the use of more irregular or contract workers, part-time and casual employees rose from around 13.4 per cent in 1988–9 to an average of 15.5 per cent between 1992 and 1994. Though the absolute number of such employees peaked in 1991, they fell at a slower rate than overall civil service employments, so that irregular employees reached 16.1 per cent of the total by 1996.

These figures also indicate a slow but steady 'feminization' of the regular, full-time civil service. This was accompanied by a gradual 'aging' of the service, indicated by an increasing proportion of the regular civil service over 45 years old (Table 4.8), despite the VSIP program promoting early retirement.[41]

No records are available to indicate how many civil servants took voluntary early retirement or were terminated involuntarily. However, a rough measure of

Table 4.7: Composition of Employees: Regular Full-Time and by Gender

Year*	% Regular Full-Time	Regular Employees	
		% Male	*% Female*
1987	80.0	51.2	48.8
1989	79.0	50.3	49.7
1990	77.8	49.8	50.2
1991	77.1	49.3	50.7
1992	76.5	48.2	51.8
1993	76.9	48.2	51.8
1994	77.7	47.2	52.8
1995	76.3	47.1	52.9
1996	78.3	46.6	53.4

* 1988 not available.
Source: Civil Service Commission, various years.

the contribution of retirement to the downsizing can be indicated. Of the decline in total regular full-time employees of 2,964 between 1990 and 1996, 331 (or 11 per cent) were from the age group 55 +. Since 1,800–1,900 of the 45–54 age group might be expected to enter the 55 + age category from 1990 to 1996, terminations, layoffs, natural attrition, and regular and voluntary retirement in the 'early retirement' age group could have accounted for as much as three-quarters of the total downsizing of the regular full-time employees.[42] Regular full-time employees constituted almost 80 per cent of the civil service. It is probable, then, that the majority of the jobs eliminated in the civil service did occur through attrition or voluntary separation, since approximately 50 to 60 per cent of those eligible accepted voluntary separation (Irving and Pruden, 1998).

Evaluation of Fiscal Impacts

It is difficult to estimate just what the effect was on the province's accounts of downsizing and wage reductions through enforced days off. The Civil Service Commission estimates that the savings from the Filmon Fridays (compulsory days off) were $100–110 million over five or six years.[43] Our estimate is that the reduction in total civil service salaries in nominal terms from the peak in 1990 through 1996 *from all causes* was $116.4 million (the sum of the reductions below the 1990 base in total salaries paid from 1991 to 1996).[44] In annual terms this is approximately $20 million a year or, over the six-year period, around 5 per cent of the deficit that accumulated during that period. In short, the fiscal restraint exercised on the civil service played a very minor role in alleviating the fiscal crunch that the provincial government faced in the first half of the decade of the nineties. Nonetheless, it must be reiterated that the wage and employment restraint program extended to the quasi-public (health, education) sector, where the savings were almost certainly significantly greater.

The conclusion with respect to the civil service, however, is strengthened considerably when one considers the negative effects on government revenues that resulted from the reduction in salaries and jobs in the public sector. The MGEU's study of the net impact of Bill 22 may considerably underestimate the bill's impact in cutting government expenditures, but even if we reduce the MGEU's estimate by half, the contribution of the cuts in the civil service and its salaries to the fiscal position of the province remains relatively minor.[45]

Labour-Management Relations

It is not possible to separate entirely the impact on industrial relations within the civil service of the government's restrictive fiscal policy from its more broadly directed 'smaller-government' policies. Caught in the middle was the Civil Service Commission, which, as the designated management body of the province, was required to negotiate contracts with the civil service unions while implementing the government's wider agenda as it pertained to provincial employees. Nevertheless, the leadership of both the MGEU and the Civil Service Commission maintained that their relationship continued on a professional, non-confrontational, and non-political level throughout the difficult period. Paraphrasing one MGEU official:

> There has been no 'sea change' nor permanent damage or substantial impairment in relations through the period, either during the restrictive phase, or more recently as the government relented in their fear of more labour strife. It was never considered personal or anti-MGEU *per se* but rather a 'cyclical' part of the political business cycle. (Olfert and Comstock, 1998)

Despite the personal anti-labour actions of some individual government ministers, the union was willing to chalk these actions up to inexperience or incom-

Table 4.8: Age Distribution of the Regular Civil Service by Gender, Selected Years

	Less than 25 yrs Old		25-44 yrs old		45+ yrs old	
Year	Male	Female	Male	Female	Male	Female
1987	3.0%	8.0%	59.1%	66.8%	37.9%	25.2%
1990	1.8	4.6	57.9	68.9	40.3	26.5
1993	0.9	2.4	52.0	65.8	47.0	31.8
1996	0.6	1.6	46.8	59.3	52.5	39.0

Source: Civil Service Commission, various years.

petence rather than vindictiveness. According to the union leadership, it never threatened MGEU-government relations or their ultimate ability to renew productive relations. On the other hand, Commission officials were unhappy with the climate that developed at the bargaining table in the years when there was neither money nor rule flexibility to negotiate.

Furthermore, relations between the MGEU and the government broke down following the introduction of Bill 70 in 1990. Prior to this time a consultative body, the Joint Council, made up of three union and three government representatives, met regularly to discuss government plans and to hear union representations on industrial relations matters. However, with Bill 70 the relationship quickly began to deteriorate and the meetings ceased being meaningful. According to the MGEU, 'all the union's representations fell on deaf ears as the government was determined to implement its rights as it saw fit, which was a significant change from past practice' (Olfert and Comstock, 1998). As a result, the Joint Council ceased to meet and has not yet resumed meeting despite the recent improvement in relations with the relaxation of the fiscal cutbacks.

Though the MGEU and Civil Service Commission officials did not feel that the long-term labour relations climate had suffered, this feeling may not be shared by the union membership. A mail-in survey was conducted of a randomly selected sample of MGEU members.[46] Of those who responded, 83 per cent indicated that industrial relations had deteriorated over the past 10 years, with 67 per cent rating current union-management relations as poor, 30 per cent as fair, and only 6 per cent as good (no one rated the relationship as excellent). When asked why the relationship had deteriorated, the majority indicated that it resulted from government attacks on the unions and the civil service in particular.

When asked what specific event(s) marked the change in relationship, the answers were more varied. The most frequent response, mentioned by about a quarter of respondents, was the government's unilateral overruling of collective agreements and legislating days off without pay (Filmon Fridays) and wage freezes and rollbacks.[47] This variety of responses supports the conclusion that the deterioration in the industrial relations climate within the civil service was in response to an accumulation of grievances relating to the government's fiscal policies, social and economic programs, and labour relations policies rather than to any one or small number of specific events or legislative or policy measures. Finally, there was little indication that the recent thaw in the government's relations with the MGEU altered the perceptions of provincial employees, with over two-thirds of respondents indicating that they believed the government's goals had not changed over the past five years of protracted restraint.

In short, we believe that at the level of union-management relations, 'professionalism' has prevailed and relations between the Commission and the MGEU have not deteriorated significantly. At the 'shop-floor' level, however, there appears to be evidence of an increase in distrust and alienation resulting from the process of civil service downsizing and wage freezes.

Other Impacts on the Labour-Management Relationship

The restraint period had rather mixed effects on some other aspects of the labour-management relationship, specifically on pay equity and training. Pay equity had been legislated by the previous government and implemented within the civil service through a negotiated 4 per cent increase for women phased in over four years. Though this was not rolled back, the government attempted to renege on the extension of pay equity to government agencies and the quasi-public sector as mandated by the legislation. This led to a strike situation that forced the government to complete the program.

In the case of training, the impact was more complex. As we noted previously, some monies were made available to retrain specific groups of laid-off workers. However, there were big cuts in general training funds in the 1991-4 period and only recently, in the last collective agreement, has some new money been set aside for training.

More indicative of the breach in labour-management relations was the unilateral initiation by management of 'quality of working life' (QWL) schemes throughout the civil service without consultation with the MGEU or democratic representation from among the workers affected. Committees were created by management 'all over the place' to deal with issues such as restructuring and implementing the government's new philosophy as represented by the buzz words 'service first' and 'working better'. Attempts by the MGEU to negotiate QWL programs and processes at the bargaining table were rejected outright by the government as an infringement of its management rights. This is indicative of the government's (though not necessarily the Civil Service Commission's) attitude towards its major union.

Conclusion

After two years of governing with a fragile minority administration, the Manitoba Conservatives were able to form a majority government in 1990, just in time to suffer the effects of an international recession precipitated by the monetarist policies of major central banks, including the Bank of Canada. It was also the time when the public concerns over government deficits and debt were reaching a peak. The 'fiscal crisis' gave the Manitoba government a convenient rationale to downsize the public sector, cut social programs, reduce public-sector wages, privatize Crown corporations, and contract out government services—restrictive policies the public otherwise might not have tolerated. Rather than attempt to negotiate with the major public-sector unions about how and what cuts could be made, the Manitoba government unilaterally imposed wage freezes and rollbacks through legislation and simultaneously cut civil service jobs by reducing departmental budgets.

The cutbacks in the civil service must be seen in the context of the larger agenda being implemented by the government, since the actual cuts in the total civil service compensation constituted a very minor component of the fiscal recovery. By our estimates, the growth in VLT revenues between 1992 and 1997 generated almost five times the reduction in civil service compensation by the compulsory days off, wage rollbacks, and job reductions, though it must be recognized that legislated wage restraint policies also applied to most public employees outside the civil service, thus adding significantly to the budgetary savings realized from civil servants.

One aspect of the Conservatives' policies that finance ministers and the Premier repeatedly emphasized was the creation of a more 'business-friendly' climate in Manitoba. This was interpreted to mean a low tax environment and a low-wage, compliant labour force. The government used its own workforce to lead by demonstration.

Notes

1. We use the term 'neo-liberal' rather than the more fashionable, but less accurate, term 'neo-conservative' because the policies and programs that these governments advanced were based on nineteenth-century liberal economics. We distinguish the 'neo-liberal agenda' from the response to the debt and deficit debate in that neo-liberalism extends far beyond the issue of fiscal conservatism or the pragmatic response to a perceived fiscal shortfall. Rather, it attacks on ideological grounds the very commitment of the government to the provision of the welfare state and opposes government intervention and regulation of markets to correct distributional and market failures.

2. The history of the Manitoba Government Employees' Union is detailed in Doug Smith (1993), which is the major source of the following account.

3. In 1992 the MGEA changed its name to the Manitoba Government Employees' Union (MGEU). We refer to the MGEA pre-1992 and the MGEU post-1992 here.

4. The right to strike and opposition to arbitration became a trademark of Canadian unionism only after the takeover of the Canadian labour movement by the American Federation of Labor early in the last century. Prior to that time, and indeed among many Canadian unionists for several decades later, arbitration was preferred to the right to strike as the method for settling industrial disputes. In Australia and New Zealand, where the American influence was not determining, the arbitration route became the standard. As late as 1987 the issue was still current in Manitoba when many unions, though not necessarily a majority, opposed the Pawley NDP government's introduction of final-offer-selection arbitration legislation, which provided for limited rights of interest arbitration at the workers' initiative.

5. In the reopening of the 1982 contract to meet budgetary restraints, 'the Province introduced a priority staffing program to place or retrain individuals whose positions were declared redundant. . . . Another component of the program dealing with redundant employees was the use of a portion of the $10 million saved as a result of renegotiating the collective agreement as a source of funds for retraining employees. . . . As a final initiative designed to create turnover

and employment opportunities within Government, the Province introduced an early retirement incentive program. . . . We believe these examples best illustrate a comprehensive approach to a particular industrial relations issue. At all stages in the process, full consultation occurred with the major bargaining agent.' (Irving, 1986: 325–6). This set the pattern for the handling of redundancies by the Civil Service Commission during the nineties.

6. In 1986 he was replaced by Peter Olfert, who has remained as president since.

7. The result of the election was Conservatives 24 , Liberals 20, NDP 12.

8. For a discussion of the 'social democratic approach', see Phillips (1991: 121–3). 'The essence of the social democratic approach, therefore, has been *legislation*: the provisions of machinery for reconciling without violence the inherent conflict between workers and employers, and for advancing labour's interests through laws enforced through a series of quasi-judicial tribunals (labour boards, arbitration boards) and the courts. It has also sought, again by legislation, to create new individual and collective rights, including the right to some protection from the abuses of the capitalist market' (122).

9. Real rates of interest were kept at extremely high levels throughout the 1980s, peaking in 1989 and 1990. Allegations have been made that the Canadian government kept interest rates high to increase the exchange value of the Canadian dollar, a commitment that the Mulroney government made in order to overcome United States objections to the Canada-US Free Trade Agreement (FTA). Whether or not this is true, interest and exchange rates remained inordinately high, thereby dampening exports and encouraging imports to the detriment of the Canadian unemployment rate.

10. The figures in this table are from Canada, Department of Finance, *Fiscal Reference Tables*, October 1997. They differ somewhat from those in the annual publication of the Provincial Auditor, the *Consolidated Statement of Revenue and Expenditure*, though the general trends are, for the most part, the same. For purposes of disaggregating the expenditures below, the *Consolidated Statement of Revenue and Expenditure* figures are used since a comparable breakdown is not available from the *Fiscal Reference Tables*.

11. Corporate income tax receipts did not recover to their 1989 level until 1997 (Manitoba, *Report of the Provincial Auditor*, various years).

12. Note that the Provincial Auditor's figures for total expenditures are slightly higher than the those reported in the *Fiscal Reference Tables*, with the result that the percentage accounted for by payments on the debt is slightly lower in Table 4.2 than in Table 4.1, by approximately 0.5 to 0.8 per cent, except in 1977–8 and the two fiscal years from 1991 to 1993. The reason for these differences is not clear. However, there is no major discrepancy in the order of magnitude between the two series.

13. The *Fiscal Reference Tables* tell a similar story. The only major dip in aggregate federal transfers is in the period 1992–4.

14. According to the CANSIM data, the decline in total government employment was considerably less, approximately 5 per cent over the comparable period.

15. The election was a disaster for the NDP, going from government (and 29 seats) to third-party status (12 seats) and losing 14 seats to the Liberals. The party's share of the popular vote dropped to under 24 per cent. The Conservatives, however, also lost seats to the surging Liberals, who trailed the Tories by only four seats to become the official opposition, thus leaving the Conservatives in a minority government position.

16. One exception was the government's move to privatize Manitoba Data Services, a profitable Crown corporation processing primarily provincial government data, in which there were some MGEA members. The MGEA unsuccessfully fought the sale. There were other battles between the government and the labour movement generally. One was over Final Offer Selection (FOS) arbitration brought in by the previous NDP administration. Here the Conservatives had the support of the Liberals, who also opposed FOS. However, attempts by the Conservatives to repeal the legislation in 1989 were defeated by a filibuster and legislative manoeuvring by the NDP.

17. The relocation program was postponed in March 1991, not because of union opposition but because of fiscal restraint. Relocation proved to be an expensive election promise.

18. The Liberals were reduced to seven seats. The party had begun to flounder soon after the 1988 election, largely due to inexperience of most of the new members. Indeed, the more seasoned members of the NDP led the opposition in Question Period and they were also able to split the Liberals over the issue of FOS arbitration.

19. The Act affected the civil service and employees of various Crown corporations, as well as employees of health and social services. Nurses, government-employed doctors, lab and X-ray technicians, teachers, school, municipal, and university employees, judges, and MLAs were excluded.

20. The major arbitration award, which included the narrow interpretation, is not reported. However, a summary is included in Manitoba Labour Relations Board (1993: AA93–04–014), Province of Manitoba and the MGEA, 30 April (Ibrahim Award). The chair of the Arbitration Board was Martin Friedman, QC, and this award was cited in all the other bumping cases that went to arbitration.

21. The inclusion of provincial court judges under this legislation was challenged in the courts. The primary issue of contention was the independence of the courts from the political party of the day. The challenge was ultimately heard by the Supreme Court of Canada, which decided against the provincial government, and the judges were reimbursed for lost wages. The other staff who had to be present (such as court clerks) were, however, not reimbursed.

22. In early 1995, the Minister of Finance, Eric Stefanson, claimed that the savings in the first two years of the days-off-without-pay program were $22 million and 500 jobs.

23. There was little support for this suggestion in a subsequent survey of union members, discussed later in the chapter. Also, all unions (including the MGEU) affected by the compulsory days-off-without-pay legislation negotiated an end to them as soon as the legislation expired.

24. The 18-month contract from October 1994 to March 1996 synchronized the MGEU contract with the government's fiscal year. The MGEU did not resort to arbitration in the first contract because the first half of the period covered by the contract was subject to Bill 22 and, in any case, only a few months remained before the second contract had to be negotiated. In the second contract, a policy decision was taken to go the strike route. When the strike vote failed, the union was forced to accept the government's last offer.

25. One reason for the failure to achieve a majority in favour of a strike may have been uncertainty in the minds of many civil servants of the legality of strike action. The only previous government strike, by corrections staff, was settled before its legality could be determined by the courts.

26. Smith (1993: 268–9) goes on to say: 'If this [neo-liberal] agenda were to be implemented in Manitoba, people could expect to see cuts in the civil service, the abrogation of public sector bargaining, a centralization of public services, a reduction in the powers of municipal governments and school boards, repeal of labour legislation, reductions in social benefits, and privatization of government information services. To the degree to which these things have been accomplished, it would be fair to say the Filmon government was attempting to implement the New Right agenda.'

27. Drache and Glasbeek (1992: 192–3) have argued that in many jurisdictions government opposition to and restrictions on their own unions were designed to 'send an unmistakable message to the private sector . . . to be tough with trade unions [and even] to undermine them'.

28. Estimate provided by Peter Olfert, president of the MGEU.

29. Manitoba Civil Service Commission negotiators said that, despite the MGEU request for arbitration, no preparations were made to set up the machinery and the threat of arbitration had never been a factor in their relations with the union (Irving and Pruden, 1998).

30. Olfert and Comstock (1998); Irving and Pruden (1998).

31. Loxley (1995: 19) notes, 'budgets are important in helping *manage* economies, helping smooth out the inevitable boom and bust cycles of capitalism, and building infrastructure to maintain or enhance the quality of life.'

32. This restriction does not apply to user charges and a host of other taxes that the Conservatives raised both before and after the Act was introduced. Loxley (1995: 20, 54) argues that the net effect of the legislation was regressive by ensuring that the tax burden was shifted onto the poor.

33. Requests from the City of Winnipeg for new sources of funding to offset falling provincial transfers and rising property taxes were met by repeated refusals from the provincial government, which continually suggested that if Winnipeg would only treat its workers as the province had treated its employees, the city would not need new revenues.

34. The industrial relations literature on the inherent conservatism of the civil service and of professionals to unionize and to take collective action is quite large. For Canada, see Thompson (1982: 385, 394–5); Ponak (1982: 351–2);

Ponak and Thompson (1989); Crispo (1978: 143 ff.) However, the most recent evidence is that professional and white-collar government employees are in fact among the most likely employees to join unions. Nationally in 1998, union coverage among professionals, such as nurses and teachers, was reported as 51.5 per cent, among clerical workers, 30.6 per cent compared to the average union density of 33.0 per cent. On an industry basis, government services had a density of 70.5 per cent, more than double the average rate (Akyeampong, 1998: 36–7). However, this does not imply that such professional, white-collar, and government service workers are as militant or ready to resort to industrial action as blue-collar workers in the traditional union sectors.

35. The Corrections Division had gone on an unofficial strike, the legality of which was never resolved, in 1977. Lottery workers and home-care and nursing-home workers struck for extended periods in 1996.

36. Smith (1993: 276) notes, for instance, that 'in 1991 the Coalition for Fairness brought together over 25 unions [including the MGEA] that were affected by the government's wage freeze. The association also mounted a media campaign before the 1991 budget to highlight to the public the government programs that were at risk. This was followed by a radio campaign that enumerated the services being reduced. In 1992 the union mounted a media relations campaign designed to remind people of the variety of services they received from government employees.' Further, the association organized a national conference on health care and, in conjunction with the Canadian Union of Public Employees (CUPE) conducted a public education campaign opposing cuts to health care.

37. The government adopted the tactic of having the committee hold hearings all night. As a result, many of those who had signed up to make presentations were unable to do so. There is little indication that the government majority on the committee or the government itself paid any attention to the presentations made in any case.

38. However, this has not extended to some of the government services that were spun off as 'profit making' agencies (such as the government post office) where management has become less accommodative, particularly of people with behavioural and attitudinal problems (Buckley and Turcan, 1998).

39. What the government's involvement was in the initiation of these programs and whether they comprised part of any coherent human resource management policy is impossible to say. Attempts to arrange an interview with the minister responsible for the civil service during much of this period, to explore this and related questions, were unsuccessful. On the other hand, the general pattern of the adjustment program appears similar to that worked out in the early 1980s between the Pawley government and the MGEA (see Irving, 1986: 325–6).

40. The rise in lottery profits was largely the result of expanded VLT gambling, which increased revenues from $5 million in 1992 to $124 million in 1997 (Manitoba, *Financial Statements* 1988–94; *Public Accounts,* 1994–7).

41. Although not included in Table 4.8, the proportion of males over 55 years declined slightly over the period. This was more than offset by the rise in the

proportion of males in the 45–54 age group. However, the proportion of females age over 55 years actually increased over the period.

42. This is based on the assumption that 60 per cent of the employees in the age group 45–54 in 1990 would be age 55 + six years later. Even if the 45–54 age group was skewed toward the lower end of the age group, the majority of the downsizing must have come from the oldest age group(s) who were not replaced by younger workers (i.e., if only 40 per cent of the employees 45–54 stayed to enter the 55 + age group in 1996, the reduction in employment in the 55 + group would account for over half of the total decline in the regular full-time workforce).

43. Interestingly, that is considerably less than the government 'earned' in *each* of the years 1995 to 1997 from VLTs.

44. In real terms, the decrease was considerably greater, $415 million.

45. The relatively minor role of civil service salaries in the fiscal position of the province reinforces our conclusion that the civil service cuts were just part of a much larger agenda involving the reduction of the public sector and the creation of a labour cost (low real wage) and anti-union environment favourable to attracting business. This conclusion does not rest entirely on the evaluation of the government's approach to its own employees. The Conservative administration also introduced changes in 1996 to the Labour Relations Act and the Essential Services Act designed to weaken organized labour's bargaining power and to restrict its political and social activity. See also Drache and Glasbeek (1992: 192–3).

46. One hundred fifty survey forms were mailed and 35 responses were received, a return rate of 23.3 per cent. Three or four of those who responded indicated that they were new or recent employees and therefore could not respond to any or all of the questions. The results of the survey were compatible with anecdotal evidence of impaired industrial relations gathered in the course of the study. However, given the relatively low response rate and the bias inherent in voluntary response surveys, the results should be interpreted with caution and considered as indicative rather than conclusive.

47. It should be noted that not all the respondents were opposed to Filmon Fridays, although only two indicated this was a favourable way of implementing civil service salary cutbacks. This is a much smaller number than would be expected given the Civil Service Commission's sanguine view of the popularity of Filmon Fridays.

References

Akyeampong, Ernest. 1998. 'The Rise of Unionization Among Women', *Perspectives*, Statistics Canada (Winter).

Canada, Department of Finance. 1997. *Fiscal Reference Tables*. Ottawa.

Crispo, John.1978. *The Canadian Industrial Relations System*. Toronto: McGraw-Hill Ryerson.

Drache, Daniel, and Harry Glasbeek. 1992. *The Changing Workplace*. Toronto: Lorimer.

Godard, John. 1998. 'Manitoba: Beyond Class Struggle?', Faculty of Management, University of Manitoba, unpublished paper.

Irving, Gerry. 1986. 'Industrial Relations: The Manitoba Experience', in Mark Thompson, ed., *Is There a New Industrial Relations*, Proceedings of the 23rd Annual Meeting of the Canadian Industrial Relations Association (Winnipeg: CIRA), 323–32.

Loxley, John. 1995. 'Balanced Budget Legislation or Bad Budget Legislation?', *Canadian Dimension* (Dec.-Jan.): 19–20, 54.

Manitoba. *Financial Statements of Boards, Commissions and Government Agencies*. 1989–94. Winnipeg.

——. *Manitoba Budget Highlights*. 1988–97. Winnipeg.

——. *Public Accounts*. 1988–97. Winnipeg.

——. 1991. Public Sector Compensation Management Act (Bill 70). Winnipeg.

——. 1993. Public Sector Reduced Work Week and Compensation Management Act (Bill 22). Winnipeg.

——. *Report of the Provincial Auditor: Summary Financial Statements*. 1988–97. Winnipeg.

Manitoba Civil Service Commission. 1988–97. *Annual Reports*. Winnipeg.

Manitoba Government Employees' Union. 1991–7. 'Summaries' of Collective Agreements.

——. 1993. 'Tax Savings Under Bill 22', unpublished study.

Manitoba Labour Board. 1993. *Compendium of Grievance Arbitration Decisions*. Winnipeg.

Mimoto, H., and P. Cross. 1991. 'The Growth of the Federal Debt', *Canadian Economic Observer* (June).

O'Connor, James. 1973. *The Fiscal Crisis of the State*. New York: St Martin's Press.

Phillips, Paul. 1991. 'Spinning a Web of Rules', in Errol Black and Jim Silver, eds, *Hard Bargains* (Winnipeg: Manitoba Labour Education Centre).

Ponak, Allen. 1982. 'Public-Sector Collective Bargaining', in John Anderson and Morley Gunderson, eds, *Union-Management Relations in Canada* (Don Mills, Ont.: Addison-Wesley).

—— and Mark Thompson. 1989. 'Public Sector Collective Bargaining', in John Anderson and Morley Gunderson, eds, *Union-Management Relations in Canada*, 2nd edn (Don Mills, Ont.: Addison-Wesley).

Smith, Doug. 1993. *Lives in the Public Service: A History of the Manitoba Government Employees' Union*. Winnipeg: Manitoba Labour Education Centre.

Statistics Canada, CANSIM matrices 2863, 2866.

Thompson, Mark. 1982. 'Collective Bargaining by Professionals', in John Anderson and Morley Gunderson, eds, *Union-Management Relations in Canada* (Don Mills, Ont.: Addison-Wesley).

Interviews

Bruce Buckley and Terry Turcan, Staff Representatives, MGEU, 11 Mar. 1998.

Gary Doer, former President of MGEA and current provincial NDP leader, 12 Mar. 1998.

Gerry Irving, Assistant Deputy Minister, and Bob Pruden, Director, Negotiation Services, Labour Relations Division, Manitoba Civil Service Commission, 9 Mar. 1998.

Peter Olfert, President, and Bill Comstock, Director, Negotiation Services, MGEU, 25 Feb. 1998.

Chapter 5

The Logic of Union Quiescence: The Alberta Case

Yonatan Reshef

Worldwide, governments are trying to balance their budgets and eliminate their debts. Since 1993, in North America, Alberta has been on the forefront of these efforts, even viewed by some as a trailblazer (Farnsworth, 1995; Fund, 1995). Upon election in June 1993, Premier Ralph Klein and his Progressive Conservative government embarked on an ambitious plan, popularly known as the 'Klein Revolution'. The target was to eliminate the provincial debt by 2010 and balance the budget within four years without raising taxes. The major vehicles to its achievement were unprecedented budget cuts and public-sector restructuring.[1]

But not everyone was ready to surrender to the Klein Revolution. The day after Albertans handed a majority mandate to Klein, union leaders were confident that, in the coming months, workers across the province would unite against Klein's policies, that 'the government would cave in and the labour movement would rise as a major political force in Alberta' (Feschuk and Mitchell, 1994). 'You are headed for one of the biggest labour battles that you've ever seen in this province', declared the newly elected president of the largest union in Alberta, the Alberta Union of Provincial Employees (AUPE) (Coulter, 1993). Given the organizational muscle of AUPE, as well as of other public-sector unions in health care and education, labour militancy was a real prospect.

More than five years later, unions have failed to influence the Klein Revolution in any significant way. Instead, union leaders have created a credibility gap between their initial rhetoric and subsequent practices. To explore the sources of this gap, this chapter focuses on union responses to the Klein government policies and the forces shaping these responses. Specifically, I am asking why AUPE did not mount any collective action to influence the political discourse in Alberta between 1993 and 1998. Though the relationship between the government and AUPE is my major focus, occasionally I will refer to the actions of health-care and education unions during the Klein Revolution, to broaden the discussion and put it in perspective.

For the purpose of this study, collective action is a political expression organized by unions outside the physical and political boundaries of a particular workplace or bargaining unit. The action encompasses a large number of participants who challenge the government's definition of 'what is the public interest', in an attempt to protect public goods that may be associated with their work (Johnston, 1994: 13). Data for this study were collected through semi-structured interviews and archival material. I conducted in-depth interviews with 40 union and 15 management/government personnel.[2]

Industrial Relations in a Conservative Province

A Conservative Climate

In the immediate pre- and post-World War I years, most Alberta labour leaders were leaning towards radicalism and heavy political involvement. Alberta was home to some of the most radical labour and political movements and birthplace of both the One Big Union (OBU), in 1919, and the Co-operative Commonwealth Federation (CCF), in 1932. This radicalism eventually faltered and failed (see Geddes, 1990). Nowadays, Alberta unions' industrial relations approach is based on a conservative, business unionism philosophy. Their focus of activity is the workplace, where members' immediate economic interests are protected chiefly through collective bargaining. Not surprisingly, business unionism fits the unions' conservative environment.

Alberta's conservatism 'is accepted as a matter of faith by most Canadians' (Ponak, Reshef, and Taras, 1998: 1). The conservative Social Credit Party governed the province from 1935 to 1971. Since then, the Progressive Conservative Party has dominated the political scene in Alberta. In 1993, the labour-oriented New Democratic Party (NDP) was eliminated from the legislature (it won two seats in the 83-seat legislature in the 1997 election). The 1997 election cemented a 26-year hold of power by the Progressive Conservatives, who increased their seats from 54 to 63. The landslide victory came in the wake of the Klein Revolution and, thus, should be seen as a vote of confidence in the government and its direction. It should come as no surprise that the Reform Party, the most right-of-centre of current federal political parties, originated in Alberta.

Several examples illustrate the province's fiscal conservatism. Until recently, the province's $5.00-an-hour minimum wage was the lowest in Canada;[3] its total per capita expenditures on health decreased from $2,495 in 1993 to $2,317 (estimated) in 1997, well below the national average of $2,528 (Alberta Health, 1998); and the government has set a target for per capita provincial expenditure of 5 per cent below the average of the other nine provinces (Government of Alberta, 1997a, 1998, 1999). From 1995–6 to 1997–8 the government's per capita expenditure was approximately 91.0 per cent of the average of the other nine provinces.

The oil and gas industry, with its culture of rugged individualism and *laissez-faire* ideology, has played an important role in shaping the province's conservative climate (Harrison and Laxer, 1995: 5). To a large extent the fortunes of this industry dictate the fortunes of the province. 'It is significant that the industry is entrepreneurial, paternalistic, and predominantly non-union' (Ponak, Reshef, and Taras, 1998: 2). Moreover, Alberta lacks a significant manufacturing base, the traditional bastion of trade unionism. In 1995, the manufacturing sector employed 8.0 per cent of the total labour force (Statistics Canada, 1995: B31). The comparable figure for January 1999 was 8.5 per cent (Alberta Advanced Education and Career Development, 1999).

Interestingly, in industrial relations, general conservatism has been mixed with local populism. Although according to a recent national poll Albertans are the most accepting of the right of managers of profitable companies to lay off employees and out-source in-house operations (*Maclean's*, 1996–7: 26, 27), in practice, Albertans do not automatically support profitable companies pursuing greater profits at the expense of employees. In May–June 1997, the United Food and Commercial Workers mobilized 10,000 Safeway workers to strike the company's 75 stores. Though the stores remained open during the 75-day strike, customers largely stayed away and sales revenue fell by more than half. And, in 1995, the public supported an illegal strike by some 120 laundry workers. Apparently, Albertans possess a basic sense of fairness, and they do not hesitate to express themselves when they perceive it to have been violated.

Generally, however, Albertans are not supportive of trade unions. In a survey of 1,240 Albertans, 68.4 per cent responded that they would not join a union if one existed in their workplace (Fong, Kinzel, and Odynak, 1995). In addition, 75.0 per cent of the respondents disagreed with the statement, 'Unions in the public sector (government, health care, education) should be directly involved in decision-making about budget cuts.' Low attitudinal support for unions and few manufacturing establishments have translated into low unionization levels, which since the early 1980s have been the lowest in Canada (Coates, Arrowsmith, and Courchene, 1989: 36; Statistics Canada, 1990, 1992; Akyeampong, 1997). In 1997, unionization reached its lowest level, 22.1 per cent, since its 1983 peak of 32.3 per cent. Between 1983 and 1996, private-sector unionization dropped from 16.0 to 13.8 per cent, whereas unionization in public administration plummeted from 79.3 to 58.6 per cent (Alberta Labour, 1986, 1998). Broader public-sector unionization remained stable at 63.7 per cent.

The Legal Environment

Labour law has long been recognized as an important formal expression of the socio-political climate in a particular society (Cohen, 1961), and Alberta's labour laws reflect its conservative leaning. Although the labour laws generally follow prevailing Canadian models, a 1986 national survey of some 10,000 entrepreneurs deemed Alberta the province with the least pro-labour legal system in

Canada (Languedoc, 1986). In the public sector, Alberta requires interest dispute arbitration for firefighters, police officers, civil servants, hospital employees, and employees in government enterprises, granting only teachers and civic employees the right to strike. University and college teachers, however, are respectively covered by the Universities Act and the Colleges Act, which mandate the creation of academic staff associations as the only legal bargaining agent and prohibit strikes. This situation has been recognized as the most restrictive in Canada's public sector (Gunderson and Hyatt, 1996: 253).

The comprehensive legislation governing industrial relations in the civil service, the Public Service Employee Relations Act (PSERA), came into effect on 22 September 1977. While generally patterned on Alberta's private-sector legislation, the Act prohibited strikes and lockouts and substituted binding arbitration of interest disputes. Section 55 of the PSERA stipulates three criteria arbitrators must consider in rendering a decision: wages and benefits in private and public and unionized and non-unionized employment; the continuity and stability of private and public employment; and the province's fiscal policies.

The PSERA created a single bargaining agent for all civil service employees, the Alberta Union of Provincial Employees (AUPE), and indicated that civil service employees constitute a single bargaining unit. In reality, however, the AUPE negotiates one master agreement and subsidiary agreements for its 10 local units.[4] The PSERA upholds the right of management to make staffing decisions based on merit rather than the seniority criterion preferred by most unions. Specifically, s. 48(2) of the Act forbids negotiation over employee selection, appointment, promotion, transfer, or training.

The early 1980s provided two examples of Alberta's conservative legal system in action. First, in 1982, the government extended the ban on strikes and lockouts. In the wake of several strikes by nurses, the government introduced the Health Services Continuation Act. It made any strike or lockout involving nurses illegal and called for an arbitration tribunal to prepare a binding collective agreement. In 1983 the government introduced the Labour Statutes Amendment Act (Bill 44), which repealed the Health Services Continuation Act. Bill 44 prohibited strikes and lockouts by any employee/employer group in approved hospitals; introduced compulsory arbitration to deal with impasses in negotiations between hospitals and their employees; and established criteria for determining wages and benefits under compulsory arbitration. These criteria replicate the constraints put on arbitrators by the PSERA with one modification. Instead of heeding the province's fiscal policies in rendering decisions, arbitrators must consider the 'general economic conditions in Alberta' (Section 99[a] [iii]).

Second, in the spring and summer of 1982, Alberta's construction unions and contractors concluded more than 30 collective agreements giving workers record pay increases (Fisher and Kushner, 1986). Unfortunately, the parties were unaware that a deep economic crisis was looming. Within a few months, largely due to declining oil prices and high interest rates, two megaprojects (Cold Lake and Alsands) were cancelled. This triggered a chain reaction of postponements and cancellations of hundreds of projects of all sizes by the end of that summer. Unemployment quickly soared to unprecedented levels. Wishing to capitalize on the situation, union contractors were looking for ways to get out of existing collective agreements. Altering terms and conditions of employment 24 hours after the commencement of a lockout became a popular tactic among contractors. In 1984, the Alberta Labour Relations Board upheld the legality of the 24-hour lockout.

In summary, until 1993, Alberta unions operated within a conservative yet relatively stable environment. In the civil service, the government never seriously jeopardized the AUPE's vested interests in job security and organizational survival. This would change profoundly with the 1993 election and the advent of the Klein Revolution.

The Changing Context of Industrial Relations

The 1993 provincial election was fought over which political party would reduce public spending the most. Upon election, Premier Ralph Klein and his Progressive Conservative government began to fulfil their campaign promises by introducing across-the-board reductions in provincial funding to all government departments. Over four years, the government would cut basic education by 5.6 per cent, higher education by 15.3 per cent, health care by 17.7 per cent, and general welfare by 19.1 per cent. Other departments would take average budget cuts of 20 per cent. Alberta wiped out the deficit in less than three years by reducing its level of provincial spending to an exceptionally low level, 'by a considerable measure, the lowest per capita in Canada' (McMillan, 1996: 15). In 1995, these reductions amounted to a drop of 27.4 per cent in real per capita expenditures in government services (McMillan and Warrack, 1995: 149).

In its battle to put the province permanently back on solid financial ground, in 1995 the government enacted the Balanced Budget and Debt Retirement Act, which forbade the government from bringing down a budget with a planned deficit. The Act outlined procedures the budget planning process must follow to prevent unplanned deficits and required that any budget surplus be directed at paying down the provincial debt. The Act did not sanction any penalty if the government strayed from this course of action.

In early 1998, posting a $2.73 billion budget surplus, the government made a payment of $2.6 billion on the net debt. However, this is after taking into account one-time spending of $390 million on health care, education, and public works. Without those expenses, the surplus would have been more than $3 billion. The surplus for 1998–9 was a much more modest $672 million. In 1999, Alberta became the only province in Canada with no remaining net debt (the current $14 billion gross debt is matched by an amount in the Heritage Savings Trust Fund, established decades ago during the boom years). In early 1999, the government enacted the Fiscal Responsibility Act, which requires that Alberta's accumulated debt ($14 billion) be eliminated in 25 years, and sets five-year milestones to ensure progress.

The above developments were important landmarks in the Klein government's campaign to promote the 'Alberta Advantage', which implied that flexible labour policies, privatization, and low overall labour costs were an effective industrial strategy. This strategy and associated processes reshaped the industrial relations scene in Alberta.

Workforce Reduction

A massive workforce reduction through layoffs, voluntary severance, and early retirement figured prominently in the Klein Revolution. Between 1994 and 1997, provincial civil service permanent full-time and long-term wage employees were reduced by 23.5 per cent, from 27,705 to 21,193 (Alberta Personnel Administration Office, 1995, 1996, 1997).[5] Using a different definition of employee, Statistics Canada (1998: 19, 38) reports that between 1992 and 1996 Alberta recorded a civil service decline of 27.3 per cent, the largest of any province.[6] In addition, between 1993 and 1995 the Alberta health-care workforce declined by 21.2 per cent, from 65,512 to 51,639 employees (Alberta Health, 1994, 1995). In education, by early 1997 there were about 1,500 fewer teachers than three years earlier, or about 5.0 per cent of the 1993 teaching workforce (Johnsrude, 1997). Not surprisingly, as Table 5.1 reports, between 1992 and 1997 the four major Alberta public-sector unions suffered membership losses.

Wage Rollbacks

A compensation rollback for public-sector managers and front-line employees facilitated the Alberta government effort to balance the budget and eliminate the

Table 5.1: Union Membership, 1992–1997

Unions*	Union Membership		Membership Change (%)
	1992	*1997*	
Alberta Union of Provincial Employees (AUPE)	48,246	36,910	−23.5
United Nurses of Alberta (UNA)**	14,000	12,500	−10.7
Alberta Teachers Association (ATA)	30,858	29,358	−4.9
Canadian Union of Public Employees (CUPE)	27,881	26,878	−3.6

*These four unions are the biggest unions in Alberta with one exception. UNA is the fifth biggest union, following the 18,000-member United Food and Commercial Workers.

**In 1997, UNA's membership grew to more than 16,000 following its 15 October merger with the Staff Nurses Association of Alberta (SNAA).

Sources: HRDC (1992, 1997); personal communications with ATA, UNA, and CUPE.

provincial debt. In October 1993, the government asked all health-care employees voluntarily to take a 5 per cent pay cut. Soon, the request was extended to all other public-sector employees. In November 1993, the government announced that the salary budgets for health, education, advanced education, and public administration were being cut by 5 per cent. Consequently, in 1994, all public-sector employees were expected to take a 5 per cent wage rollback followed by a two-year wage freeze. Unions were expected voluntarily to negotiate the rollbacks with the respective employers. However, according to the interviewed union leaders, there was a real possibility that the government would impose the rollbacks if the unions failed to negotiate them. During the negotiations themselves, employers threatened unions with more layoffs if they did not accept the required 5 per cent, and sometimes even deeper, rollbacks. Most unions negotiated the –5,0,0 framework, hoping to ensure their members' job security. Two AUPE local presidents explain:

> The reason why we buckled under the pressure to take that 5 per cent [wage cut] was because we were promised at the time that more members would not lose their jobs. We were told over and over again by a well-oiled provincial machine that we were in big trouble financially and that we had to take this rollback. So, we said, OK, we better help out the province. We don't want to get other members fired. . . . So we gave in. . . . They [government personnel] really sold that whole concept: do your part; just do this little 5 per cent and things will be fine!

An AUPE officer adds that 'the government never put it in writing, but the government made it pretty clear through negotiations and through its public statements at the time that the alternative to the rollbacks was massive job losses.' A government official explains that 'the pitch was fine. If you don't take the minus five then we're going to have to lay off *more* people so we can achieve that saving. There's going to be downsizing, yes there is.' Thus, the government never suggested that the –5,0,0 framework would come in lieu of downsizing. The rollback would merely reduce its scope.

Following additional developments described below, the union leaders realized that the Klein government was determined to impose its agenda and they could do little to stop it:

> There was very little you could say that would make sense as to 'how do we react to all this?!' The load of public thinking as well as the reckless exercise of power that Ralph Klein is engaged in. And so, at the time the 5 per cent was imposed, all of that was working against any member who thought they had any power to do anything about it. . . . The Klein government had demonstrated its resolve. It had demonstrated that it was going to bulldoze ahead with its plans and its policies, regardless of opposition. And at that point [when demanding the 5.0 per cent wage rollback] they were still riding high in the polls, and they felt that they were invincible. And maybe in a political sense they were. So, I think that realization probably coloured a lot of the decisions that were being made by the union leaders.

The government did not instruct unions and managers how to implement the rollbacks. The expectation was that reduced budgets would compel the parties, jointly and creatively, to restructure and streamline operations. As one government official explains:

> We [government] are not telling you [unions/managers] how to achieve it [the 5 per cent wage reduction], but we're telling you what our fiscal expectations are. You folks can sort out during the life of your collective bargaining how you're going to achieve your cutbacks. And those cutbacks, in a bargaining sense, lead to many many areas of restructuring. Because it wasn't just from a monetary perspective but it was how they organized and designed their work.

In 1994, the AUPE's three-year collective agreement contained a 2.3 per cent rollback of wages. Another 1.2 per cent reduction was obtained by employees taking three days off without pay, and an additional 1.6 per cent reduction was obtained by employees taking four statutory days off without pay. This agreement contained a 'sunset clause' stating that the 1.6 per cent wage reduction would be restored on 1 September 1997.

The erosion of unionized civil servants' wages had begun before the Klein Revolution, in 1986 (AUPE, 1996). Despite a 10 per cent raise over the previous two years, by 1992 real wages had fallen to about 95 per cent of the 1986 levels. After 1993 that decline accelerated. Between 1993 and 1997 the average annual salary of permanent full-time government employees dropped by 1.94 per cent, from $39,901 to $39,126 (Personnel Administration Office, 1993, 1997). Table 5.2 presents changes in unionized civil service workers' real wages as percentages of 1986 wages.

In 1997–8, the AUPE's main bargaining thrust was to restore the 1994–5 wage losses. By July 1999, the following wage settlement was accepted by all but one of the union's local units.[7] As of 31 August 1997 the employees received a 1.6 per cent wage increase representing that part of the 5 per cent rollback subject to a 'sunset' clause in the 1994 agreement. The employees received another 2.3

Table 5.2: Unionized Civil Servants' Real Wages as Percentage of 1986 Wages

Years	Consumer Price Index Change(%)*	Real Wages as Percentage of 1986 Wages	% Wage Increase
1992	1.5	95.4	0.00
1993	1.1	94.3	0.00
1994	1.5	88.3	−5.00
1995	2.3	86.3	0.00
1996	2.1	83.9	0.00

*Percentage change from the previous year, for Alberta.
Source: AUPE (1996).

per cent increase as of 1 September 1997, equal to the portion of the rollback removed from the salary grid. The remaining 1.2 per cent, which corresponds to three unpaid days off between Christmas and New Year's, was restored on 1 January 1998. On 1 September 1998, employees received an additional wage increase of 2.25 per cent, their first *real* wage increase since 1986. (Note that AUPE members did get *nominal* wage increases between 1986 and 1993.) For the first time, a 2.0 per cent 'achievement bonus' was given to every local unit member upon ratification of the agreement. Management may wish to tie this lump sum to employee performance during the next bargaining round, scheduled for 1 September 1999.[8]

Civil Service Restructuring

A comprehensive restructuring of the civil service was a major component of the Klein Revolution, driven by a business planning approach, privatization of government services, work design, and human resources management (HRM) innovation. Following the 1993 budget, each government agency developed a three-year business plan indicating its needs, goals, achievement tactics, and performance measures. The business plans are meant to reflect the government's commitment to 'transparency' and 'accountability' by defining concrete goals and clearly describing strategies for their achievement. The business plans should also facilitate the government's scheme to minimize its role in the marketplace, or in Klein's parlance, to 'get out of the business of business'. To date, the Klein government has privatized several services, such as highway maintenance, payrolls, automobile licensing and registries, corporate records, boiler inspection, and treasury branches.

The following case of the Alberta Transportation and Utilities (AT&U) department is an example of how restructuring was achieved (Rastin, 1999). The main goals of the 1995 restructuring effort were to:

1. generate $3.2 million per year in savings;
2. outsource 100 per cent of the engineering design process to the private sector;
3. reduce the number of full-time equivalent (FTE) positions to 112 from the existing 333;
4. create performance measures to evaluate the out-sourced engineering design process.

The restructuring team achieved or exceeded the four targets. For example, the number of FTE positions was reduced to 73. Human resources personnel within AT&U actively assisted those laid off through training, counselling, and attempting to relocate the employees to other government jobs. The remaining employees no longer engage in design production or research and development activities, but conduct design review and set technical standards. The department's mission, vision, goals, and performance measures are stated in a three-year business plan. At the beginning of a plan's three-year cycle, front-line employees meet with their supervisors to set goals and learning needs. During the following three years, employees meet with their supervisors three times a year to assess their situation vis-à-vis their plans. To improve everyone's performance, the Personnel Administration Office (1997) introduced a number of HRM innovations, such as 360-degree feedback,[9] teamwork, and skill improvement. Accordingly, AT&U employee qualifications now emphasize flexibility, commitment, and ability to work in teams, learn new skills, and make decisions. The AUPE was kept informed of the changes but did not play an active role in this restructuring effort.

A recent HRM innovation occurred in February 1998, when the government introduced the previously mentioned achievement bonuses. According to the government, achievement bonuses should recognize that there has been a fundamental change in public service performance. Employees are finding new and better ways of doing things and they should be evaluated, recognized, and rewarded accordingly. The AUPE supports the initiative, although the 1998 bonuses were not tied to employee performance, but were given to all local unit members upon ratification of their sub-agreement.

No systematic evidence is available on the penetration of the new HRM initiatives and their effects on employee performance, job satisfaction, and industrial relations. However, performance indicators and employee satisfaction measures suggest that these initiatives are beginning to bear fruit (Personnel Administration Office, 1999). Table 5.3 reports the results of two recent government surveys of employee attitudes towards the HRM innovation (Government of Alberta, 1997b, 1999). In 1997, employees were also asked, 'Thinking back over the last two years, would you say the quality of service provided by Government of Alberta employees has . . .?' Forty-nine per cent of the respondents answered 'decreased', 16 per cent answered 'increased', and 34 per cent replied 'remained the same'. Finally, employees were asked, 'Thinking back over the last two years, would you say employees have become . . .?' Thirty-two per cent of the respondents answered 'more effective', 28 per cent answered 'less effective', and 39 per cent answered 'remained the same'.[10]

The above information suggests that, by and large, employees are satisfied with most elements of the new HRM system. In the 1997 sample, however, respondents did not think that the HRM innovation had improved service quality. In both samples, employees are more satisfied with opportunities they have to expand their knowledge and skills than with opportunities to get involved in business improvements. Employees are least satisfied with the recognition they get for their contribution to progress on business goals. Importantly, the 1998 figures for the last two items show improvement over the comparable 1997 figures. Continuous improvement in these categories is important in order to avoid having knowledgeable and skilled employees who are frustrated with their limited opportunities to participate in business improvement.

Table 5.3: Government Employees' Agreement with Selected Statements

Statement	% Agreed 1997	% Agreed 1998	% Neutral 1997	% Neutral 1998	% Disagreed 1997	% Disagreed 1998
1. You actively work to expand your knowledge and skills.	96	93	2	3	3	3
2. You know and understand how your work contributes to the achievement of department business plan.	77	77	6	7	16	15
3. You have acquired or developed the knowledge and skills over the past two years which has [sic] made you more competitive in the job market.	70	79	6	7	22	13
4. Your organization provides the support you need to acquire or develop knowledge and skills in your current job.	73	76	4	7	22	18
5. Your organization helps you know and understand how your work contributes to the achievement of your department business plan.	62	62	8	12	30	26
6. Your organization provides support to help you acquire or develop knowledge and skills that would make you more competitive in the job market.	61	69	9	8	31	22
7. Your organization asks for employee input when they plan business improvements.	48	54	8	11	44	35
8. Your organization provides recognition for your contribution to progress on business goals.	45	50	10	12	46	37

1997: n = 750.
1998: n = 2,312.
Source: Government of Alberta (1997a, 1999).

Enrolling the Public

A series of opinion polls indicated that Albertans had serious concerns about the impact of Klein's policies on the quality of education and health care (Hughes, Lowe, and McKinnon, 1996). Yet at the same time, a majority of Albertans supported Klein and his agenda in two consecutive elections, in 1993 and 1997. The ability of Albertans to separate Klein from at least some of his policies remains one of the most fascinating phenomena of his administration.

Clearly, Klein's message to the public was highly effective. In the end, as several union leaders admit, most of the public accepted Klein's argument that Alberta had an expenditure problem and not, as the unions were arguing, a revenue problem. A top AUPE executive concedes that in 1993-4, 'there was a very important debate that took place, and we lost that debate, lock, stock and barrel. And that was the debate over the debt and deficit. What they were and what they meant.'

Round tables were a major process the government used to spread and popularize its message. Participants from all walks of life were expected to advise the government on where and how much to cut, restructure, and streamline. Critics have suggested, however, that these fora were orchestrated, their outcome a *fait accomplis* (Lisac, 1995: 144-59). Two provincial union presidents explain:

> We feel that the round tables that took place throughout the province were a farce. The answers were already decided before they even took place. And they were so orchestrated by the government that you really didn't have any input. . . . There was no intent by the government to structure them in any way that the feedback would be representative. They were strictly to present a front by the government, so that they could say they were listening to Albertans.

'What this [process] did was create a mythic voice of Alberta—a united, one-dimensional Alberta' (Lisac, 1995: 145). Whenever union leaders tried to challenge this voice, they were labelled as 'special interest groups'. An AUPE officer notes that 'the Klein government has done a very good job at making it seem . . . that somehow if it is the unions that are speaking up, then it is only out of self-interest.' Unions were delegitimized, their view rendered irrelevant, and their message marginalized.

It is important to stress that managers hold a very different view:

> I guess we are inside and looking at the perspective of collaboration with the unions; looking at a Premier who has been open to listening to the unions, having them come in and deal with him directly; very much listening to what their concerns are. So looking at [the unions'] view as being irrelevant and their message marginalized or delegitimized, all of those things just don't feel true.

Managers explain that whereas unions were not involved in policy-making, they did participate in policy implementation. For example, together with managers, union leaders designed transition and support arrangements for displaced workers. And, as mentioned before, unions negotiated the implementation of the 5 per cent pay cut. One manager uses the latter example to make the point that:

> we still had to negotiate the minus five and it finally was negotiated and it was ratified by all members so how can one say . . . that [the unions] were marginalized and [that they] aren't as effective as they were before. There was a lot of give and take. We ended up with an agreement that was tough for everybody.

Union Responses to the Klein Revolution

The developments described above were too profound to allow the AUPE to adopt a 'wait and see' strategy. To weather the storm and remain a viable force in society, the AUPE had to countervail the forces unleashed by the Klein Revolution. Union responses to the Klein Revolution occurred within the parameters of a traditional industrial relations system that emphasizes collective bargaining as the foremost mechanism to advance member interests. Union response options were shaped by an ongoing interaction between the external environment and developments within the AUPE's internal environment resulting directly from Alberta government policies, as well as structural and philosophical characteristics of the AUPE (and most other North American unions). To simplify the presentation, the two sets of factors are discussed separately.

The AUPE's Internal Environment
Fear
Witnessing the torrent of layoffs around them, employees soon feared for their own job security. 'The first thing you have to remember', explains an AUPE officer, 'is that the political climate in Alberta in 1993, and I don't think it is overstating it, was hysteria.' The effect of member fears on union leaders' representational capacity has received no research attention in industrial relations. I propose that members' fears for their own, colleagues', and relatives' jobs and livelihood significantly undercut union leaders' abilities to mobilize collective protests. Several AUPE officers lend preliminary support for this relationship:

> In the end of 1993, many members [who initially were opposed to the cuts] started [arguing] that it was okay to accept the 5 per cent [wage rollback], by the spring/summer of '94, it was 'please accept,' almost 'we demand that you accept the 5 per cent regression to save jobs'. . . . So when the general membership, their number-one priority is keeping their jobs, it's very difficult to go to the bargaining table and say, 'My people are going to walk,' because everybody knows they're not. . . . One [thing] that [fear] does is reduce any chance of member militancy; it is off the agenda now. . . . People don't want to make waves because, in spite of the economic conditions in Alberta, and how Alberta seems to be held up as a model

for the rest of the country to follow, people are still worried about job security and concerned about keeping a job. That is still people's greatest concern.

It is important to bear in mind that front-line employees were not the only casualties of the Klein Revolution. Managers, at all levels, also bore the brunt of the cocktail of restructuring, downsizing, budget cuts, and wage rollbacks. For example, following restructuring, many managers had to reapply for their own old positions. A government official notes that:

> in education, health care, and government services there has been tremendous change. Restructuring, remingling different people, reorganizing different departments. Your world becomes topsy turvy. Leadership and the challenges there, the new leaders of the [regional health] authorities, the new leaders in the school system, have been on a tremendous learning curve. So it's not only the compensation issues, the workload issues, but your whole environment is all shook up. It's very distressing and it adds to the dissatisfaction or the concern [of managers].

A detailed account of the effects of managers' uncertainty of their own future on industrial relations is beyond the scope of this study. In a nutshell, it destabilized industrial relations, for example, by thwarting the AUPE's and other unions' efforts to engage government and management personnel in tripartite negotiations over wage rollbacks and workforce transition. Some managers thought that they should not negotiate special deals with the unions, given the managers' uncertain future. Others preferred to 'lie low', thereby hopefully enhancing their job security.

Member Support of the Government

Influenced by the spirit of the day, some union members felt it their civic duty to contribute to the collective effort to restore fiscal order to the house of Alberta. As one provincial union leader admits:

> Well, the Klein propaganda is a very effective piece of propaganda. They do their PR well, and they won that debate. And we still have members saying to us that they don't want the 5 per cent [pay cut] back, because they don't think that the economic circumstances are justified, in spite of the fact that the government this year [1997] is going to bring in somewhere near a $3 billion surplus when everything is counted. . . . With the deficit, and the debt, and everything else . . . the right wing has been pumping that particular message out. And the [public] bought into it. There was a deficit, and they felt that, yup, we've got to tighten our belts, and we have to do this.

Moreover, as one AUPE officer succinctly explains, 'there is no question that union members in Alberta are Albertans and so they have the same culture and political background as the rest of the province.' Since 1993, most Albertans, including many union members, have accepted the government's argument that Alberta has an expenditure rather than a revenue problem and endorsed the prescribed remedies.

Union leaders thus faced the unenviable task of catering to two very different interest groups, as an AUPE executive describes:

> So on one end you've got the people who definitely are just terribly upset by what they see as this far right wing agenda. And then you have the other people who are very much in support of it. And you represent all of them and all of them pay fees so you walk this very fine line and that's partly what has driven us in taking the approaches that we have taken.

Clearly, under such circumstances, union solidarity, a cornerstone of collective actions, is elusive.

Confusion

The blueprint for the Klein Revolution was drafted, at least partially, by Roger Douglas.[11] As Minister of Finance in the fourth Labour government of New Zealand, Douglas presided over some of the most far-reaching structural reforms that country has ever experienced. Among other things, he suggests:

> Vested interests seeking to preserve vast privileges will always argue for a slower pace of change. It gives them more time to mobilize public opinion against the reforms. . . . If you take your next decision while opponents are still struggling to mobilize against the last one, you will continually capture the high ground of national interest and force them to fight uphill. (Douglas, 1993: 223, 225)

The Alberta government took this advice to heart. An AUPE officer, relaying what she heard from a senior government official, provides some evidence that the pace of the Alberta government reforms was well planned:

> He said, 'we were told we would have strikes, massive strikes. There were no strikes. We were all amazed, so we kept going.' And he said, 'But when we examined why this was so effective, what we saw was you hit them fast, you purposely exclude special interest groups or anyone who's going to be making noise, and you move fast enough so that your opposition can never get a breath enough to come back at you. And then by the time when they do, you say, well, it's done now.' And that's why the government was so effective.

Indeed, in 1993, '[n]o one was prepared for the fast, furious, and severe assault on the public sector that transpired' (Taylor, 1995: 313). Union leaders were no exception. Like other stakeholders, they failed to anticipate that the government had both the resolve and the public support to make fundamental and rapid changes, and the determination to 'not blink' in imposing this agenda.[12] An Alberta Federation of Labour officer admits that 'I don't think we were well prepared. No, not entirely. Certainly we didn't see it to the extent that it took place. . . . The cuts came so fast that they left many unions with their heads spinning. They weren't prepared for the scope and the pace of the change.' Other union officers echo this sentiment and emphasize the effect of the government strategy on the membership:

Was our membership prepared for it? Absolutely not. There was total unwillingness to accept it. I recall very clearly in the fall of '93 when we set our proposals for bargaining for '94, my membership was even less accepting of this coming along, less accepting of that possibility than I was. . . . Part of the philosophy and agenda of this government was to hit 'em hard and hit 'em fast. And hit them so hard and hit them so fast that they just scatter. And that's exactly what happened and for the most part it would be fair to say that most working people ran for cover, in fear of raising their heads because they'd get shot off. And if I sit over here and don't say anything and maybe they'll forget I'm here.

A provincial union president succinctly captures the situation: 'I think they're trying to keep us running in all directions.' This made it difficult for union members and leaders to cope with the pace and scope of the changes. Union members hoped that by keeping quiet they would keep their jobs. Meanwhile, having to put out many simultaneous local fires undermined union leaders' capabilities to plan and support collective actions.

Inter-union Relationship

Whereas the pace and scope of the changes caught unions unprepared and confused, over time one would expect increasing union co-ordination and concerted action as a means to introducing a labour perspective into the government's agenda. However, long-established union rivalry frustrated efforts to create a lasting and effective united front. Alberta public-sector unions are highly fragmented. For example, in health care there are no less than eight unions (nine until the October 1997 merger of SNAA and UNA). Competition over membership, commonplace before 1993, has been intensified following the restructuring (regionalization) of health care. Hospital support staff are represented by the AUPE and CUPE, licensed practical nurses by the Canadian Health Care Guild (CHCG) and the AUPE, and, until recently, registered nurses by UNA and the SNAA. Even in the civil service, where the AUPE is the sole bargaining agent for some 15,000 government employees, until 1997 there were 12 different local units. While at present it is difficult to assess the effect of this structure on the solidarity of the AUPE, one should not assume the latter's automatic existence.

Managers capitalized on, and also intensified, these rivalries. For example, during the 1994 wage negotiations some managers demanded more than the stipulated 5 per cent wage rollback as a quid pro quo for job security. This in turn pitted unions against each other as weaker unions, notwithstanding pressures from their stronger counterparts, succumbed to employer and member pressures to sign a deal. As one provincial union president explains:

Then you get to the bargaining table, and the employers, in health care, are saying, 'Well, the Premier said 5 per cent but our budgets are such that 5 per cent is not going to do', and that's why huge concessions [were extracted] out of groups such as CUPE. . . . therefore you have to give up your benefits and even more of your layoff and your recall rights and all of that kind of stuff. It wasn't limited to 5 per cent. . . . This gave far more to the employers than government ever publicly admitted they were seeking. It created a divide-and-conquer mentality amongst unions and amongst individual employees.

Naturally, union rivalries undermined the likelihood of concerted union action. One provincial union leader aptly summarizes the overall situation:

public-sector unions are far too busy fighting amongst themselves when the real fight is against the employers, and more specifically, against government policy. I think that the politicians and the employers have been very successful in diverting our attention from the real place where we need to put our energies. They have us fighting [among ourselves]. It's most unfortunate, and a huge waste of time.

Perhaps the most opportune occasion for concerted action occurred in November 1995 during the 10-day strike by laundry workers in two Calgary hospitals. A full analysis of this intriguing event is beyond the scope of this study. Briefly, this illegal strike involved 120 laundry workers who were, more or less, equally divided between two bargaining units represented by the AUPE and CUPE. After conceding wage rollbacks of up to 28 per cent during the previous bargaining round, the laundry employees were told that, soon, they would lose their jobs to two private companies, one in Edmonton and the other in Calgary. Frustrated and realizing that they had nothing to lose, CUPE laundry workers called in sick, practically starting an illegal strike. The following day, AUPE workers at another hospital joined them.

The AUPE, CUPE, and other public-sector unions tried to capitalize on the public support this strike attracted and translate the laundry workers' particular adversity into a collective grievance that would spread throughout the province. However, the government acted fast and effectively. After 10 days, the government intervened with a financial package that made it possible for the Calgary Regional Health Authority to agree to an 18-month moratorium on contracting out and to the precedent of providing severance pay to laundry workers once the moratorium ended. The last of these laundry jobs were eliminated in February 1998. Importantly, this was the first occasion that the Klein government strayed from it's 'no blink' policy. Conceding that 'we're taking a bit of a detour', Klein announced that the government was cancelling a scheduled $53 million cut in health care (*Maclean's*, 1995: 41).

Several union leaders thought that union fragmentation was a major reason for their inability to convert the laundry workers' local complaint into a collective grievance. A CUPE executive explains:

We were hopeful that other health-care unions would join in, not just token participate by sending a few elected representatives down, but by actually walking out on the streets with us and shutting facilities down. It would have had to happen only for a day or two and we would have won the day. But UNA chose not, the leadership chose not to lead the membership out. Many of their members wanted to come but didn't want to defy their own leadership. The Canadian Health Care Guild didn't show anyway. Health Sciences was there in spirit and in body and were beginning to walk with us. But the support at one point in time just didn't occur.

A UNA executive agrees:

quite honestly there was not the will there, amongst at least my membership, to go for a general strike [during the laundry workers' strike]. . . . You don't have one group go out on strike and end up in a general strike the next day. It takes time to build. And it was starting to build. I'm not trying to rationalize it or excuse it. By and large our membership in the hospital industry is not élitist, but they haven't asked other unions to join our strikes. We've had four hospital strikes [in the 1980s], one became illegal, another started out and was illegal in 1988. We've never said, 'Don't cross our picket lines.' We've never said, 'Don't go to work because we're not at work.'

A more recent opportunity to deliver a co-ordinated labour message to the government and the public occurred during the 1997 Growth Summit. The Growth Summit process began in January 1997 and culminated in September 1997 with the two-day Summit, involving hundreds of Albertans who participated in more than 40 mini-summits held to discuss reinvestment priorities and policies. The September Summit brought together 102 delegates for two days of information exchange and a debate over reinvestment in the public sector. Six sectoral groups addressed issues in government, social economy, MASH (municipalities, academic institutions, schools, and hospitals), business and industry, energy, and agriculture and rural development. Union representatives were part of MASH. Originally, 10 union representatives were invited to participate in the Summit. For various reasons, the Alberta Federation of Labour and its constituent unions, such as the AUPE, rejected the invitation and held their own Conference on Alberta's Social and Economic Future (Alberta Federation of Labour, 1997). Representatives from non-affiliated unions did participate in the Growth Summit, but obviously they could not speak on behalf of all Alberta labour.

Clearly, the Klein government benefited from inter-union divisions. The Conservatives both enhanced and capitalized on existing divisions, although it appears to have been a fortunate coincidence for the government rather than a premeditated divide-and-conquer strategy.

The AUPE's Inherent Characteristics

Government policies and associated management practices created formidable obstacles to union collective action. However, union abilities to influence the evolution of the Klein Revolution were further undermined by the following inherent factors.

Philosophy

As mentioned before, business unionism is the dominant paradigm of the Alberta labour movement. A major assumption underlying business unionism is that the economic and political spheres are, and should remain, separate (Murray and Reshef, 1988). Consequently, most of the social dialogue between unions and employers occurs in the labour market, mainly through collective bargaining. The centrality of collective bargaining becomes all the more pronounced for a union like the AUPE, where workers are forbidden to strike and a formative experience of a defining collective struggle does not exist.

Business unionism, at least partially, informed the AUPE and other union leaders' responses to the Klein government. For example, when offered the opportunity to negotiate over the rollbacks, the leaders initially resisted but eventually grabbed it. As Taylor (1995) has correctly noted, Klein was savvy in offering the unions the negotiation option, thereby creating a comfort zone that catered to the unions' industrial relations paradigm and established modes of operation. Bargaining over the wage cuts allowed the Klein government to chart short- and long-term paths for the unions. In the short term, unions would focus their attention, energy, and dwindling resources on negotiating the implementation of the pay cuts and their aftermath at the expense of addressing the policies themselves. An AUPE officer observes:

> What it [negotiating the wage rollbacks and their human resources consequences] did was put the battle at the bargaining table. The battle was not the fight that probably could have been against the provincial legislators. It went down to the bargaining table, and it was a scrap between the union and the employer.

In the long run, the government had all but ensured that during the next bargaining round the unions would be thrown into another bargaining vortex, this time to recoup the 1994–5 wage losses. An AUPE executive explains that in 1998:

> a lot of people knew that it [not getting satisfactory wage increases] was in fact a problem with the province, because now they're looking at the problem of recovery. So the fight is on again, and guess where the fight is again. The fight is at the bargaining table between the employer and the union. And some areas, that I can't mention, both parties would like to see the money come back, but the employer is saying we don't have it. How can we give it to you?

In 1997, the first bargaining round following the 1994–5 wage rollbacks, 213 agreements were signed in the public sector, 34 of them in public administration. The average agreement would last three years and provide a 1.7 per cent wage increase per year (Alberta Labour, 1998). Only 9.9 per cent of these 213 agreements included wage increases of 5.0 per cent or more. As mentioned before, AUPE civil service members received their first *real* wage increase since 1986.

Bargaining over wage rollbacks also helped the government secure union consent for its policies. As one local union president laments:

One of the evils of our collective bargaining process is that it manufactures consent, right? People who are ostensibly involved in the rule-making feel somehow morally obligated to follow those rules, which is why voluntarism is a pillar of our collective bargaining system. So public policy is made by unions doing their business.

Instead of defying the government, union leaders inadvertently became implicated in the making of the Klein Revolution.

Leadership

To challenge the Klein government agenda, union leaders had to develop an alternative vision about how to eliminate the deficit problem and mobilize wide support for the new vision, so that it becomes independent of their special interest group status. During the Klein Revolution, Alberta union leaders never articulated an alternative scenario that would challenge the government line, emphasize a labour perspective, and give the unions a unique independent presence in society. Consequently, the leaders could not, in Offe and Wiesenthal's parlance (1980: 81), inspire 'willingness to act' in unionized and non-unionized Albertans. Two AUPE officers relate the situation to the leaders' long-established conservative paradigm:

we're starting to see the consequences of 40 years of business unionism, which is explicitly anti-political and says, all the union does is what the law says it does, which is to negotiate collective agreements. There is no political or social dimension. You don't even have ongoing relationships with other unions as a matter of fact. You simply exist as little business units and you come together once a year at a convention and pat each other on the backs, have a few drinks and then go home, and anything else is some sort of socialist nonsense. . . . one of the things business unionism does is it creates cultures in which union leadership voluntarily gives up the particular kind of weapon of mass protest and massive industrial action, and once you've given it up it's very hard to get it back because you justify that by creating an ideology around conservative unionism which tells members they shouldn't be doing this.

My own analysis suggests that union leaders perceive themselves mainly as administrators, rather than prophets or agitators who strive to lead their organizations through new realities using novel actions. As such, they chose to confront the aftermath of Klein's policies rather than the policies themselves, and to do so mainly within the familiar surroundings of the bargaining table. Interviewed union leaders were unanimous that they did not have any other choice. Most of them were convinced that mobilizing collective protests was beyond their capacity and mandate:

I have not seen an instance where a trade union leader has successfully mobilized anything. I know that sounds audacious, but I challenge anyone to give me an instance where that has happened. Everyone from Jean-Claude Perot [former president of the Canadian Union of Postal Workers] to Bob White [former president of the National Automobile, Aerospace, Transportation and General Workers Union of Canada (CAW), and also former president of the Canadian Labour Congress], and all those people, were simply acting as leaders to try to take and orchestrate and fashion whatever militancy was there into some sort of workable plan, so that they could do their jobs with the other party, be that at the bargaining table or at the grievance table or anywhere else. So I don't think [names of two presidents] or the trade union movement is capable of mobilizing anything in this province. . . . [Collective protests] won't be union organized. It will be for a hundred workers who have had enough and who say, today is the day. And then it will gain momentum in that manner. I don't think we're ever going to have the union coalitions sit down at a table and say 'Okay, on October 5, we're going to walk out.' There's got to be an issue that will precipitate it and it's going to build rather than just stop.

During the turbulent years of the Klein Revolution, most union leaders felt that their best efforts should have been directed towards keeping their houses in order by working within the existing system, not against it. 'During this exact period of time', offers one union executive, 'I think the unions were just trying to maintain the membership base, protect the members' jobs and that's about it.' And another AUPE executive adds that union leaders were 'trying to bring some of the downside of the Alberta Advantage to the public. Right now, that's probably (other than the service to union members) the biggest role that labour is playing and can play.' Consequently, the leaders scanned their internal and external environments, assessed the likely success of alternative actions, and chose the most workable orthodox response. Perhaps, as the following results of a recent survey of approximately 1,000 Albertans show, playing by the long-established rules of the game was the more prudent tactic (Drixler, 1998).

Table 5.4 presents mean comparisons for the responses of unionized and non-unionized Albertans to four questions about collective action and unions.[13] The evidence suggests that the majority of the respondents would not support a province-wide strike as a means to influence socio-economic policies. Note that while the differences between the mean responses are statistically significant, even the unionized respondents are not overly supportive of a province-wide strike, which is, of course, but one form of collective action. Interestingly, the average non-union respondent is virtually neutral on whether unions are special interest groups that do not represent the average respondent's interest. Moreover, a majority of the respondents believe that unions should participate in government decision-making on reinvestment in public services. However, the data do not indicate whether unions should be partners in the decision-making process, advise governments of their concerns, or merely be informed of reinvestment decisions.

It is noteworthy that a few AUPE leaders, deeply frustrated with their own behaviours during the Klein Revolution, condemned themselves for having 'neither the resources, nor the skills, nor the motivation to mount a sustained

Table 5.4: Attitudinal Survey, December 1997

Item[a]	Mean[b] Response		Disagree[c] (%)		Neutral[d] (%)		Agree[e] (%)	
	Non-union	Union	Non-union	Union	Non-union	Union	Non-union	Union
1. A Province-wide strike will speed up reinvestment in public services.	3.10	3.65	60.8	42.3	10.1	16.4	29.2	41.3
2. I would support a province-wide strike.	2.82	3.82	67.6	49.4	7.7	8.5	24.6	42.1
3. Public-sector unions are special interest groups.	4.08	3.25	39.1	61.5	16.6	14.6	44.2	23.9
4. Public-sector unions should be involved in government decisions about reinvestment in public services.	4.16	4.85	34.1	21.7	15.3	16.8	50.6	61.5

Note: There were 831 non-union respondents and 151 union respondents to these questions.

[a]The four items are 7-point scales where '1' is 'strongly disagree' and '7' is 'strongly agree'. The full text of the items is available in note 13.

[b]Mean differences for the four comparisons are significant at the $p < .01$, two-tailed test.

[c]An aggregate sum of categories 1–3.

[d]The fourth category.

[e]An aggregate sum of categories 5–7.

Source: Drixler (1998).

campaign of any kind' to undermine the Klein Revolution. However, given the basic conservatism of Alberta in general and many of their members in particular, the union leaders' behaviours might be justifiable. The recent Ontario experience raises doubts that well-organized collective action could have derailed the Klein Revolution.

In summary, a blend of structural, cognitive, and cultural factors further undermined the public-sector unions' capacity to respond in unison to the Klein government policies. Labour leaders chose to deal with the consequences of the government policies through collective bargaining rather than to attack the policies themselves.

The Logic of Union Quiescence

Long-established business unionism philosophy and years of operating within a relatively stable conservative environment had taken their toll on union members' and leaders' abilities to go beyond established practices and expertise. Consequently, between 1993 and 1998, both groups lacked the scripts, or sequence of behavioural events, necessary to reconfigure their resources and behaviours to carry out collective action. Given that in the post-World War II era Alberta unions never have been particularly strong or politically militant, their responses to the Klein Revolution were consistent with their past performance.

Union and member solidarity, a key to collective action, was significantly eroded during the Klein Revolution. Wittingly or not, the government showed a remarkable capacity to capitalize on and intensify union rivalries and member divisions and fears. In doing so, it sapped the unions of any vitality and resolve they might still have had to pursue collective action. Competition over membership became more intensive during the Klein years, undermining the unions' capacity to act in concert. Member divisions further diminished the prospects for mobilization. Some union members supported the government agenda whereas others thought that, as responsible citizens, they ought to contribute to the collective good as defined by the government. For many other members, layoffs and pay cuts created deep-seated economic uncertainty that fixed their attention on daily survival, leaving them little disposed to collective action. Apparently, fear created a well-disciplined workforce, thereby undermining union leaders' representational capacity. As one union leader aptly notes, 'If you can't convince people that they can act upon the world and succeed, then you can't lead them.'

Lacking the will and ability to mobilize and driven by business unionism, members and leaders resorted to institutionalized means of action, namely, a local strike and collective bargaining. Collective bargaining seems to have furthered the government cause rather than the union efforts to countervail it. Strikes may have a similar effect, as a union research officer admits: 'Now many employers see [strikes] as an opportunity. If they had cutbacks in funding, they see a three-month strike or whatever as an opportunity to balance their books and save money, because the funding goes on.' It appears that unions wishing to influence policy-making will have to explore different ways of applying their resources and expertise. For example, unions may wish to cultivate alliances with other interest groups who are disenchanted with government policies and feel that they cannot influence the policies on their own.

Notwithstanding the 1993–8 events, the AUPE and other Alberta public-sector unions are still players in industrial relations. Their interaction with management will continue to centre on negotiating wages and working conditions within parameters, legal and financial, set by the government, but the long-term effect of the Klein Revolution on the parties' relationship is unclear. Currently, union and management personnel hold different views about the future. AUPE officers are pessimistic about their relationship with the Alberta politicians:

> I think it's irreparable as far as this government's concerned. I don't think there will ever be an ability for them to re-establish trust. So, it's not, I don't particularly see, as long as this government's in power that the relationship with labour is going to be improved or that there will be any sense of trust restored. . . . You've got a workforce now that is deeply, deeply cynical. . . . The legacy is individuals feeling misused and abused because there has not been an ongoing defence of workers. There is a great sense of betrayal, and a feeling of ongoing coercion.

Union interviewees are ambivalent about current and future interactions with management personnel. A few believe that 'the relationship is terminally poisoned.' Generally, however, this sentiment applies to dealings with senior level bureaucrats. Other union leaders are taking a more charitable stance, explaining that their locals 'looked at it [wage rollbacks and layoffs] as it really wasn't our employer's [fault]. It was the government's.' This position applies to mid- and low-level managers with whom union leaders maintain a close continuous working relationship.

Government personnel are more optimistic about their future working relationship with union leaders and members. They recognize that 'restructuring and downsizing have created high levels of uncertainty and job insecurity' among employees (Personnel Administration Office, 1997: 7). Managers are concerned with employee morale, but they believe it will improve in the long run. To address the problem, the government has launched several HRM initiatives, such as recognition programs, corporate learning strategy, and workforce adjustment assistance. These initiatives are intended to provide employees with the support they need to adjust to changing circumstances and prepare the Alberta public service for future challenges. Generally, government employees have responded favourably to these efforts. In 1998, 77 per cent of non-managerial employees were 'very satisfied' or 'somewhat satisfied' with their work (Government of Alberta, 1999).

To be able to deal successfully with future industrial relations developments, union leaders and members should come to grips with their behaviours during the Klein Revolution. Why have they not been able to claim part of the monopoly the government commands over the definition of the public interest? Can unions mobilize against the current political terrain? Why did unions not forge alliances with any of the groups that emerged immediately after the 1993 election to protest cuts to education, health, and other government services? Should unions rethink their strategies and underlying philosophy?

This soul-searching requires that the AUPE as well as other Alberta unions reassess their *raison d'être*. If unions see the Klein Revolution as the dawning of a new age of conservatism that jeopardizes their vested interests in job security and organizational survival and threatens past achievements, then the unions must find a way to counteract this development or else they risk fading into the background of society. If unions feel that the Klein Revolution is merely an episodic phenomenon, a temporary aberration that does not require them to adopt new assumptions and behaviours, they still must develop a rationale demonstrating that they do not simply lack imagination and foresight. Either way, Alberta unions should not carry on as before.

Notes

I am indebted to Nicole Lyotier and Nancy Cranston for their excellent research assistance, to Ross Bradford for helpful comments, and to all the interviewees for their time and willingness to share valuable information.

1. Throughout the study, the term 'public sector' includes education and related services, hospitals and related health care, urban transit, telephones, welfare organizations, public administration, and publicly owned broadcasting, telecommunications and utility services. 'Public administration' denotes provincial and local government employees, whereas 'civil service' refers to government employees.

2. Fifty-two interviews were face to face and three were conducted over the phone. Interviews ranged in length from 35 to 70 minutes, with the average interview lasting 45 minutes.

3. In June 1998, the government approved a 90-cent-an-hour increase in the province's $5.00-an-hour minimum wage. The increase was phased in beginning with a $.40 increase effective 1 October 1998, with further increases of $.25 on 1 April 1999 and $.25 on 1 October 1999. This brought the province's minimum wage to $5.90. The minimum wage was phased in to provide businesses time to prepare for the increase. The change placed Alberta's minimum wage behind Saskatchewan and Manitoba ($6.00), Northwest Territories ($6.50), Ontario ($6.85), Quebec ($6.90), British Columbia ($7.15), and Yukon ($7.20). The adjustment to the minimum wage also included the removal of the student differential. Previously, the minimum wage for students under 18 years of age was $.50 less than the minimum wage for those over 18. Effective 1 October 1998, Alberta has one minimum wage for all workers.

4. Until 31 December 1996, the number of local units was 12.

5. Long-term wage employees are those who have accumulated 2,850 work hours over two years, and are thus entitled to the same benefits received by full-time permanent employees.

6. According to Statistics Canada (1998: 102), an employee is any person drawing pay for services rendered or for paid absence, and for whom the employer is required to provide a Revenue Canada T-4 Supplementary Form.

7. The remaining group, representing medical and rehabilitative services, applied for interest arbitration. In October 1999, the arbitration board ruling imposed the same wage settlement accept by the other AUPE units.

8. Since the bonus is not an integral part of the collective agreement but is attached in a 'Letter of Understanding', management can abandon it in subsequent bargaining rounds.

9. 360-degree feedback, also known as multi-rater assessment, is the process in which an individual is evaluated by representatives of several groups with whom the individual interacts, such as his or her top managers, supervisors, co-workers, clients, suppliers, and one's self. Subsequently, the individual receives a confidential report that details a gap analysis between self-perception and the perceptions of others. Because each rater offers a new, unique view, the process should produce a much more complete picture of an employee's performance than the traditional supervisor-subordinate performance evaluation.

10. Unfortunately, these questions were not asked in the 1998 survey.

11. During the early days of the Klein Revolution, Douglas visited Alberta and presented his thoughts on restructuring the government to the government. His book, *Unfinished Business*, was 'required reading' for the architects of the Klein Revolution.

12. 'Don't blink, public confidence rests on your composure' is the eighth principle in Douglas's (1993) recipe for change.

13. This is the full text of the four items:
    a. A province-wide strike by public-sector unions will speed up reinvestment in public services such as health care and education in Alberta.
    b. I would support a province-wide strike by public-sector unions to speed up reinvestment in public services such as health care and education in Alberta.
    c. Public-sector unions are special interest groups that do not represent my interest.
    d. Public-sector unions should be directly involved in government decisions about reinvestment.

References

Akyeampong, Ernest B. 1997. 'A Statistical Portrait of the Trade Union Movement', *Perspectives on Labour and Income* 9 (Winter): 45–54.

Alberta Advanced Education and Career Development. 1999. *Labour Force Statistics*. Edmonton.

Alberta Federation of Labour. 1997. *Investing in Tomorrow*. Edmonton.

Alberta Health. 1994, 1995. *Health Workforce in Alberta*. Edmonton.

———. 1998. *Annual Report: 1996-1997*. Edmonton, Alberta.

Alberta Labour. 1986. *Membership in Labour Organizations in Alberta, 1985*. Edmonton.

———. 1987. *Labour Legislation Review Committee: Final Report*. Edmonton.

———. 1996, 1997a, 1998. *Labour Statistics*. Edmonton.

———. 1997b. *Annual Report: 1996-97*. Edmonton.

Alberta Personnel Administration Office. 1995, 1996, 1997. *Public Service Commissioner's Annual Report: Profile of the Alberta Public Service*. Edmonton.

AUPE. 1996. *General Services: Bargaining Conference*. Edmonton.

Coates, Mary Lou, David Arrowsmith, and Melanie Courchene. 1989. *The Current Industrial Relations Scene in Canada, 1989*. Kingston, Ont.: Industrial Relations Centre, Queen's University.

Cohen, Sanford, 1961. 'An Analytical Framework for Labor Relations Law', *Industrial and Labor Relations Review* 41: 350-62.

Coulter, Diana, 1993. 'Worst Labor Strife Ever Seen in Cuts', *Edmonton Journal*, 25 Nov., A6.

Douglas, Roger. 1993. *Unfinished Business*. Auckland, New Zealand: Random House.

Drixler, Cathy. 1998. *The 1997 Alberta Survey: Sampling Report*. Population Research Laboratory, Department of Sociology, University of Alberta, Edmonton.

Farnsworth, Clyde H. 1995. 'Budget Cuts Paying Off for Premier of Alberta', *New York Times*, 1 Jan.

Feschuk, Scott, and Alanna Mitchell. 1994. 'Klein Juggernaut has Unions Quaking', *Globe and Mail*, 2 Nov., A13.

Fisher, E.G., and Stephen Kushner. 1986. 'Alberta's Construction Labour Relations During the Recent Downturn', *Relations Industrielles* 41: 778-99.

Fong, Donna, Cliff Kinzel, and Dave Odynak. 1995. *The Alberta Survey (A): Sampling Report*. Population Research Laboratory, Department of Sociology, University of Alberta, Edmonton.

Fund, John. 1995. 'Learning from Canada's Reagan', *Wall Street Journal*, 23 Feb.

Geddes, Elaine F. 1990. 'Alberta Labor Legislation under the Social Credit Government: 1935-1947', Master's thesis, University of Alberta.

Government of Alberta. 1997a, 1998. *Measuring Up: The Annual Report on the Performance of the Government of Alberta*. Edmonton.

———. 1997b. *1997 Surveys of Albertans and Employees*. Edmonton.

———. 1999. *Core Human Resources Measures Project: 1998 Survey of Employees—Detailed Report*. Edmonton.

Gunderson, Morley, and Douglas Hyatt. 1996. 'Canadian Public Sector Employment Relations in Transition', in Dale Belman, Gunderson, and Hyatt, eds, *Public Sector Employment* (Madison, Wis.: IRRA): 243-81.

Harrison, Trevor, and Gordon Laxer. 1995. 'Introduction', in Harrison and Laxer, eds, *The Trojan Horse: Alberta and the Future of Canada* (Montreal: Black Rose Books), 1-19.

HRDC. 1992, 1997. *Directory of Labour Organizations in Canada*. Ottawa: Minister of Supply and Services.

Hughes, Karen D., Graham S. Lowe, and Allison L. McKinnon. 1996. 'Public Attitudes Toward Budget Cuts in Alberta: Biting the Bullet or Feeling the Pain?', *Canadian Public Policy* 22: 268-84.

Johnsrude, Larry. 1997. 'Why Women are less In-Kleined to Vote for Ralph', *Edmonton Journal*, 2 Feb., F1.

Johnston, Paul. 1994. *Success Where Others Fail: Social Movement Unionism and the Public Workplace*. Ithaca, NY: ILR.

Languedoc, Colin. 1986. 'Entrepreneurs Pick Labor Headaches', *Financial Post*, 1 Dec., 21.

Lisac, Mark. 1995. *The Klein Revolution*. Edmonton: NeWest.

Maclean's. 1995. 'Ralph Klein Blinks: Faced with Labor Strife, Alberta Backs Off Health Cuts', 108, 49 (4 Dec.): 41.

———. 1996-7. 'Haves & Have-nots: Canadians Look for Corporate Conscience', 109, 53 (30 Dec.-6 Jan.): 26, 37.

McMillan, Melville L. 1996. *Leading the Way or Missing the Mark? The Klein Government's Fiscal Plan*. Edmonton: Western Centre for Economic Research, University of Alberta.

——— and Allan Warrack. 1995. 'One-Track (Thinking) Towards Deficit Reduction', in Trevor Harrison and Gordon Laxer, eds, *The Trojan Horse: Alberta and the Future of Canada* (Montreal: Black Rose Books), 134–62.

Murray, Alan I., and Yonatan Reshef. 1988. 'American Manufacturing Unions' Stasis: A Paradigmatic Perspective', *Academy of Management Review* 13: 639-52.

Personnel Administration Office. 1993, 1997. *A Guide to Human Resource Initiatives in the Alberta Public Service*. Edmonton: Client Relations Branch.

———. 1999. *Final Report to External Review Team*. Edmonton.

Ponak, Allen, Yonatan Reshef, and Daphne Taras. 1998. 'Alberta: Industrial Relations in a Conservative Climate', working paper, University of Calgary.

Rastin, Sandra. 1999. *Outsourcing of the Engineering Design Process in the Alberta Transportation and Utilities Department: A Case Study*. Ottawa: Canadian Policy Research Networks.

Statistics Canada. 1995. *Labour Force Annual Averages*. Catalogue no. 71–220-XPB.

———. 1998. *Public Sector Employment and Wages and Salaries, 1996*. Catalogue no. 72–209-XPB.

Taylor, Jeff. 1995. 'Labour in the Klein Revolution', in Trevor Harrison and Gordon Laxer, eds, *The Trojan Horse: Alberta and the Future of Canada* (Montreal: Black Rose Books), 301–14.

Chapter 6

Labour Relations in the BC Public Service: Blowing in the Political Wind

Mark Thompson

Introduction

Labour relations in the British Columbia public service have varied from relatively co-operative to highly confrontational. The changes have reflected the province's political climate. The conservative Social Credit Party governed from 1952 to 1972 and resisted pressure from provincial employees to grant them bargaining rights. When the New Democratic Party was elected in 1972, British Columbia established collective bargaining in the provincial public service, one of the last provinces in the country to do so. Acting under legislation based on the private sector, the parties quickly embraced traditional public-sector industrial relations. When the Social Credit Party returned to power in 1975 it did not make substantial changes in labour relations in its first term. The parties, i.e., professional managers and union leaders, exhibited an appetite for cooperation, but political events intervened. During the early 1980s, the government swung to the right and attempted to amend the public service collective agreement by legislation as part of a broader program of government restraint. Labour and its political allies were able to resist most of the collective agreement changes, although reductions in social programs occurred. Economic conditions were important, but the government's political direction, philosophy, and views of the significance of labour relations (harmonious or conflictual) ultimately determined government's course of action. The Social Credit government was at least comfortable with confrontation, and four consecutive collective agreements were negotiated after a strike.

When the NDP returned to power in 1991, it clearly preferred labour-management co-operation. Labour relations in the public service during this period were relatively harmonious, but this harmony was perceived by the public as expensive, i.e., overly generous to employees and contributing to growth in the size of government. In fact, after an initial period of high settlements and a highly publicized (and expensive) accord in the health sector, the employer was quite restrained in bargaining. The government was anxious to demonstrate that it could resist public-sector union demands without provoking a new round of confrontations. In 1998 it offered labour a combination of modest settlements in bargaining supplemented by other gains for labour outside of the collective agreement, principally, enhanced retirement packages made available by actuarial surpluses in the provincial pension fund. The failure of the Ontario Social Contract negotiations and subsequent defeat of the Ontario NDP government were powerful incentives to both parties to resolve their differences. Despite its efforts to establish a new climate for relations with its own employees, the NDP government has been unable to establish a long-term commitment to co-operation by either labour or line management. Opportunities for gains by labour outside of collective bargaining are likely to be limited in the future. Given the close links between public-sector industrial relations and provincial politics, co-operative efforts under way in the late 1990s probably would not survive a change in government.

Context of Labour Relations in the Public Service

Industrial relations in British Columbia are characterized by close ties between labour relations and partisan politics. Since the 1930s, the New Democrats (or the Co-operative Commonwealth Federation) have been a major factor in provincial politics and have normally been supported by at least one-third of the electorate. Organized labour has backed the NDP and maintained close ties to the party. The NDP's strong power base in turn stimulated the formation of right-of-centre coalitions formed to defeat it. Since labour was identified with the NDP, business interests supported the Social Credit Party from the 1950s through the 1980s and then the Liberal Party (which is separate from the federal Liberal Party) in the 1990s. After an overwhelming electoral defeat in 1991, the Social Credit Party disappeared. The BC Liberal Party then assumed its right-wing position in provincial politics. Neither the Conservatives nor the federal Liberals have gathered substantial support in provincial politics since the early 1950s, leaving little room on the political spectrum for parties based on broad consensus (see Thompson and Bemmels, 1998). The NDP, led by Dave Barrett, took power for the first time in 1972 but held office only until in 1975. Social Credit, first under William Bennett and then William Vander Zalm, retained control of the government until 1991, when Mike Harcourt, a moderate New Democrat, led the party to victory. Harcourt was Premier until 1995, when Glen Clark, a more traditional New Democrat with close ties to private-sector unions, succeeded him as leader. Clark subsequently won the 1996 election in an upset generated by a three-way split among the conservative opposition.

Prior to 1972, provincial government employees had no bargaining rights. The labour movement, in particular the BC Government Employees' Association, which represented a large proportion of public service workers, pressed for the right to bargain collectively. Hospital, non-teaching school board, and municipal workers had long been covered by collective bargaining legislation. The right-wing Social Credit government of Premier W.A.C. Bennett, which held power from 1952 to 1972, refused to enact bargaining legislation. Instead, the public service commission advised the government, which established wages, salaries, and working conditions unilaterally.

After the 1972 election, change occurred quickly. Premier Dave Barrett immediately appointed a five-person Commission of Inquiry into Employer-Employee Relations in the Public Service of British Columbia. The Commission's mandate was to recommend how collective bargaining could 'best be introduced into the public service of British Columbia' (Higgins et al., 1972). Not surprisingly, the commission quickly recommended full bargaining rights for government employees.

The government accepted most of the commission's recommendations and enacted the Public Service Labour Relations Act (PSLRA) in 1973, making British Columbia one of the last provinces to pass such legislation. In most respects the PSLRA was in the mainstream of Canadian public-sector labour legislation of the time. Rather than passing a comprehensive labour relations statute for the public service, the PSLRA incorporated many features of the Labour Code, the private-sector relations statute enacted at about the same time. In addition, two features of the PSLRA stood out. It mandated three bargaining units for the entire public service—one for registered nurses, another for other licensed professionals, and a third for all other employees. The certification process following passage of the law resulted in certificates for two small bargaining units, represented by different unions, and a certificate for the third unit, which includes the overwhelming majority of all public service employees. The BC Government Employees' Union (BCGEU), successor to the Government Employees' Association, was chosen as the bargaining agent for the general bargaining unit in the provincial government. The second notable feature was the requirement that each bargaining unit have two collective agreements—a master agreement including all of the terms and conditions of employment to all employees in the bargaining unit, and a second 'subsidy' (*sic*) agreement for each occupational group to include terms and conditions of employment specific to the occupational group. Since 1973, the formal legislative structure of labour relations in the public service has not changed greatly. In 1975, the Labour Code was amended to provide for the designation of essential services by the Labour Relations Board to prevent immediate and serious danger to health, life, or safety. By extension, these provisions applied to the public service and have been invoked from time to time (Kelliher, 1983).

According to the terms of the two laws, government employees have the right to strike and the employer can lock out, both under a regime of providing essential services. The parties are free to bargain on a wide range of issues, with the notable exclusion of pensions (treated under separate legislation), 'the principle of merit and its application in the appointment and promotion of employees', the organization, establishment, and administration of ministries, and the application of the classification system (Public Service Labour Relations Act, s. 13). In practice, the parties have negotiated language in the master agreement that attempts to achieve the same procedures for recruitment and promotions found in contracts negotiated under other legislation. However, the bargaining restriction over the organization of ministries has been used to prohibit the union from negotiating workload or crew sizes and remains a contentious issue between the parties. The PSLRA provides for the exclusion of several categories of employees from the bargaining unit. Although the number of persons in excluded positions is greater than in other jurisdictions (Korbin, 1993), the main functions of government have not been able to operate during strikes by the major union representing government employees.

The most notable legislative enactments since 1973 have been ad hoc wage control measures. These measures, imposed by the government unilaterally, caused high levels of labour-management conflict. After joining the federal Anti-Inflation Program in 1975–8, the province imposed public-sector wage controls early in 1982, the first province to take such action. The primary target of the measure was the BCGEU, whose collective agreement expired in the spring of that year after three years of wage increases generally below the rate of inflation. The union resisted the restraints unsuccessfully, despite a brief strike. The following year the William Bennett government introduced an overall government restraint program, which included several bills specifically aimed at the BCGEU, including one to remove a prohibition against layoffs in the collective agreement.

These measures aroused a storm of protest (discussed below) by public-sector unions generally and by the BCGEU in particular. Another strike occurred. Ultimately, the formal bargaining system was preserved, but the government maintained spending restrictions. Since that time, public-sector wage controls, under various names and administrative arrangements, have been the norm in British Columbia, except for the 1988–91 period. The Bennett government introduced a Compensation Stabilization Program that essentially lasted until 1988. The government introduced a new program early in 1991. When the New Democrats were elected, they eliminated controls on collective bargaining in 1991 but substituted a system of wage 'guidelines' for employers across the broader public sector. At first the guidelines were transmitted to management with relatively little public awareness, but early in 1998 the Minister of Finance, prior to a major round of bargaining, called attention to them. The guideline system did not have any formal enforcement mechanism, relying instead on the spending authority of the provincial government to ensure that individual employers observed the limits.

From 1983 through 1991, when the Social Credit Party was defeated, relations between the government and the BCGEU were less confrontational but still quite adversarial. In addition to the strikes in 1982 and 1983, stoppages occurred in the two subsequent rounds of negotiations in 1986 and 1988. When the government announced a major program of privatization in the late 1980s the union resisted through litigation, political action, and negotiations. Ultimately, the government did shift a number of functions to the private sector, most notably bridge and highway maintenance, but without the major conflict that marked the

1982–3 period. Moreover, the BCGEU campaigned successfully to limit privatization of liquor sales (Murray, 1993). During most of the 1980s, public-sector compensation restraint was an overriding theme of government. While these measures have generated tensions between the parties, the government has avoided direct attacks on the collective bargaining system in the public service. The Vander Zalm government did pass highly interventionist labour legislation in 1987, but it was not directly aimed at the public service (although one measure effectively stripped bridge and highway maintenance workers of their successor rights). In the late 1980s, the government sought concessions from the union with limited success. During the early 1990s, the province was relatively prosperous, so arguments for concessions were not persuasive in economic terms. Governments did not press such demands, preferring to rely on wage controls and contracting out to achieve their fiscal objectives. Some collective agreements have provided for reduced entitlements, but these have been in the context of other gains and trade-offs in negotiations.

The context of industrial relations in the public service generally has not promoted co-operation. The BCGEU obtained bargaining rights only after a change in government. Although the union remained formally non-partisan, it was an active member of the BC Federation of Labour, which vigorously supported the New Democrats. During its time in power from 1972 to 1975, the NDP government sought innovation in labour relations generally, but it was not in power long enough to put its mark on labour relations in the public service. The parties thus started their relationship with traditional labour-management roles, despite any political will to engage in co-operation. Subsequently, the Social Credit Party regarded the BCGEU with suspicion, if not hostility. When the Social Credit government swung to the right during the 1982–3 recession, the BCGEU and the government were in direct confrontation. From then on, the undercurrent of partisan politics inhibited general efforts to promote co-operation, despite any appetite by senior officials on either side for a different style of labour-management relations.

Fiscal State of the Province, 1990–1997

The fiscal state of the provincial government became a major political issue in the mid-1990s. Sensitive to charges that the NDP could not manage public finances, NDP leader Mike Harcourt ran for office pledging to balance the budget over his term in office. He retreated from this promise somewhat after taking office in 1991, on the grounds that public finances were in worse condition than his predecessor had indicated. His government also faced reductions in federal transfer payments. The Harcourt government did not achieve its fiscal objective, despite a relatively strong economy. Whatever its spending priorities, the NDP government of the 1990s faced the problems of inadequate public-sector infrastructure that were the result of a decade of population growth that was double the Canadian average.

Harcourt's successor, Glen Clark, a former Minister of Finance, promised in his 1996 election campaign that the government would balance its budget during the coming fiscal year. After the election it became apparent that the government could not balance the budget while using the same reporting standards as its predecessors. The official opposition charged repeatedly that Clark had lied about the financial situation of the province, and Clark acknowledged that his credibility rested in part on his ability to balance the provincial budget. Throughout his term of office, Clark attempted to present an image of fiscal conservatism while remaining faithful to NDP principles of social activism. By the end of 1998 the government was running a deficit, which grew worse with the collapse of Asian markets on which the province relied. In its 1999 budget, the Clark government abandoned all pretense of balancing the provincial budget, projecting a $900 million deficit.

Table 6.1 presents the official data on revenues and expenditures for the provincial government in the 1990s. Revenue includes net contributions from Crown corporations, and expenditures exclude some capital projects funded through borrowed money to be repaid over time. Conventional wisdom in the province is that the government has run deficits for seven years, although government data show a tiny surplus in 1994–5. Popular perception aside, the overall picture is one of restrained spending, especially in the second half of the decade, but no major deficits relative to the gross domestic product (GDP).

Table 6.2, which shows BC's economic performance, also indicates that the province was not in a state of fiscal crisis. Gross domestic product and population rose every year between 1991 and 1997. Per capita income increased every year except 1996. Certainly, some of the increases in spending for public administration during the decade would be tied to increased population and economic activity. Prior to 1997, at least, pressures to restrain government spending were as much political as economic, as other governments moved from deficit to surplus positions.

Employer Representation

Since the advent of collective bargaining in the 1970s, the government has been represented by various agencies, all of them reporting to Treasury Board. Collective bargaining functions have been highly centralized during this period, but responsibility for other human resources functions has varied. Organizational changes typically have involved other human resource management functions. During the restraint era of the 1980s, human resources functions were decentralized and fiscal controls were exercised through restrictions on the number of employees in each ministry. As will be discussed below, the limits on the number of employees were only partially effective.

After a report by a commission of inquiry into the public sector, a major reorganization of the human resources/industrial relations functions occurred in

Table 6.1: British Columbia Revenue and Expenditure, 1990–1996 Fiscal Years ($ million)

Year	Revenue	Expenditure	Balance	Per cent, GDP
1990–1	$16,934.9	$17,359.7	($424.8)	0.6
1991–2	17,529.9	19,472.6	(1,942.7)	2.9
1992–3	18,884.1	20,530.5	(1,646.4)	2.4
1993–4	21,178.0	22,116.1	(938.1)	1.3
1994–5	23,217.6	23,190.6	27.0	0.0
1995–6	22,505.0	22,418.0	(413.0)	0.6
1996–7	23,199.0	23,914.0	(715.0)	0.6

Sources: Statistics Canada, *Public Sector Finance 1995/96*, Catalogue no. 69–212–XPB; Government of British Columbia, *Public Accounts, Annual Report 1996–97*; Brian Bemmels, Janice Foley, and Mark Thompson, *Profile of Work and the Economy of British Columbia* (Vancouver: Centre for Labour and Management Studies, Faculty of Commerce and Business Administration, University of British Columbia, 1998).

1994. A thrust of the commission's report was to centralize the administration of human resources in the broader public sector (Korbin, 1993). For the public service, the logic of the reorganization of the public sector was the creation of the Public Service Employee Relations Commission. It provides a range of human resources management services to ministries and agencies on a centralized basis, oversees all labour negotiations, and advises ministries on the interpretation of collective agreements. It also carries out classification systems, workforce adjustment services, central payroll services, and the like. Individual

Table 6.2: British Columbia Economic Performance

Year	Population (000s)	Change from Previous Year	GDP per capita (constant dollars)	Change in GDP per capita
1990	3,300	—	23,876	—
1991	3,380	+2.9	24,099	+0.9
1992	3,477	+2.7	24,935	+3.5
1993	3,576	+2.6	25,518	+2.3
1994	3,671	+2.6	26,847	+5.2
1995	3,766	+2.6	27,091	+0.9
1996	3,858	+2.4	24,822	−0.9
1997	3,933	+2.0	27,171	+1.3

Source: Brian Bemmels, Janice Foley, and Mark Thompson. *Profile of Work and the Economy in British Columbia* (Vancouver: Centre for Labour and Management Studies, Faculty of Commerce and Business Administration, University of British Columbia, 1998).

ministries have labour relations staff to deal with issues arising from component agreements and lower-level grievance procedures. All negotiations and major labour relations decisions are taken by the commission, however.

Size and Shape of the BC Public Service, 1990–1997

The size of the British Columbia public service has been politically controversial. The Harcourt and Clark governments portrayed themselves as avoiding new hiring. The opposition accused them of catering to their public-sector union supporters by increasing the public payroll. As with the budget, it is difficult to determine how much growth occurred in the public service in the 1990s. Absolute employment in the public service rose by 4,100 employees, or 10.4 per cent, between 1990 and 1997, while the ratio of population per employee rose from 83.1 to 89.6 during that period (Statistics Canada, 1998). Nonetheless, this contrasts with the national trend towards absolute reductions in the size of the public service.

The public service in British Columbia is typical for Canadian provinces with few exceptions. Relative to its population, provincial government employment has fallen slightly since 1981. Overall, the ratio of provincial government employees to the population is slightly below the national average, a fact related to the size of the population, since Ontario, Alberta, and Quebec have similar ratios (British Columbia, Ministry of Finance and Corporate Relations, 1998). The health-care and education sectors are small. The majority of psychiatric patients have been discharged from provincial facilities. Responsibility for their care was transferred to local agencies. A comprehensive reorganization of the health sector has caused other provincial health services to move to regional health boards, which do not employ members of the public service. Local school boards have always had control over public education. The province contracts with individual boards to provide services for categories of students with special needs, such as the visually or hearing-impaired. The first community colleges grew out of local school boards and colleges have remained separate from the provincial government. Except for a small number of highly specialized institutions, all post-secondary education is provided by local boards or agencies funded by the provincial government. Liquor sales are dominated by provincial facilities, however, and employees are members of the public service.

In the past, the size of the public service and the scope of government functions have been controversial, reflecting the polarized politics of the province. Despite their political differences, successive provincial governments have maintained a relatively stable public service by shifting functions to the private sector on an incremental basis. Between 1983 and 1992, the number of bargaining unit employees in the public service shrank by 14.7 per cent. The number of managers rose by 54.4 per cent in the same period, partially because of the need to monitor services contracted to the private sector. Between 1985 and 1993, the use of 'consultant' contracted services grew by 322 per cent while public service salaries grew about 36 per cent (Korbin, 1993). Privatization became a major political issue in 1987–8, when Premier William Vander Zalm announced plans to transform the provincial government from a provider of services to a 'guarantor' of services. Using consultants who had worked for the government of Margaret Thatcher in the United Kingdom, the government proposed wholesale elimination of services. These actions provoked widespread protests by labour and had repercussions in bargaining, discussed below.

Since a collective agreement was in place, the BCGEU responded politically. It launched a public relations campaign to oppose privatization. It enlisted the support of local political leaders and even small business groups that could be affected by a reduction in the levels of highway maintenance. Ultimately, pressure generated by the BCGEU and other political problems caused Vander Zalm to abandon most of his privatization initiative, but only after privatizing highway and bridge maintenance services and several other small support units, including computer services and prison chaplaincies (Thompson, 1993). The announced 'transformation' of the public service did not occur, and the policy was not resurrected. The Vander Zalm government also made a political commitment to reduce the number of public servants. Unwilling to cut services to match its promised staff cuts, the government resorted to hiring individuals as contractors, thereby reducing the count of government employees. Ultimately, this policy was found to have violated both the BCGEU collective agreement and the Public Service Act.

When the NDP returned to power it made no effort to recapture any privatized or contracted services for the public service. In the meantime, the BCGEU had retained representation rights for the largest group of workers affected by the Vander Zalm privatization—highway maintenance employees—and successfully negotiated compensation outside of government restrictions.

During the 1990s, both the Social Credit and NDP governments increased contracting out of social services, a policy not announced by the government or the subject of any public comment by the union most directly affected, the BCGEU. Exact data on this trend are not available, in part because of several changes in the configuration of the ministries involved. In 1995, for instance, the Auditor General identified a total of $524 million in spending on grants to non-governmental organizations in social services. The total for the government was $1,524 million, not including educational institutions or hospitals (British Columbia, Office of the Auditor General, 1995). One of the major contractors for social services is the Ministry for Children and Families. Between 1997–8 and 1998–9, grants and contributions to non-governmental agencies within the ministry budget grew from $1.041 billion to $1.109 billion, while the ministry's total budget increased from $1.364 billion to $1.427 billion. In other words, the ministry budget increased by 4.6 per cent, but virtually all of that increase was taken up by private contractors or other service providers. Direct spending by the ministry increased by 0.3 per cent (British Columbia Ministry of Finance and Corporate Relations, 1998). Privately, government officials acknowledged that the government was relying more heavily on private-sector service providers for social services, putting government employees more in the role of supervisors or quality monitors rather than direct service providers.

The BCGEU responded to this policy by attempting to organize employees of service providers. Job rights were not affected by the transfer of functions, so political pressures within the union to resist contracting out were modest. Moreover, the union's organizing efforts were generally successful. Between 1993 and 1997, the BCGEU obtained certifications for 185 bargaining units. It and other unions certified 534 bargaining units in the health and social services sector, covering almost 13,000 employees (British Columbia Labour Relations Board, 1994-8). During the same period, the BCGEU grew from 51,000 to 53,000 members.

Collective Bargaining in the BC Public Service

The three bargaining units established by the Public Service Labour Relations Act in 1973 have remained intact. The BCGEU represents the bulk of all public service employees. Its members work in virtually every unit of the provincial government. The nurses' bargaining unit, much reduced in size by the transfer of psychiatric patients to other caregivers, is represented through a joint certificate of the Union of Psychiatric Nurses (affiliated to the BCGEU) and the BC Nurses' Union. An independent union, the Professional Employees' Association, represents licensed professionals.

Because of its size and pervasive influence in the public service, the BCGEU has dominated collective bargaining in the public service since negotiations first took place. In the 1990s the BCGEU has settled first, with the smaller unions following suit. There has been no serious effort in the 1980s or 1990s to challenge the hegemony of the BCGEU in setting patterns for bargaining in the public service. Consequently, the focus here is exclusively on labour-management relations involving the BCGEU.

By 1998, the BCGEU had approximately 67,000 members (including affiliated unions not connected to the public service) and had renamed itself the BC Government and Service Employees' Union to emphasize the expansion of its membership beyond the public service. Approximately 20 per cent of its members were not employed in the government at all, some having retained membership after privatization of government functions. The union has always had strong central leadership, first under an appointed general secretary and later with a full-time president. When collective bargaining arrived in the BC public service, both political and economic factors favoured labour's position. The government of the day was anxious to improve the caliber of the public service and to set a good example with labour relations and other features of the employment relationship. Compensation increases were relatively generous. In fact, the BCGEU settlements set the pattern for the rest of the public sector. This experience was common for provincial bargaining in Canada, especially during the early years of full collective bargaining.

The period of unfettered bargaining was shorter in British Columbia than in most other jurisdictions. British Columbia was one of the last provinces to enact bargaining legislation for the public service, and in 1982 it was the first to enact provincial wage controls. In the interim, the federal Anti-Inflation Policy effectively limited bargaining between 1975 and 1978 for the BCGEU as it did for other public-sector workers (Fryer, 1995).

The 1980s were a tumultuous period for the public sector in British Columbia, and in particular the public service. In 1983, newly re-elected Premier William Bennett launched a campaign to reduce the size of the public service and to weaken the BCGEU's power. He tabled a 'restraint program', a package of 26 bills that included a measure to eliminate the right of government employee unions to negotiate almost any subject except wages and gave public sector employers the right to fire employees after the expiration of collective agreements. Other bills reduced the scope of human rights legislation and cut social services (Palmer, 1987).

These measures provoked a vigorous reaction, uniting public-sector unions and community groups. A community coalition, funded largely by the BCGEU, spearheaded protests against the government's program. The BCGEU was in negotiations with the provincial government, which put it into the forefront of the protests against the government's restraint package. In addition, its members were most threatened by proposed cutbacks in public services and the termination provisions in the government's legislative package.

Under the threat of a province-wide general strike, the government and the labour movement reached compromise on the issues raised by the restraint package. The 1982 wage control program was extended, which obviously affected the BCGEU negotiations, but other attacks on the union's status were withdrawn. The government proceeded with most of the reductions in public services it had announced (Thompson, 1985). The lasting effect on labour relations in the public service was not legal, but political. For example, one of the persons whose job was eliminated as a result of the restraint package was John Shields, a children's welfare officer and the first vice-president of the BCGEU. He successfully sought reinstatement and was elected president of the union in 1985. Despite his experience in the 1983 confrontation, Shields emphasized the need to work cooperatively with the employer to improve the quality of the public service (Shields, 1998).

During the remainder of the 1980s through the early 1990s, relations between the government and its unionized employees were sullen and quite adversarial. The province continued with its compensation restraint program until 1987 and reimposed it in 1991. Government took aggressive postures towards its employees in bargaining. The unions resisted to the point of striking. Ultimately, changes to collective agreements were modest. During the 1986 round of negotiations, the government demanded longer hours of work, exclusion of some employees from union membership, and reductions in fringe benefits. The union approached the newly elected Premier Vander Zalm, who expressed a desire to end confrontation. After a brief strike by clerical workers and the threat of leg-islation to ban strikes during the 1986 World's Fair, the parties settled for a mod-est wage increase and changes in sick-leave provisions.

Late in 1987, Premier Vander Zalm announced his plan to eliminate as much of the public service as possible, replacing the direct provision of services by a system of contracting out or privatization. Under these conditions, neither party had much interest in labour-management co-operation. Negotiations in 1988 took place against the background of the government's privatization campaign. The BCGEU demanded protection for members affected by privatization and a wage increase to compensate for losses suffered under the government's wage control program. Bargaining was protracted and resulted in a strike by the entire BCGEU bargaining unit except for members whose services had been designated as essential. Ironically, the parties agreed on provisions to permit employees fac-ing layoff due to contracting out or other causes to bid for other jobs in the gov-ernment or accept severance packages. The sticking point in bargaining became the wage package. With the assistance of a prominent mediator, the parties agreed on a compromise wage settlement consistent with the general pattern for the province at the time.

Public-sector unions, in particular the BCGEU, were strong (and open) sup-porters of the NDP during and after the 1991 election. For the BCGEU, this was a reversal of past practice, as the union had always officially been non-partisan. Individual members of the BCGEU and staff personnel had been active in the NDP campaign in many ridings. The president of the party was a senior staff official of the BCGEU during most of the Harcourt government. While Harcourt personal-ly was not particularly close to the labour movement, his leadership style emphasized consensus and he recognized the labour movement's role in his vic-tory. Thus, he immediately weakened the formal wage control program (and subsequently abolished it). He also called a meeting of senior managers and public service union leaders to discuss the improvement of labour relations in the public service.

The provincial government also continued a program to reorganize the health-care sector begun by Social Credit. With encouragement from the gov-ernment, the parties in health care negotiated an accord to facilitate reductions in staff levels in many acute-care facilities and the redeployment of redundant personnel. At the time, the accord was hailed as a major success by government and labour. Employers complained that the accord was too expensive and had to be forced to accept it. Subsequently, employer fears were confirmed, but the government absorbed most of the extra costs. Early in the tenure of the Harcourt government, however, the health-care accord was seen as a model of labour-management co-operation.

Another result of the change in government was a dramatic improvement in the collective bargaining success of the BCGEU. As Table 6.3 indicates, the public service employees fared well in their initial round of bargaining with the new government, compared with the economy as a whole. The initial round of nego-

Table 6.3: Wage Settlements, BCGEU and Provincial Average, 1992–1997

Date	BCGEU Compensation Increase	Year	Average of All Collective Agreements Compensation Increase
1 Aug. 1992	6.0%	1992	3.88%
6 Dec. 1992	2.0%	1993	3.01%
1 Feb. 1993	3.3% (reclassification)		
2 Mar. 1994	0% salary; 1.5% fringes	1994	2.03%
27 Mar. 1995	1.5%	1995	1.47%
30 Nov. 1997	1.0%	1996	0.71%
		1997	0.91%

Source: BC Labour Relations Board, *Collective Bargaining Information Monthly Summary*, various issues; collective agreements, *The Provincial*, various issues.

tiations produced two increases in compensation that were 4 per cent (double) above the provincial average, followed by two additional increases in 1993 that were virtually identical to the average for all collective agreements. The settlements were structured to favour BCGEU members in the lower pay grades, thereby diminishing the impact on the entire wage scale. At the time, the BCGEU settlements were attacked as generous and politically motivated. Without taking sides in the debate, it is proper to observe that the provincial economy was strong in the early 1990s and the BCGEU had been under wage restraint almost continuously for nearly a decade. Whether the increases were overly generous or a 'catch up' for years of restraint, the initial round of bargaining prepared the parties for co-operative efforts in the future.

Bargaining was not the only change in the public service in the wake of the NDP's election. Premier Harcourt appointed Judith Korbin, (a former union official and vice-president of Canadian Airlines), as a one-person commission to examine ways of enhancing the delivery of public services 'through an independent, professional public service' and to examine 'the personnel and labour relations environment' for bodies operated or funded by the provincial government (Korbin, 1992).

One of the motives for appointing the Korbin Commission was the disruption in the public service caused by Vander Zalm's policies. Early in its work, the commission concluded that the improper use of contract employees had been widespread during the previous government, which had sought to reduce the number of persons employed in the public service. However, the commission also examined compensation and bargaining structures in the broader public sector and found substantial variation in the terms and conditions of employment, especially in managerial positions.

Korbin favoured centralized controls of expenditures for the public sector. She recommended a stronger role for the provincial government in the determination of public-sector compensation generally, and she endorsed the service- and results-oriented managerial style known as 'new public management'. In addition, she proposed the establishment of centralized bargaining structures in most of the public sector.

The government implemented most of Korbin's recommendations as they related to the public service. 'Contractors' were returned to the public service, adding to the number of public servants recorded for statistical purposes. New public-sector employers' legislation was passed. The management structure in the provincial government described above was a result of the Korbin Commission. The new Act had only limited effects on the government service, which had been highly centralized since bargaining began in the 1970s. It encouraged centralized bargaining in other elements of the public sector. A Public Sector Employers' Council was formed to co-ordinate bargaining for most components of the public sector in the province, establishing an explicit role for the provincial government in collective bargaining, compensation, and human resources management for the first time. For the public service, the formation of the Council did not represent a substantial change, but the Korbin Report did provide additional stimulus to the parties in the provincial government to seek greater areas of co-operation.

Past Efforts at Labour-Management Co-operation

Despite the dramatic history of labour relations in the public service, the parties had discussed the goal of labour-management co-operation, at least at the senior levels, on several occasions. The 1979 master agreement included a provision calling for a joint committee representing the employer and union in each ministry. The terms of reference were general—the discussion of matters not subject to collective bargaining or grievances. During the same period the parties agreed to solicit suggestions from employees for improving service to the public or other clients, with the understanding that no job losses would result. Responses from the bargaining unit were frequently positive. Liquor board employees, for instance, proposed changing the handling procedures for bottled goods to reduce costs, a move that would reduce the number of hours worked per store, largely through a reduction in the use of casual labour. Accounting procedures for small expenses were simplified and control systems decentralized. While these were minor changes, they did indicate a willingness of the parties to work co-operatively.

The 1983 restraint package and resultant disruption of labour relations generally put an end to these efforts. The union in particular could not be seen to be abetting the government's efforts to reduce the size of the public sector. In a slightly calmer political climate, the parties reintroduced the joint committees in the 1986 master agreement, and they continued through the 1998 contract. The terms of reference were expanded to include measures to reduce the consumption of non-renewable resources and consultations about the effects of the reorganization of a ministry that resulted in redundancies, relocations, or reclassifications of staff. But the continuing atmosphere of confrontation between the BCGEU and senior politicians, in particular Premiers Bennett and Vander Zalm, obviously limited the success of these endeavours. Subsequently, the parties recognized the value of joint committees for dealing with ministry-specific issues.

Shortly after the election of the Harcourt government in 1991, the BCGEU and the government established a joint committee to replace the existing job evaluation plan with a gender-neutral system. Ironically, the Vander Zalm government had made the political decision to introduce pay equity into the provincial public service. The BCGEU signed a memorandum of agreement with the Vander Zalm government in 1989. Under the New Democrats, a joint committee was struck, and consultants were engaged to report to the committee rather than to either of the parties. An extensive program of consultation and communications was launched. The union, at least, found this effort successful, especially compared with other jurisdictions where changes to job evaluation required much longer periods of discussion. Apart from the parties' views, the implementation of pay equity in the provincial public service has been relatively free of controversy (Pratt, 1996).

The issue of formal labour-management co-operation on a broader level arose again after the 1991 election. The provincial government endorsed the conclusions of the Korbin Commission, which stressed the need for improved service delivery and basically stated the case for the so-called 'new public management'. Premier Harcourt convened a forum in March 1993 on improvement in the public service. The Premier, several members of his cabinet, managers at all levels, and representatives of the four unions attended. Harcourt and Korbin were co-chairs. John Shields of the BCGEU strongly supported a public service open to changing social needs, efficient delivery of services, and empowerment of employees charged with delivering services (Korbin, 1993). Given the political history of the province, there was a common theme that the public had to perceive that it was receiving high levels of service from the government at reasonable cost. The BCGEU acknowledged that it should co-operate in efforts to improve the performance of the provincial government to forestall any future efforts to reduce the size of the public service when a right-wing government replaced the NDP. The early success of the health-care accord was also an example of gains the parties could obtain through co-operation. The parties agreed on an agenda, which ultimately was incorporated into the master agreement between the government and the BCGEU (Shields, 1998).

The so-called 'Partnership Agreement' was a memorandum of understanding entitled 'Delivering Quality Services to the Public'. The agreement called for the parties to work jointly to improve the delivery of services by the government, improve the organization of work, reduce unnecessary procedures, and the like. It provided for a Partnership Council at the provincial level with representatives from senior government management and the private sector, plus an elaborate system of joint committees in each ministry down to the work site level to examine all work systems in the public service and seek improvements in the methods of delivery (Rankin, 1997).

The Partnership Agreement received high-level and public support from the parties. The president of the BCGEU and the Premier's deputy minister both made strong statements in favour of the agreement. Committees were established with time limits to report on their progress by April 1995. The Partnership Council established a reporting system to monitor initiatives within each ministry.

Despite the enthusiasm for the Partnership Agreement, it failed (Shields, 1998; MacArthur, 1997). A report issued in August 1996 identified 32 projects as 'registered', and 13 of these were in a single ministry, where the union leadership and management worked effectively. Some of the successes of this period included the organization of community justice centres with employees of several ministries, the decentralization of the Ministry of Health, the organization of a new Ministry for Children and Family Services, and the decentralization of government information and permits authority. However, these changes were relatively modest, and when the parties signed the 12th Master Agreement in 1998, the Partnership Agreement was not renewed.

Predictably, the parties' views on the causes of the failure of the Partnership Agreement differed. Both agreed that the agreement did not cause a change in the culture of the public service. A number of projects were successful and a climate of co-operation was encouraged. Officially, the BCGEU blamed middle management for resisting any sharing of power with employees, especially when the union was involved. The president of the union alluded to managers who had a political agenda different from the government's (Shields, 1998). Privately, senior managers agreed that both management and union representatives were to blame. As one individual explained the experience, the agreement required commitment from both union and management representatives in each ministry, and few ministries had such enthusiasm from both sides (Rankin, 1997).

In addition, there was tension between the government and the BCGEU. During the 1994 negotiations, the government had committed itself to job security for members of the public service. Indeed, with the return of contractors to the public service, the size of the public service rose slightly. After Glen Clark became Premier and won re-election for the NDP, he announced cuts of 3,500 jobs in the public service. The BCGEU regarded this action as a betrayal of a commitment by the previous government and protested vigorously. Tensions between John Shields from the BCGEU (who had not supported Clark's election as leader) and the Premier rose. Eventually, the union negotiated transfer and early retirement provisions for employees affected, and no employee who would accept a transfer was subject to being laid off. Public-sector pension funds in British Columbia, as in other jurisdictions, were in a surplus position, so it was relatively inexpensive for the government to offer early retirement packages. Ministries not involved in the delivery of social services, such as Agriculture and Highways, experienced major reductions in their staff complements and service delivery. Although there were no forced layoffs, the government's actions damaged the climate of co-operation promised by the Partnership Agreement.

The demise of the Partnership Agreement did not end the parties' efforts to find a mechanism for co-operation. An inquiry into the government's child protection services provided added impetus for their efforts. In the wake of the tragic death of a child at the hands of his mother who had received assistance from the Ministry of Social Services, the government appointed a commission of inquiry into the circumstances of his death. The inquiry not only examined the events surrounding the death of the child but looked at the entire child welfare system in the Ministry of Social Services. The commissioner noted the elimination of child welfare workers in the 1983 restraint program and found that the government had tried to maintain services through greater use of contractors. As a result, the government had lost the ability to assure that children at risk received proper care (Gove, 1995).

The commission recommended a sweeping reorganization of child protection services, involving the consolidation of functions from five different ministries, the installation of a comprehensive system of case management, and the formation of two new ministries. Implementation of the commissioner's recommendations revealed that social workers had excessive caseloads, although there was no agreement on the appropriate caseload. With support from the BCGEU, the government appointed a senior official (who ironically had been an architect of the Social Credit government's privatizing and downsizing program) and the president of the BCGEU as co-chairs of a committee to review workloads in child protection functions and recommend improvements in service delivery. Operating under tight deadlines imposed by the Premier, the committee prepared a report with comprehensive recommendations to reorganize the delivery of child protection and support services. While the committee was working, issues of workloads of social workers arose and several isolated wildcat strikes by child protection workers occurred. The committee recommended an increase in the number of social workers in its 1997 report. The government accepted its recommendations, including the hiring of additional social workers and the establishment of training programs for social workers already on staff.

The BCGEU hailed the work of the committee as a successful example of labour-management co-operation in a highly charged political atmosphere. Senior representatives of the parties in effect had collaborated to overhaul a function of the provincial government (Shields 1998). It should be noted, however, that the commission had recommended that additional resources be devoted to child services, a relatively unusual circumstance in a period of government restraint.

Dual-Track Negotiations

Against this background, the parties negotiated a new master agreement in 1998. In February of that year, the Minister of Finance announced that the government would not fund any increase in wages in the public sector before the year 2000, in effect declaring that public-sector unions were expected to accept a two-year salary freeze followed by a 2 per cent increase. The announcement was carefully phrased to avoid the language of a wage control program, although the effect was the same. The lack of public protest by labour organizations pointed to at least tacit acceptance of the limits by the senior leadership of the labour movement.

At the same time, the government offered to discuss changes in public policies with public-sector unions that might improve the status of their members after conventional collective bargaining ended. Tony Penniket, the former NDP government leader of the Yukon, was appointed to represent the government in these discussions. The existence of this second track for negotiations was an obvious incentive for public-sector labour organizations to accept a rather stringent wage control program. In addition, both the government and public-sector unions were conscious of the consequences of the failed Social Contract negotiations in Ontario, which contributed to the defeat of the NDP government there. The parties shared an unstated concern that the Liberal opposition in British Columbia appeared ready to follow the lead of Ontario's Harris government in reducing the size and entitlements of the public sector if it were elected.

This approach was new to Canadian public-sector industrial relations but attracted little attention from the public or interest groups. Limits on public-sector compensation imposed by ministers of finance have been common in Canadian federal and provincial governments since 1982–3. The offer to discuss public policy issues was an innovation in Canada and recalled corporatist negotiations between labour and government in the 1970s and 1980s in other countries. While there have been discussions between government and labour (or other interest groups) in the past in Canada, there appears to be little precedent for such an arrangement at any level of government. Labour governments in Europe and Australia have made 'accords' or 'social contracts' with national labour organizations, covering terms and conditions of employment as well as social policy. None of these was restricted to the public sector, however (Treu et al., 1987; Beaumont, 1995).

The parties in the broader public sector of British Columbia created bargaining structures to facilitate dual track negotiations. These structures contrasted with the highly fragmented arrangements that faced the government and labour in the Ontario Social Contract negotiations (Hebdon and Warrian, 1999). Although the BC public sector contains hundreds of separate employers, implementation of the Korbin Report built on a tradition of province-wide bargaining to centralize negotiations before the dual-track round began. The parties were organized into approximately six sectoral 'tables' (the education sector included at least three distinct sets of negotiations). Settlements occurred sequentially, starting with teachers, followed by the public service and health care. Although it imposed a two-year wage freeze, the government did not seek concessions except in the context of cost-neutral exchanges (i.e., reductions in fringe benefit costs were reflected in other entitlements). Nor did the government seek a reduction in the absolute size of the public sector. Economic developments for the province after the January 1998 announcement were almost universally bad throughout the remainder of the year, so the parties had little appetite for labour conflict. This attitude reflected the tone of labour relations in the province generally. The number of labour disputes during this period was lower than at any period since World War II.

The BCGEU entered negotiations with job security as its most important priority, although it also sought a wage increase. In the wake of the Korbin recommendations, public-sector bargaining was more centralized than ever before in British Columbia. The first test of the new bargaining system was the BC Teachers' Federation and a broader public-sector employers' association representing the province's school boards, who were bargaining on a province-wide basis for the second time. After a relatively short round of negotiations, the union agreed to a package with the wage freezes as provided in the government's program. The second track of bargaining produced a government commitment to increase educational spending and amendments to the legislation governing teachers' pensions to offer inducements to early retirement. The parties estimated that these two measures would create 6,000 new openings for teachers, about 12 per cent of the teaching labour force, within a short period. This package obviously reduced the average salary level for many school districts, as senior teachers were replaced by more junior staff. While the union accepted the package, the trustees' association rejected it, claiming that the government would not provide sufficient funds to meet the obligations in the agreement. The provincial government then imposed the settlement on the employers.

The BCGEU was the second union to settle. It also ratified a collective agreement providing for a two-year wage freeze, followed by a 2 per cent increase in 2001. The contract also provided for a new system of labour-management cooperation. The Partnership Agreement was abandoned in favour of a process to identify 'operational efficiencies', which the parties labelled 'gain-sharing'. The new master agreement provided for ministry joint committees to report to the Minister of Finance on operational efficiencies that will result in savings to the government. These committees had originated less formally by agreement between the government and the BCGEU two years earlier. The ministry joint committees are to consider proposals that:

(a) streamline the decision-making process within government;
(b) identify redundant work practices and recommend improvements;
(c) enhance the delivery of services to the public in an efficient and cost-effective manner;
(d) reduce the requirement of rules, reports, and other bureaucratic requirements that contribute to unnecessary administrative work;
(e) advise on the appropriate use of information technology to support public service objectives and assist in efficient work performance;
(f) identify contracts for services that can be performed by employees in a more cost-effective manner or that are in the public interest to be provided by employees.

Savings are to be allocated equally to the government and the employees. The mechanisms for sharing of savings were not specified, but must be approved by the Auditor General.

This provision was part of a larger package that included benefits from the dual-track bargaining system, which emphasized job security. All regular employees with three years' seniority have significant protection against layoffs, although not against transfers. Amendments to the public service pension plan enhanced the pensions of employees after 1 April 2000, and the employees' contributions to the pension plan were reduced by 1 per cent from November 1998 to April 2000. All employees received a one-time 'efficiency gain payment' of $200. Implementation of pay equity was continued.

From the government perspective, this settlement was relatively inexpensive—a two-year wage freeze with other benefits basically coming from actuarial surpluses in the public service pension fund. The settlement represents a continuation of previous efforts to improve service delivery and reduce costs in the provincial public service. Politically, the NDP government is almost guaranteed a period of peace with the largest public-sector union in the province until after another election. In terms of labour-management co-operation, the gain-sharing provisions of the agreement are the most significant. Past accomplishments have been modest, and it is difficult to predict greater success in the 1998–2001 period, although the continuing pressure from the right-wing Liberal Party and the business community to reduce government spending demonstrated the need for efficiencies in the public service.

Conclusion

This review of labour-management co-operation in the BC public service reveals several continuing themes. At the senior levels of the civil service and the BCGEU there has been a traditional appetite for co-operation on improvements to service delivery. Strong central leadership in the union and the two-tier bargaining structure have promoted this approach to labour relations. BCGEU leaders have been able to undertake these rather risky initiatives with little fear of membership resistance. The bargaining structure, which did not correspond to units of government, further limited the ability of groups within the union to resist co-operation. The joint ministry committees established in 1979 continued to function, and the parties apparently found value in their operation. The 1998 gain-sharing provisions resemble less formal measures adopted in the early 1980s, for example. The short-lived Partnership Agreement was an ambitious effort to change the culture of the public service and was strongly supported by senior government and labour officials. This agreement failed in part because of the high expectations of the parties, especially the BCGEU, about managers' commitment to cultural change and because of a gulf between the government and senior levels of the public service.

Historically, co-operative initiatives have been thwarted by political events. The Bennett government showed no appetite for co-operation after 1983. It concentrated on reducing the size of the public service by eliminating functions and by reductions in staff. Similarly, Vander Zalm's focus was on privatization and contracting out. While it is not clear that the BCGEU would have co-operated with either Social Credit government to improve the public service, the premiers' political positions made such actions unlikely, if not impossible.

Ironically, the attacks on the public service by the Bennett and Vander Zalm governments also created a climate favouring co-operation when the NDP took office. The Harcourt government was relatively moderate and hoped to win the approval, if not the support, of the business community. Thus, it did not reverse the privatization measures, a number of which had proven to be successful and reinforced the role of the private sector while not upsetting patterns of labour relations. Nonetheless, the Harcourt government and the BCGEU shared a commitment to improving the public service as a reflection of the NDP's preference for an active state role in provincial life and a political realization that government should be seen to be efficient and responsive to avoid future attacks from the political right. The Korbin Commission revealed many irregularities in the management of public service staff levels under Vander Zalm, which the NDP government was legally obliged to rectify, as well as poor management of compensation and human resources in the broader public sector. The BCGEU strategy was to co-operate with management in an effort to demonstrate that the public sector could be effective and efficient, a position that could survive a change in government. Public-sector unions and the NDP were painfully aware of the costs of a major confrontation with an NDP government in Ontario and made every effort to avoid public disputes. Thus, the two-year wage freeze imposed on all of the broader public sector in 1998 was accepted without substantial protest, presumably because public-sector unions wanted to avoid damaging the NDP's chances for re-election with consequences similar to what happened in Ontario.

While provincial politics in British Columbia are more polarized than in other jurisdictions (Blake, 1985), the experience of the public service illustrates that co-operation is difficult, if not impossible, with a right-wing government in power. Ideologically, the Social Credit Party was not interested in co-operation (although it did take part in limited initiatives). But its response to economic pressures was to reduce the functions and size of the public service and to try to eliminate the legal and constitutional rights enjoyed by the BCGEU and its members. Major disputes arose over job security. While relations between the NDP and the BCGEU have not been uniformly smooth, the numerous personal and political ties between the two groups facilitated co-operation. In its two terms in office during the 1990s the NDP appointed a large number of persons with party connections to senior levels in the public service, another factor promoting co-operation. At the same time, the New Democrats in British Columbia attempted to be seen as responsible or even tough managers of the public service to promote a positive business climate, while retaining labour's political support. Ultimately, it did nei-

ther. Business remained hostile to the government, and labour grudgingly accepted the centralized controls over collective bargaining. The example of Ontario's
failed public-sector labour relations was a powerful one for both the government
and the BCGEU, however, as each feared the consequences of the election of a
right-wing government that would attack the public sector and union rights as the
Harris government had done.

No government sought major concessions from the BCGEU after 1988. Perhaps
the disruptions caused by the Bennett restraint program served to warn governments, regardless of ideology, to avoid wholesale attacks on public-sector
unions, and the resistance of BCGEU was sufficient to blunt more limited efforts
to obtain concessions. In any case, after the recession of the early 1980s the
province was relatively prosperous and has never had a particularly large public
sector. Thus, the element of crisis behind the efforts of other provincial governments to secure concessions in the 1990s was not present.

Despite the attempts at co-operation in the 1990s, there is no substantial evidence of the new public management philosophy either in the delivery of public services or in the conduct of labour relations. The parties do point with pride
to isolated examples of improvements in direct services to the public, such as the
location of motor vehicle licensing offices in shopping malls with the same hours
of operation as retail establishments. But there has been no wholesale change in
the culture of the public service and no sign that such a change is a serious
objective of either of the parties.

On the other hand, the parties have demonstrated that they can improve efficiencies and respond to challenges, such as the successful reorganization of
child protection services. The predominant theme of Canadian industrial relations in the 1990s has been one of adaptation rather than transformation.
Evidence of adoption of the new public management techniques in any element
of the Canadian public sector is scarce (Thompson, 1998). The British Columbia
experience with labour-management co-operation illustrates this situation. Most
of all, the experience there demonstrates the links between broader political
developments and labour relations in the public service.

References

Beaumont, P.B. 1995. 'Canadian Public Sector Industrial Relations in a Wider Setting', in
    Gene Swimmer and Mark Thompson, eds, *Public Sector Collective Bargaining in
    Canada: Beginning of the End or End of the Beginning?* (Kingston, Ont.: Queen's
    University, IRC Press), 408–29.
British Columbia, Labour Relations Board. *Annual Report*, various years.
——, Ministry of Finance and Corporate Relations. 1998. *BC Stats: Business Indicators*,
    Feb.
——, Office of the Auditor General. 1995. *Report of the Auditor General*. Victoria: Office
    of the Auditor General.

Fryer, John L. 1995. 'Provincial Public Sector Labour Relations', in Gene Swimmer and Mark Thompson, eds, *Public Sector Collective Bargaining in Canada: Beginning of the End or End of the Beginning?* (Kingston, Ont.: Queen's University, IRC Press), 341–67.

Hebdon, Robert, and Peter Warrian. 1999. 'Coercive Bargaining: Public Sector Restructuring under the Ontario Social Contract, 1993–1996', *Industrial and Labor Relations Review* 52, 2: 196–212.

Kelliher, Stephen. 1984. 'Ten Years with the "Dullest Bill": The Evolution of Policy and Practice under the Labour Code', in Joseph M. Weiler and Peter A. Gall, eds, *The Labour Code of British Columbia in the 1980's* (Vancouver: Carswell Legal Publications), 5–24.

Korbin, Judith. 1992. *Interim Report*. Victoria: Commission of Inquiry into the Public Service and the Public Sector.

———. 1993. *Final Report*, vol. 1, *The Public Service of British Columbia*. Victoria: Commission of Inquiry into the Public Service and the Public Sector.

McArthur, Doug. 1997. 'Speaking Notes, Institute of Public Administration of Canada', 23 Oct.

Murray, Gregor. 1993. 'The Changing Nature of Public Sector Unionism: A Case Study of the BC Government Employees' Union, 1974–1991', in Thomas Kuttner, ed., *The Industrial Relations System: Future Trends and Developments*, Proceedings of the XXIXth Conference of the Canadian Industrial Relations Association (Fredericton: University of New Brunswick Law Journal), 651–60.

Palmer, Bryan D. 1987. *Solidarity: The Rise and Fall of an Opposition in British Columbia*. Vancouver: New Star Books.

Pratt, Patrice. 1996. 'Innovative Partnering: Lessons from the Public Sector: Provincial Government Experience', Labour Management Symposium, 10 Oct.

Rankin, Tom. 1997. 'Renewing Renewal: A Report to the Partnership Council', report to BC Government Partnership Council, 1 Dec.

Shields, John. 1998. 'Restructuring to Enhance Service Delivery', speech delivered to the Conference Board of Canada, Public Sector Executives Network, 27 Feb.

Thompson, Mark. 1985. 'Restraint and Labour Relations: The Case of British Columbia', *Canadian Public Policy* 11: 171–9.

———. 1993. 'The Impact of Privatization and Contracting Out: Evidence from British Columbia', in Thomas Kuttner, ed., *The Industrial Relations System: Future Trends and Developments*, Proceedings of the XXIXth Conference of the Canadian Industrial Relations Association, (Fredericton: University of New Brunswick Law Journal), 633–45.

———. 1998. 'Canadian Public Sector Industrial Relations: Adapting to Change', paper presented to the 11th World Congress of Industrial Relations, Bologna, Italy, 23–5 Sept.

——— and Brian Bemmels. 1998. 'Industrial Relations in British Columbia: The Parties Match the Mountains', unpublished ms.

Treu, Tiziano, et al. 1987. *Public Service Labour Relations: Recent Trends and Future Prospects*. Geneva: International Labour Office.

Chapter 7

Restructuring Federal Public-Sector Human Resources

Gene Swimmer and Sandra Bach

Introduction

In this chapter we analyse the context, process, and outcomes related to the restructuring of human resources and labour relations in the federal public service since 1990, a period constituting the most significant changes since the origin of collective bargaining in 1967. Although there have been previous examples of governments downsizing the federal public service, significant and large-scale federal government restructuring did not begin until the current decade. The process was initiated by the Conservatives, but was really shaped and accelerated by the Chrétien Liberal government. From both governments' perspective, the impetus for change was twofold. First, the expanding government deficit had to be addressed through spending reductions, which included public service compensation. Second, a philosophical change about the role of government emphasized policy rather than the delivery of public services (with service delivery delegated to parapublic and private-sector agencies). Federal unions were not impressed by either argument, pointing out that government compensation is a minute part of federal spending and that 'reinventing government' is just a rationale for cutting vital public services. Notwithstanding union concerns, massive changes were developed and implemented on what must be characterized as a unilateral basis, with unions relegated to a consulting role or being forced to bargain under the clear threat of legislation. Between 1991 and 1997, normal collective bargaining was effectively cancelled.

While bargaining was suspended, there remained a forum for negotiating changes at the service-wide level, known as the National Joint Council (NJC). On three different occasions the government tried to negotiate modifications to the job security provisions covering all federal public employees in order to help implement its downsizing. Complete agreement with the public service unions was not possible, and the government resorted to legislation in the first two instances. Nonetheless, the unions co-operated with management and succeeded in minimizing layoffs through joint adjustment committees and other less formal fora.

Despite the government's heavy-handed process, federal public employees did not fare that badly on the wage side compared to their provincial counterparts, as there were no wage rollbacks or unpaid days required. The biggest changes took place in employment and job security, where the number of formal federal government employees fell by 53,000 from 1993 to 1998. Reflecting the government's new mission, these were not across-the-board reductions—so-called 'knowledge workers' were largely spared, at the expense of administrative support and operational positions. As a result, the largest federal public service union, the Public Service Alliance of Canada (Alliance), lost 21 per cent of its membership, compared to losses of less than 7 per cent for unions representing professional groups. The survivors of this downsizing exercise are left with watered-down job security, although it is still probably superior to much of the private sector.

While 1997 was marked by the beginning of balanced budgetary accounts and future government surpluses, as well as the resumption of collective bargaining (after a six-year absence), the nature and form of federal staff relations have not yet solidified. Government positions relating to employment security, wages, and conditions of work may be influenced by the mitigating fiscal pressures, but the overall management approach towards labour relations remains to be seen. Although government officials acknowledge the need for greater employee commitment and co-operation, not only to enhance the quality of services provided but to cope with increased workloads, they do not appear to see the linkages between these workplace factors and macro-level labour relations policies.

The Labour Relations Environment

Before delving into the restructuring of the federal public service during the current Liberal regime, it is important to summarize the labour relations environment that developed over the previous years. In 1944 the federal government established the National Joint Council as a forum for discussion of compensation with the existing employee associations. Any agreement among the parties was forwarded to the cabinet, but this was purely advisory. Collective bargaining was enshrined for federal public employees with the passage of the Public Sector Staff Relations Act (PSSRA) in 1967. It included standard certification rules, based on approximately 80 occupationally defined bargaining units that cut across government departments. Within three years the entire public service was organized, often by the newly reconstituted staff association that represented the employees in pre-1967 NJC consultations.

The Act differed from private-sector legislation in two areas: dispute resolution and scope of bargaining. Unions were given the choice, exercised at the beginning of each bargaining round, of having a subsequent dispute resolved by interest arbitration or the right to strike by 'non-essential' workers. Over time, many bargaining agents rejected arbitration, after learning that the conciliation-strike route led to superior settlements, even for groups unlikely to strike. The Liberals, governing party for virtually the entire 1970–84 period as bargaining evolved, responded with several policies to devalue the conciliation-strike route, including greater designation of essential workers who would have to work during a strike and wage controls (Swimmer, 1995). Nonetheless, by the mid-1980s the arbitration route was largely the domain of professionals, who found the possibility of a strike abhorrent or ineffective, or of groups who had almost all members classified as essential.

The Act also narrowed the scope of bargaining, meaning that many issues that would be negotiable in the private sector were management's unilateral right. Based on the principle that public policy should not be determined at the bargaining table, any issue that would require an Act of Parliament (except for the appropriation of funds) could not be negotiated. This precluded any aspect of the merit system or pensions from negotiation. Another section of the Act granted management the unilateral right to organize the public service and classify the positions therein. Despite these legislative proscriptions, the parties occasionally consulted and/or negotiated agreements covering these issues.

Since the advent of collective bargaining, the NJC has evolved into a forum for resolving service-wide issues of concern between the employer and unions. There is no formal dispute resolution process, so any agreements are voluntary. An agreed-upon directive becomes part of all collective agreements. Unless the parties agree to a change, the status quo remains. In the mid-1980s, the NJC rose in prominence when the Conservative government used the process to negotiate aspects of service-wide job security.[1]

The major player on the union side is the Public Service Alliance of Canada, which represents most non-professional employees. From its inception, following the merger of two employee associations, the Alliance has been the largest bargaining agent in the federal public sector, currently representing over 120,000 employees. Despite its association origins, the Alliance has become increasingly militant over the past 30 years. In 1991, the union launched one of the biggest public-sector strikes in Canadian history.

The next largest labour group is the Professional Institute of the Public Service of Canada (PIPSC), currently representing about 30,000 professionals in the public service. The PIPSC has historically been less militant, generally choosing to forgo the right to strike in favour of arbitration. The third largest union is the Social Sciences Employees Association (SSEA), made up of two professional groups that broke away from the Alliance and PIPSC and representing 5,000 employees. This organization has always chosen the arbitration route, and given its history, relations with the other two unions have often been strained. There are another 13 smaller unions with memberships of 2,500 or less.

As is commonly the situation in the public sector, there are three layers of management. The formal employer for purposes of collective bargaining is the Treasury Board, which was responsible for negotiating 80 contracts until the move to co-ordinated bargaining in the mid-1980s. Day-to-day operations are overseen by departmental managers who are responsible, among other things, for administering the collective agreement. The approach and mandate of these two levels of management towards staff relations are ultimately shaped and determined by the third layer, the government of the day.

The Fiscal Environment

When the Conservative government under Brian Mulroney was elected in 1984, concerns were developing about the federal government's level of indebtedness. Over the previous decade the federal debt had soared from $27 billion to $183 billion. Despite the stated goals of deficit reduction during the Conservative reign, large annual deficits were the norm, reaching $42 billion in the 1993–4 fiscal year (see Table 7.1). By then, the federal debt exceeded $508 billion (which amounted to 69 per cent of gross domestic product). This occurred despite increases in personal income taxes and the introduction of the federal Goods and Services Tax. The Bank of Canada's high interest rate policy in the late 1980s increased debt-servicing costs and the 1990–1 recession simultaneously reduced tax revenues and increased social expenditures such as unemployment insurance. As will be discussed subsequently, in 1991 the government imposed compensation restraints on the federal public service in the name of deficit reduction, despite the fact that federal compensation amounted to less than 12 per cent of government spending.

In 1993, the newly elected Liberal government pledged to reduce and eventually eliminate the deficit. Faced with a populace committed to reducing government indebtedness and no effective left-of-centre opposition party, the Liberals were able to live up to their promise by attacking expenditures rather than increasing taxes. They reduced program spending dramatically, from $120 billion in 1993–4 to $107 billion in 1997–8 (at about 12 per cent of GDP, program spending was at its lowest level since 1950), by removing or devolving federal programs and through cuts in provincial transfer payments. Federal compensation was also reduced by $2.4 billion over the same period through imposed salary freezes and layoffs. The contribution of compensation restraint to deficit reduction was minimal, however, considering that the annual difference between expenditure and revenue fell by $45 billion. Much more important were high levels of economic growth, which increased tax revenues by more than $35 billion, allowing the Liberals in the 1997–8 fiscal year to deliver a $3.5 billion budget surplus, the first federal surplus in 28 years.

Labour Relations under the Conservative Government

Following through on a widely quoted campaign statement to give public servants 'pink slips and running shoes', Brian Mulroney's government announced in 1985 that 15,000 permanent positions within the federal government would be cut over the next five years. It was originally presumed that specific programs would be targeted based on recommendations of the Nielson Task Force on Program Review, but the government's refusal to act on the recommendations

Table 7.1: Aspects of Federal Finances in Billions of Current Dollars

	1984–5	1987–8	1990–1	1993–4	1994–5	1995–6	1996–7	1997–8
Total revenue	$71.1[c]	$97.6	$119.4	$116.0	$123.3	$130.3	$140.9	$153.2
Total expenditure[a]	$109.5	$125.4	$151.4	$158.0	$160.8	$158.9	$149.8	$150.4
Program spending[b]	$87.1	$96.5	$108.8	$120.0	$118.7	$112.0	$104.8	$106.7
(% GDP)	19.0%	16.9%	16.0%	15.3%	14.7%	13.8%	12.4%	12.1%
Compensation	$12.7	$14.6	$17.4	$19.0	$18.8	$18.3	$17.9	$16.6
(% total expenditure)	13.5%	13.2%	11.8%	11.8%	11.7%	11.1%	11.4%	11.0%
Deficit (surplus)	$38.4	$27.8	$32.0	$42.0	$37.5	$28.6	$8.9	($3.5)
(% GDP)	8.4%	4.9%	4.7%	5.7%	4.8%	3.5%	1.1%	(0.4%)
Debt	$208.0	$301.1	$390.8	$508.2	$545.7	$574.3	$583.2	$579.7
(% GDP)	45.4%	52.6%	57.6%	69.3%	70.1%	70.7%	69.1%	65.8

[a]Total expenditure includes all direct government spending, transfers to other levels of government, contingency funds, and public debt charges.
[b]Program spending excludes public debt charges and contingency funds.
[c]Dollar figures have been rounded.
Sources: Finance Canada, *Fiscal Reference Tables (1 and 2), 1997;* 1997–8 figures come from Government of Canada, *Public Accounts of Canada, 1998,* vol. 1; Finance Canada, *Main Estimates, Part II,* Summary Tables, Budgetary Main Estimates by Standard Object of Expenditure (various years); CANSIM Matrix 1901 (expenditure based GDP at market prices).

turned this into an across-the-board exercise. Between 1985 and 1990 the number of full-time indeterminate positions fell by 15,054,[2] which could be interpreted as the Conservatives reaching their goal. Most of the staff reductions were accomplished through attrition, with only 1,200 layoffs. At the same time, there were substantial increases in part-time indeterminate, term, and casual positions. Lee and Hobbs (1996: 341) estimated that full-time equivalent employment fell by less than 4,700 during the five-year period. It should be noted that between 1990 and their electoral defeat in 1993, the Conservatives actually increased total employment by at least 5,000 jobs.

The Mulroney government also established a renewal initiative, known as Public Service 2000,[3] aimed at simplifying the personnel system, reducing central agency controls to increase the power and accountability of departments, and empowering workers to deliver programs efficiently. Task forces headed by deputy ministers made recommendations on aspects of human resource management. The federal unions, although conceding the need for change, condemned the program from the start because it was developed and presented as an 'unabashedly management-driven exercise'. Some of the task force recommendations resulted in legislative changes to the PSSRA and the Public Service Employment Act. One of the more important amendments allowed employees to be 'deployed' between jobs at the same classification level without a job competition. While deployments greatly simplify staffing, the process reduces the number of job competitions available to employees and greatly limits the right of appeal by other employees. Unions complain that the merit principle has been compromised through this process. And at the same time, they see one of their potential services to members—appealing job competitions—being wiped out. While the name 'PS2000' fell into disfavour by 1993, proposals such as a simplified 'universal job classification system' and a reduction in the number of bargaining units survived the Conservative regime and have been implemented (or are due to come on stream) during the Chrétien Liberal mandate.

Despite their rhetoric, the Conservatives were largely responsible for enhancing the job security of the federal public employees. In an attempt to foster co-operation with the unions about downsizing, the government instructed Treasury Board to negotiate aspects of job security on a service-wide basis at the NJC (Swimmer and Kinaschuk, 1992). The parties agreed to a 'Workforce Adjustment Policy' in 1985, which was extended for another three years in 1988. Although management retained the unilateral right to determine which indeterminate employees would be declared surplus, these staff would now be entitled to six months' layoff notice (which could be taken as a payment-in-lieu), retraining up to one year, and salary protection for one year when accepting a job at a lower pay rate. Another section of the policy required departments to cease contracting out services if this would 'facilitate deployment of permanent employees affected by workforce adjustment'. In 1990, the Alliance successfully argued in court that the intent of the clause prohibited contracting out if layoffs would result or if there were surplus federal employees capable of doing the work.

Unknowingly, the Conservatives agreed to a plan that effectively removed their ability to contract out, a right they were intent on getting back when the NJC agreement expired in 1991.

Faced with a greater budget deficit ($32 billion) than originally forecast as a result of a deepening recession, the 1991 federal budget called for a freeze in the total federal wage bill and established the wage guidelines that for every 1 per cent wage increase, 2,000 jobs would be eliminated. The government's position was subsequently refined to 0 per cent and 3 per cent wage maxima for two years, at a time when private- and public-sector settlements were in the 4–5 per cent range (see Table 7.2). The government was prepared to end strikes or roll back arbitration awards through legislation in order to maintain its wage guidelines. The government position eventually led to a confrontation with the Alliance, which began a nationwide legal strike of non-designated members in September 1991. The strike, the largest in federal public service history, lasted for almost three weeks before its legislated end, with as many as 70,000 staying off work each day. The imposed settlement was only slightly better than the government's wage guideline, including a $500 signing bonus for 30 per cent of its lowest-paid union members and minor benefit improvements. On the other hand, the union proved it could get the workers out and wound up with fairly sympathetic public opinion.

During most of this period, NJC negotiations were continuing to amend the workforce adjustment policy. An agreement was reached in late November 1991

Table 7.2: Average Percentage Wage Increases for Major Collective Agreements

Year	Local Admin.	Health, Educ. and Welfare	Provincial Admin.	Federal Admin.	Public Sector	Private Sector	National CPI*
1990	4.9	5.5	6.5	5.3	5.6	5.7	4.8
1991	4.9	3.8	3.7	1.7	3.4	4.2	5.6
1992	3.3	1.7	2.1	—	2.0	2.6	1.5
1993	0.8	0.7	0.4	0.0	0.6	0.8	1.8
1994	0.7	–0.3	0.1	0.0	0.0	1.3	0.2
1995	0.6	0.5	0.8	0.0	0.6	1.4	2.1
1996	0.7	0.5	0.3	0.0	0.5	1.9	1.6
Average 1990–6	2.3	1.8	2.0	1.2	1.8	2.6	2.5

*Not seasonally adjusted.
Note: These rates do not include wage rollbacks or unpaid days that were not included in collective agreements.
Sources: Human Resources Development Canada, Workforce Information Directorate, *Major Wage Settlements*, various years; Statistics Canada, *Consumer Price Index*, Catalogue no. 62–001, various years.

that bestowed ironclad job security on indeterminate employees in return for allowing the government to contract out. The new Workforce Adjustment Directive (WFAD) entitled all indeterminate employees declared surplus to the guarantee of a 'reasonable job offer', usually in the same geographic area and at the same classification level. The surplus period was extended indefinitely until such a job offer had been made, and if the job offered was at a lower classification level, the employee's current salary was protected indefinitely. In cases where surplus status resulted from contracting out, employees could also resign and receive 6–12 months of extra severance pay (see Table 7.3 for details). The government apparently made these concessions because with 20,000 term employees and annual attrition of another 10,000, it retained substantial flexibility to contract out, cut, or devolve programs.

Daryl Bean, president of the Alliance, claimed that the job security breakthroughs were a tangible result of the September strike, while the Treasury Board President, Gilles Loiselle, said that these proposals had been offered before the strike. There has been much debate about whether the union was putting a positive spin on a strike that was mainly a moral victory. The fact is that job security was not an issue in the strike, but there were important differences between the government's formal pre-strike proposal and the eventual agreement. One of our respondents insists that the WFAD was virtually all there in August. Regardless of what really occurred, the Alliance version is now an ingrained part of that union's culture and internal politics.

Despite the controls on federal public service compensation and higher tax rates, the Conservative government's fiscal woes continued. The continuing recession reduced tax revenues and meant that the government would again exceed its projected deficit for 1992–3. As a partial solution, in December 1992, the government extended collective agreements for two years, meaning that wage increases were limited to 3 per cent for the 1991–5 period. This was the last straw for the Alliance, which earmarked an additional $1.25 million for the upcoming election campaign to oust the Conservatives.

Labour Relations under the Liberal Government

In October 1993, the Liberals under the leadership of Jean Chrétien were elected with a solid majority, while the Conservatives were humiliated at the polls. Federal public-sector employees and their union leaders were close to euphoric about the prospect of a return to Liberal rule. Chrétien repeatedly made statements about his appreciation of the federal bureaucracy, in sharp contradiction to the Conservatives' negative rhetoric. In addition, he indicated that, if elected, the Liberals would not extend the Tory wage freeze or unilaterally dismantle the WFAD.[4] Even the most cynical union leaders, with memories of Liberal-imposed wage controls in the early 1970s, were cautiously optimistic that labour relations would become more harmonious.

Table 7.3: Workforce Adjustment Policy Changes in the 1990s

Date	Policy Changes	Specific Benefits/Changes
November 1991	Workforce Adjustment Directive Agreement (WFAD) comes into effect.	Essentially lifetime job security for federal public servants; those declared 'surplus' to be guaranteed a 'reasonable job offer' (RJO) within same geographic area and classification level. Up to 12 months' additional severance pay for resignation, if employee is 'surplus' because of contracting out.
2 February 1995	Final offer given to unions through the National Joint Council prior to the 1995 budget; Alliance rejects the offer and, given rules of unanimity, offer is rejected.	Suspension of the WFAD for departments affected by downsizing; extension of geographic range for an RJO; greater allowances for contracting out; creation of early departure (EDI) and early retirement incentive (ERI) packages.
27 February 1995	The federal government announces workforce reductions of 45,000 federal civil servants over a three-year period; legislates its final offer.	WFAD revised. Those in 'most-affected departments' lose job security in return for benefits of the incentive packages. Those choosing to remain 'surplus' to be taken off the payroll after 60 days if a job not located, remaining on the list (with benefits) and receiving a severance package one year later.
7 February 1996	Deal signed between the Government and 20 per cent of the federal unions. The Alliance and the SSEA are warned that a less generous deal may be legislated if they don't sign.	The WFAD is changed so that the RJO could include the transfer of public servants to the private sector at 85 per cent of their wage rates.

| 7 March 1996 | Government legislates changes to the WFAD through the Budget (including changes to the RJO). WFAD revised to create Type 1, Type 2, and Type 3 employment transition (ASD) arrangements. Both Type 1 and 2 constitute a 'reasonable job offer'. Those employees not accepting a Type 1 or 2 RJO are given four months' termination notice. A Type 3 employment offer is not considered an RJO, and if declared surplus, they receive other benefits under the WFAD. | Those unions not signing the government's February offer receive less benefits (12 months' salary top-up if commercialized position 15 per cent less than previous wages, as opposed to 18–24 months for other unions). Type 1 arrangements include union successor rights and transfer of collective agreements to the new employer, guarantee of two-year minimum employment, and benefit, severance, and pension arrangements similar to those of the federal government. Type 2 arrangements require the average salary in the transferred service to be at least 85 per cent of the previous salary, a two-year employment guarantee, and benefits, severance, and pension arrangements similar to those of the federal government. Employees accepting a Type 2 offer receive a three month transition payment plus salary top-up for 18 months (24 months if the individual's salary is less than 80 per cent of previous salary). If an employee receives a Type 3 transferred job (fewer benefits and guaranteed conditions than Types 1 or 2), he or she receives a salary top-up for 12 months, plus a six-month transition payment. |
| 14 May 1998 | The WFAD is again altered through the NJC, coming into effect on 23 June. The amended WFAD applies only to signatory unions, which does not include the Alliance, the SSEA and the Dockworkers. | Changes to the RJO include the choice of a time-limited (52-week) offer of indeterminate employment, after which period they would be laid off and subject to severance and other benefits (including similar benefits to transferred ASD employees) or a transition support measure (plus severance) for 10–34 weeks or an education allowance of up to $7,000 (plus severance); $385 of financial planning advice is also extended. The alternation/swap process is written into the WFAD. |

Table 7.3 continued

Date	Policy Changes	Specific Benefits/Changes
29 August 1998	The Alliance and Treasury Board agree to a new WFAD to cover Alliance members at the bargaining table.	The Alliance's WFAD encompasses all the changes agreed to by the other unions and Treasury Board in 1996 and 1998, plus other provisions: a. a surplus employee on a time-limited RJO can offer to resign in return for a lump-sum severance payment; b. department must give union 180 days of intention to use ASD; parties must then strike a joint committee to negotiate human resource elements of the transfer; c. use of normal grievance procedure to resolve disputes, as opposed to NJC procedures.
September 1998	The SSEA is the only union not covered by the amended WFADs. The 1998 changes were not ratified by the membership after collective agreements had been signed for the SSEA groups. The SSEA still has access to an unlimited RJO, as per the 1991 WFAD, except in cases of alternative service delivery where the 1996 WFAD applies.	

Although many had hoped the Liberals would end the wage freeze once elect-ed, union leaders were not surprised with the government's announcement that the legislated wage freeze would remain in place until 1995, under the Tories' timetable. The unions understood that the Liberals had to institute some policies to reduce the deficit, which stood at approximately $42 billion for the 1993-4 fiscal year. Though the government never 'opened up' the books, the deputy minister of finance made an NJC presentation about Canada's deficit and debt position relative to its trading partners. The union view was that with compensation representing only 11.8 per cent of federal spending, down from 13.5 per cent in the mid-1980s, federal public employees were neither the cause nor the solution to the deficit problem (see Table 7.1).

With the first Liberal budget less than a week away, Treasury Board President Art Eggleton announced the government's plans to reduce departmental operating budgets by $1 billion over the next few years. Although there would undoubtedly be job reductions (unions were predicting as many as 40,000 lost positions), he claimed that there would be no large-scale layoffs and that job security under the WFAD would not be changed unilaterally: 'The previous government spoke in terms of pink slips and running shoes; this government intends to work with the public service in terms of dignity, hope and satisfaction' (Howard, 1994).

Finance Minister Paul Martin's 1994 budget indicated to union leaders and members that although the rhetoric was more positive, Liberal staff relations policies were going to be at least as harsh as those of their predecessors.[5] He announced that not only would collective agreements be extended for another two years to 1997, but that increments, paid annually to about 80,000 employees (those not at the top salary step for their classification), would be frozen. The cuts were justified as a 'bottom-line fiscal requirement' because salaries actually increased by 3 per cent annually during the Tory wage freeze due to increment payments, promotions, and reclassifications.

All the union leaders we interviewed were completely caught off guard by the government's actions ('we read about it in the budget lockup'). The worst that they expected was for the government to stall and/or bargain hard at the nego-tiating table. Many also expressed that the increment freeze was particularly offensive, because it hit female, lower-paid workers hardest. Even though many leaders conceded that it would have been difficult to obtain a wage increase in bargaining, given that settlements in the public and private sectors were in the 0–1 per cent range, many non-monetary issues that had been festering for four years could have been addressed. More importantly, the legitimacy of collective bargaining would have been respected, and at the very least, increments would have continued.

Why did the government impose these policies? Certainly the money involved was not negligible: the increment freeze saved $400 million, and there was a possibility that for those groups selecting the arbitration route, the interest arbitrators would increase salaries (every 1 per cent increase in salaries across the board amounted to $130 million). Perhaps even more important was the fact that the government was going to call on all Canadians to make sacrifices, and this constituted public employees' contribution to fiscal restraint. This policy would also indicate a commitment to fiscal restraint for the benefit of bond raters. Finally, the government knew this would not be a difficult sell with the public or their own employees, as several provinces had already imposed salary rollbacks and/or unpaid days (even Ontario's NDP government). The federal plan was relatively gracious, as no money already paid to employees would be taken away.

Martin's 1994 budget also announced massive cuts in defence spending ($1.9 billion over three years) and reductions to operating funds to other departments ($468 million in 1994–5, $1.1 billion in 1995–6, and $1.6 billion in 1996–7). A significant portion of these savings would be generated through a reduction in the size of the federal public service. The numbers for defence were already known: a reduction of 8,400 civilians over four years (including 6,000 indeterminate positions), most of whom were members of the Alliance. The Liberals were aware that this could not be accommodated by normal attrition. An elaborate incentive program was developed, including up to two years' severance pay or a waiver of the pension penalty for early retirees over 50 years old, to stimulate voluntary separations and reduce the likelihood of layoffs.[6]

The budget outlined a different approach to reducing operating budgets of non-defence departments. Rather than instituting across-the-board cuts, each department was to review its programs carefully to determine whether they passed several sequential tests:

1. Does the program area or activity continue to serve a public interest?
2. Is there a legitimate and necessary role for government in this program area or activity?
3. Is the current role of the federal government appropriate, or is the program a candidate for realignment with the provinces?
4. What activities or programs should or could be transferred in whole or in part to the private or voluntary sector?
5. If the program or activity continues, how could its efficiency be improved?
6. Is the resultant package of programs and activities affordable within the fiscal restraint? If not, what programs or activities should be abandoned? (Kroeger, 1998: 17)

Programs failing to pass all tests (notwithstanding the lack of objective criteria for assessing these questions) would be candidates for removal.

The Program Review represented the Liberals' attempt at 'reinventing government', a public-sector reform that was sweeping many Western governments.[7] The basic philosophy behind these reforms is that government has grown too large and in the process has exceeded its core policy-making role, with too much emphasis on direct program delivery. There is also a presumption that private-sector management is inherently more efficient than that in the public sector, underlining the view that fewer public services should be provided directly by the government. This view would also have consequences for the provision of public services by indeterminate federal public employees.

The impact of Program Review would vary among departments and job classifications but it quickly became clear that non-professional employees, involved in program delivery, would be the most likely candidates for surplus status. These workers were invariably members of the Alliance.

The federal public service unions condemned the budget, focusing on the additional two-year wage and increment freeze, which was interpreted as reneging on an election commitment. Attempting to demonstrate a willingness for compromise, Treasury Board President Eggleton proposed union-management discussions to identify specific cost savings that could potentially be used to unfreeze wages and/or increments. This 'Efficiency Review' was greeted with scepticism by most union leaders, but they were prepared to give the process a chance. Yet it became obvious early on that these talks were not going to be fruitful. According to union interviewees, whenever unions brought up a specific way to save money, they were told that the suggestion was already built into the budget, so it did not count. At one point, when union leaders argued that the way to save money was to reduce contracting out, they were told by the politician in charge of the talks that the government could not address that area because it involved contractual obligations. This logic did not sit well with the unions, which just had their labour contracts revoked by legislation. Even the management interviewees conceded that while the Review was well-intentioned, Treasury Board never received instructions about its authority with respect to the talks. The larger political concern was that if efficiencies could be found, should public servants be the sole beneficiaries (as opposed to putting the money back into more service for the public)? By June 1994, the talks began to unravel with the withdrawal of the Alliance, followed by the PIPSC and the SSEA.

As departments continued with their Program Review exercises, rumblings began to surface about the incompatibility of the government downsizing and the WFAD. One senior manager stated that at virtually every meeting of the Program Review committee, departmental officials would point to the 'reasonable job offer' (RJO) as the reason they couldn't meet their target reductions. Although the RJO may have just been a convenient excuse for some departments, the government determined that the policy had to be modified for the Program Review process to succeed. It was reported that federal government employee annual attrition rates had fallen to 8,447 (from 13,404 in 1987) and that there were currently 10,500 employees on the 'surplus list' waiting for an RJO (May, 1994a).

In November, the government suggested that the WFAD be modified to consider a job with another level of government or the private sector (following a transfer of service) as a 'reasonable job offer'. The unions immediately expressed opposition to watering down their job security. The government also stated that if the WFAD could not be changed, it might consider buyouts and early retirement packages to increase voluntary separations. Later that same month, the Auditor

General noted that the WFAD clashed with the government's intention to down-size the public service and that the government should target particular employ-ees for reductions through incentive packages (May, 1994b).

During this period a series of secret negotiations began between senior Treasury Board officials and three union presidents over the WFAD. The manage-ment position, as mentioned above, was that the concept of the RJO had to be expanded to include jobs with other employers. Although they were prepared to negotiate on other aspects, the Treasury Board representatives made it clear that if they could not get agreement with the unions, the government would find another way to achieve what it needed. The union representatives were pushing for substantial compensation for surplus employees who would voluntarily resign or retire early, as well as for the right of an employee desiring to leave the public service to substitute for a surplus employee who wanted to stay.

Negotiations came to a head in early February 1995. There was a mutually determined formal proposal that the parties agreed to take to their constituents for ratification. The offer would involve only those nine departments that would be 'most affected' by Program Review for a three-year period. Indeterminate workers declared surplus in these departments would have the choice of a buy-out package or the acceptance of a modified RJO within 40 kilometres (previously 16 km) for a six-month period, while on full salary. If no job offer materialized, for the next 12 months the employee would be on unpaid leave, with the gov-ernment maintaining health and pension status. After 18 months, the employee would be laid off, even if an RJO never materialized.

The buyout packages were of two types: an early departure incentive (EDI) or an early retirement incentive (ERI). The EDI provided an allowance of 39 to 90 weeks of pay, depending on years of service and pension status, plus up to a $7,000 training allowance. The ERI was aimed at indeterminate employees declared surplus who were 50-60 years old with at least 10 years' service with the federal government. It involved waiving the pension penalty (which was 5 per cent for every year below the age and pensionable years requirements), plus up to a 15-week cash payment. The offer did not contain any provision for job-swapping between surplus and non-surplus employees. Apparently, the parties had agreed in principle that substitutions within departments would occur, sub-ject to management discretion. Treasury Board representatives, however, were not interested in cross-departmental substitutions and would not accept any swaps without the managers' approvals.

Two members of the union negotiating team met with all the smaller unions to brief them on the possible deal. The representatives stated that if all the unions ratified the deal, it would be easier for the Treasury Board to sell the proposal to the politicians. One union official we interviewed said that the subtext was clear: if this deal was not ratified, the government would legislate something worse. There was approval-in-principle by all but one of the unions by the end of the meeting. Later that evening, the contents of the deal were leaked to the media.

The Alliance National Board, made up of the five executive committee mem-bers, 18 component presidents,[8] and eight national directors, discussed the proposal the same evening. Like any political organization, there is a wide range of views and philosophy among its board members. The view among the more militant members was that there was no reason to accept the government's offer. Although the WFAD was up for triennial review, in the case of an impasse the directive would remain in force until collective agreements expired. The Liberals extended collective agreements by legislation, and they should be forced to pay the price of that decision. In addition, if the Liberals legislated their proposed changes to the WFAD, the matter would become a hot media issue with potential political fallout for the government. At the same time, the Alliance leaders could say to their members that they did not agree to concessions that would establish two classes of employees. Finally, accepting the proposal would have legitimized the process. Real collective bargaining does not involve one party threatening to legislate its demands.

The pragmatist board members believed that the proposed deal, if combined with job-swapping, represented a reasonable compromise and was in many ways more generous than what was being imposed on provincial government employees. No final decision was taken that evening. By the next morning, politicians and senior managers read about the deal in the *Ottawa Citizen* before their official briefings. At the same time, many Alliance officials and rank-and-file members heard about the 'secret deal'. The politically embarrassed Alliance National Board held a quick press conference, stating that the offer had been rejected. Their rejection effectively ended the negotiations.

No one will ever know whether the deal would have been accepted without the leaked story. For one thing, it is not clear that the Treasury Board officials could have delivered on job-swapping (although the government eventually accepted the concept, some two months later). Even if job substitution were available, would the Alliance National Board have signed on? As will become evident, subsequent history indicates that this probably would not have been the case.

The unions knew that some form of legislation was extremely likely. As a last-ditch attempt to keep the WFAD intact, the Alliance offered to finance and manage a registry of employees wishing to take a buyout who could swap jobs with employees declared surplus, removing the need for layoffs. The Alliance pledged it would work with the employer to minimize the impact on employee reductions arising from government's Program Review.

Treasury Board President Eggleton rejected the Alliance offer as unworkable. Managers were not about to relinquish their control by accepting the transfer of an employee arranged by the union. On 22 February he announced that the budget would include a three-year suspension of the WFAD within most-affected departments in return for new buyout packages (identical to the aborted WFAD deal—see Table 7.3). Job-swapping was not a part of the package. One week later, Finance Minister Paul Martin delivered his budget, announcing that over the next three years 45,000 public service jobs would be gone (33,000 in the core public service and the rest from Crown corporations and defence). Not all these jobs were lost, as some were transferred to other jurisdictions (i.e., approximately 8,000 Transport Canada employees were disbursed to newly created agencies such as NavCan and local airport authorities).

On 17 May 1995 Eggleton stated that the government had changed its mind on the issue of job exchanges and would introduce guidelines allowing for alternations between surplus employees and non-surplus employees willing to take a buyout package. These alternations could only be arranged once an employee was declared surplus, and would still be up to the discretion of management. The Alliance immediately took a conciliatory stance and promised to co-operate with the government on implementing the alternation process.[9] By the end of the month, Treasury Board and all the unions also signed a Memorandum of Agreement to minimize the negative impact of the Program Review downsizing on employees through the establishment of regional Joint Adjustment Committees (JACs) (Date, 1995). In some regions, the interdepartmental JAC process eventually became a major basis for arranging 'alternations'.

Why did the government do an about-face on swaps? There are several non-exclusive reasons. Union interviewees stated that the government's position was basically untenable, given that all major private-sector downsizing programs attempt to maximize voluntary attrition through universal buyout plans and job-swapping. This message was delivered by rank-and-file members across the country to their local MPs, who in turn raised the matter in the Liberal caucus. In addition, the major unions made representations to the House of Commons and Senate Finance Committees. At the same time, managers in the most-affected departments were lobbying at the bureaucratic level. They were the ones who were obliged to do the government's 'dirty work'. Job-swapping was seen as essential to keeping some degree of employee morale among the survivors of the downsizing exercise. In the end, the government decided to be accommodating, as long as costs would not soar and people with the required skills could be retained. Interestingly, central agency officials made it clear that if alternations had been part of the package from the beginning, they would have cut back on the size of the EDI and ERI payment packages. There was a feeling at Treasury Board that the Alliance wound up with a very good deal, without having to accept any accountability for the modifications to the WFAD.

Once the program was in place, the number of employees wanting to take the buyout programs greatly exceeded the government's expectations (i.e., by 15 July 1995, 4,000 workers opted for the ERI, which was the number Treasury Board thought would take it over the three-year period). With the exception of Statistics Canada, where the Chief Statistician refused to take part in the job exchange,[10] most-affected and least-affected departments co-operated with the regional JACs and individual unions to maximize the number of alternations and thereby minimize layoffs.

In December 1995 the government entered discussions with the unions about how to restructure collective bargaining, which was scheduled to return in 1997. With the ongoing developments to reduce dramatically the number of occupational classifications (currently there were 76 categories), the government wanted to push for a similar reduction in the number of bargaining units. The government's original position contained only six bargaining units and would have threatened the historical jurisdiction of many smaller unions. The smaller unions indicated that there was tremendous potential for nasty inter-union fights across the public service as rival unions scrambled to win certification votes. They eventually convinced public-sector managers and the government that it was not in anyone's interest to generate more chaos and worker anxiety while the downsizing was in progress. Although the PIPSC and the Alliance would have undoubtedly gained from the government's massive restructuring, they sided with the smaller unions for more limited consolidation. In the end, the parties agreed to a plan that established 29 bargaining units, guaranteeing all unions existing jurisdiction. Both labour and management believe the process and outcomes of these consultations were positive, but they expect that further consolidation will take place in the future with the implementation of the new job classification system.[11]

In one of the first and most visible examples of the move towards alternative service delivery, near the end of 1995 Transport Canada turned over its air navigation services to a newly created non-profit corporation, known as NavCan. Under terms of the agreement, all the former Transport employees in this area kept their salaries and benefits, and the unions involved were given successor rights. In addition, the employees received severance pay from the government, their former employer. This generous deal was widely reported in the media (and often criticized), and helped shape the government's view that the WFAD had to be further modified to more easily accommodate its plans for using alternative means of delivering services (see Corcoran, 1996; McKenna, 1996). This led to a second round of high-level WFAD consultations/negotiations between Treasury Board senior managers and the union presidents. Treasury Board representatives stated at the outset that it was politically impossible to allow workers doing the same job for a provincial government or non-profit employer to receive either severance pay or a RJO with the federal government. If there was no negotiated settlement, the Liberals would legislate. The timing was fairly obvious as Paul Martin was expected to bring down a new budget in March 1996 that would outline the government's plans with respect to alternative service delivery. At the same time, the employer took a flexible position in the area of successor rights, which was important to the unions.[12] Although management described the negotiations as non-adversarial, at least one of the union presidents described it as 'negotiating with a gun to their heads'.

In early 1996, a tentative proposal was negotiated for presentation to their respective principals. Subject to favourable responses, the parties would continue negotiations on the finer points. Three types of alternative employment arrangements were defined. In Type 1 employment transitions, the new employer would be obliged to accept the existing union and collective agreement, provide comparable fringe benefits (such as pensions and health benefits), and guarantee employment for at least two years. Type 2 transitions would provide for at least 85 per cent of the original salary, comparable benefits, and guaranteed employment for two years. In cases of Type 1 or Type 2 transitions, the new job would be deemed to be an RJO. If an employee refused to go to the new employer, she/he would only be entitled to 3-4 months' severance pay. Type 3 arrangements constituted situations where the new employer's terms and conditions were considerably inferior to the current federal employer.[13] Employees unwilling to move in these cases would still be entitled to the terms of the old WFAD, including an RJO with the federal government (see Table 7.3).

Daryl Bean, president of the Alliance, brought the proposal to his board, where it was turned down in a close vote. He was also instructed not to return to the bargaining table. Rather than allow the deal to evaporate and then be legislated, the Treasury Board and the remaining unions decided to continue negotiating. Steve Hindle, president of PIPSC, said that 'it was clear that job security will be diluted, whether we sit at the table or not, so we'd rather sit at the table to discuss what's going to be in the legislation' (May, 1996a). Bean told other union officials that he understood their position and wished them well. On 7 February 1996 Treasury Board signed an agreement with unions representing 20 per cent of federal public employees (the Alliance and the SSEA refused to sign) that was very similar to the tentative proposal.

It was not surprising that the plan was extended across the public service as part of the March 1996 budget. However, the legislation was designed so that there would be somewhat poorer severance benefits for those unions that did not accept the February 1996 agreement. For example, when an employee was transferred to a commercial employer whose salary was less than 85 per cent of the current salary, the government would top up his or her new salary for only 12 months, rather than 18 months as per the February agreement. Treasury Board President Marcel Massé stated publicly that 'penalizing the two unions will send a message that it's better to negotiate than walk away' (May, 1996b). However, it was also made clear that if the SSEA and/or the Alliance signed on to the February agreement, they would be entitled to the superior benefits. Eventually SSEA did sign on, while the Alliance refused.

Martin's 1996 budget also announced another round of Program Review cuts that would further reduce employment by 6,000 in the 1998–9 fiscal year (although the ERI and EDI plans were not being extended past 1 July 1998). Indicative of the government's commitment to alternative service delivery, he also announced that three new agencies would be established (for food inspection, national parks administration, and tax collection), with the potential of eventually affecting another 40,000 public employees.

Finally, the budget made a cryptic reference to changing compensation in a manner consistent with restraint but fair to employees. The next day, Massé explained that the freeze on compensation would end in June 1996 with the payment of increments, and collective bargaining would return in the fall. To protect the government's restraint commitments, interest arbitration would be suspended for the next three years (Government of Canada, 1996). Unions would be forced to take the strike route to back up their salary demands. This represented a 180-degree turn for the Liberals: historically, the government did its utmost to get unions to select the arbitration route, thus avoiding the risk of strikes. According to our sources, the suspension represented a compromise between the Treasury Board and Finance. Finance officials wanted a guarantee that 'catch-up' wage increases would not be negotiated so their expenditure targets could be maintained. Treasury Board officials had to concede that an arbitrator could award catch-up. Rather than remove interest arbitration permanently (Finance's proposal), the government imposed a temporary suspension.[14]

The government's decision is a tacit acknowledgement that federal compensation has fallen behind. Why else would it be afraid to have an arbitrator rule on the merits of the case?[15] This does demonstrate the government's commitment to control compensation, even at the cost of greater strike risk. It also likely indicates the government's confidence that federal public employees would be hesitant to strike, or that the public would tolerate a strike, given their support for the goal of fiscal responsibility.

Although all the union officials were extremely surprised by the announcement, its impact varied across unions. The Alliance, which has not used the arbitration route for almost two decades, was largely unaffected. The SSEA, which has always opted for arbitration, felt it had the rug pulled out from under it. SSEA officials were concerned that Treasury Board would force them into a strike situation just to avoid management concessions, let alone to obtain wage increases. The situation was similar for the PIPSC. Although some of their bargaining units were not averse to the concept of striking, several units (such as health-related occupations) have a very high proportion of employees designated as essential and, therefore, not allowed to strike. These groups would be effectively left without a dispute resolution process.

The 1997–1998 Round of Bargaining

Bargaining began in early 1997, with most groups reaching new contracts by the end of 1998. In the Liberals' first budget since their re-election to majority status in 1997, Paul Martin reiterated that the government and the Canadian public would not accept public employee settlements that included wage 'catch-up' for those years when bargaining was on hold.[16] Shortly thereafter, Marcel Massé indicated that the government was budgeting for compensation to increase by approximately 2 per cent per year for the next two years, which was superior to negotiated increases in the other public sectors, for 1997 at least (see Table 7.2). Despite the fears of some unions, the Treasury Board did not ask for wording concessions in collective agreements. Their major goal was to consolidate and standardize collective agreements without having to ratchet up to the best language from the union perspective.

In terms of visible increases, the government appeared to maintain its salary target. Most negotiated agreements have increased basic salaries by 4–5 per cent over two years. In some occupations, such as computer specialists, auditors, and technicians, where private-sector demand pushed comparable salaries way above the prevailing public service rate, the Government also agreed to lump-sum payments or additional increment steps.

The government was also concerned with voluntary attrition in the executive ranks. Based on the findings of a blue-ribbon panel it established, the Liberals announced that various executive salaries would be increased by 4–19 per cent (Advisory Committee on Senior Level Retention and Compensation, 1998). Not surprisingly, the unions reacted strongly, accusing the government of a double standard that allows for 'catch-up' for its high paid managers but denies the concept for its regular employees, who make a fraction of managerial salaries.[17]

Bargaining between the Treasury Board and the Alliance proceeded very slowly at the five separate tables. Negotiations for the largest group (covering 91,000 employees) were further complicated by an outstanding pay equity case. On 29 July 1998 the Canadian Human Rights Tribunal (1998) issued a ruling that would require the government to increase the salaries of six female-dominated occupational groups represented by the Alliance.[18] The cost of this settlement, including retroactive pay and interest back to 1985, is estimated by the Treasury Board at over $4 billion. The government subsequently appealed the case to the Federal Court.[19] The parties were faced with the daunting task of trying to negotiate prospective wage increases without compromising their positions on the pay equity appeal case. In late 1998 an agreement was reached, calling for a 4.5 per cent increase over two years plus additional pay adjustments for the female-dominated groups (for example, clerical workers will receive about $2,300 annually). These special adjustments were made without prejudice to the ongoing court case.[20]

While the formal bargaining process was proceeding, the Treasury Board approached the major unions about a third round of special negotiations around the Workforce Adjustment Directive. As the three-year suspension of the WFAD for most affected departments would come to an end on 31 March 1998, the Treasury Board was anxious to eliminate the concept of a guaranteed RJO. Treasury Board officials apparently indicated at the outset that there would not be another massive wave of downsizing, and given this new environment, the guaranteed RJO was unnecessary. The government believed that unions would be interested in trading the RJO for improved buyout packages (once the ERI and EDI expired). In the hopes of making any negotiated agreement more palatable to the Alliance national board at ratification, the Alliance and Treasury Board agreed to include an Alliance component president as part of the multi-union team. Negotiations proceeded and the parties arrived at a package to submit to the union principals in March 1998. The proposal allowed deputy heads to declare indeterminate workers surplus without an unlimited RJO in situations where they could not predict whether future jobs would be available. In these circumstances, the employee would be given a choice of a one-year time-limited RJO, payment of up to 52 weeks' salary, or an educational allowance of up to 52 weeks' salary, plus up to $7,000 in tuition fees. In return for this concession on job security, the package called for continuing the penalty waiver for surplus employees who retire between the ages of 55 and 59, transforming the ad hoc joint adjustment committees into permanent structures with ongoing budgets, and extending the priority recall period for laid off employees from two to three years (see Table 7.3).

Despite the endorsement of the component president involved in the negotiations, a slim majority of the Alliance national board rejected the proposal. Apparently, the board was not prepared to relinquish willingly the job security that was claimed as the major victory of the 1991 strike. At the same time, the issue was largely symbolic for the employer. The government was really concerned about the political embarrassment associated with a surplus employee in a remote area remaining on the payroll, without a job, rather than about the cost of the RJO.

Despite the Alliance's rejection, all other federal public service unions except the SSEA accepted the proposal.[21] The job security issue reverted to ongoing collective bargaining. Rather than resorting to legislation, the Treasury Board continued to negotiate with the Alliance, and the parties reached an agreement in late August 1998 that covered all the union's bargaining groups.[22] The new arrangement mirrors the changes to the WFAD previously agreed to by the Treasury Board and the rest of the public service unions in 1996 and 1998, but it does include a number of 'sweeteners' for the Alliance, including the ability of a surplus employee in the middle of a limited RJO to resign in return for a lump sum severance payment and a mandatory union-management committee to negotiate the human resource implications of new departmental initiatives regarding alternative service delivery.[23]

The only employees who continue to have access to an unrestricted RJO are members of the SSEA. Because the SSEA and Treasury Board had completed negotiations for new collective agreements before the 1998 proposed changes to the WFAD, the union's rejection meant that the parties revert to the status quo on labour adjustment until the next round of bargaining.[24]

By March 1999 two Alliance groups—general labour and trades and corrections—still had not settled. The first had been on rotating strikes for over a month and the second was quickly approaching a strike deadline (although only 600 of the 4,500 penitentiary guards could legally strike; the rest were designated). Rather than allow the collective bargaining process to play itself out, the government again resorted to back-to-work legislation, which not only made the strike illegal but imposed salary settlements on both union groups.[25] The Liberals justified their move on the grounds that the rotating strike of blue-collar employees had crippled grain shipments and caused a huge backlog of tax returns (May, 1999b). It could be argued that the government overturned the rules of the game for the sake of convenience rather than because of a true crisis.

Restructuring Outcomes

Employment and Job Security

Unlike in many provinces, federal salaries were not rolled back, temporarily or permanently, during the 1990s. Increments were suspended for two years, but less than half of the employees would have been entitled to such increments. Nonetheless, the federal government's total expenditures on personnel compensation fell by $2.2 billion between 1 April 1995 and 30 March 1998, reducing compensation to 11.3 per cent of federal spending.

The compensation savings largely resulted from the massive downsizing of its workforce and the removal of the once ironclad job security enjoyed by indeterminate staff. As Table 7.4 indicates, during the last four years of Conservative rule (1990–3), federal employment was either unchanged or increasing in most broad occupational categories.[26] Since 1993, the Liberals have succeeded in reducing the bureaucracy by over 53,000 employees, or 22 per cent.[27] Table 7.4 also demonstrates that the cuts were not across the board, largely as a result of the Liberals' focus on policy and regulation at the expense of program delivery. Those groups least affected have been the administration/foreign service and scientific/professional categories—the so-called knowledge workers—whose ranks dwindled by 1 per cent and 11 per cent, respectively. Meanwhile, operational, administrative support, and technical categories fell by 33–9 per cent.[28] Looked at another way, over the 1993–6 period the Alliance lost over 33,000 members (a 21 per cent reduction) in the formal federal public service, compared to the next two largest unions, PIPSC, which lost 2,000 members (7 per cent) and the SSEA, which lost only 200 members (4 per cent) (Public Service Staff Relations Board, various years). This pattern explains much of the Alliance's hostility to changes in job security.

A related outcome of the Liberals' restructuring concerns job security. What was originally billed by the government as a temporary suspension of the WFAD only in selected departments that faced major downsizing has become a permanent limitation on the concept of the reasonable job offer. The previous obligation of providing surplus employees with an RJO within the public service no longer applies when there is a position available with the alternate service provider, unless the new salary and benefits are substantially lower. In addition, department heads can opt out of an RJO in cases where they believe it is not economically feasible, by providing extra severance pay.[29] Nonetheless, in comparison with other jurisdictions, job security for indeterminate employees remains above average.

One obvious question is, could the downsizing have been accomplished without suspending the WFAD? In retrospect, given the enormous number of employees wanting to swap with those declared surplus, the answer must be affirmative. In fairness to the government, both the Treasury Board and the public-sector unions were surprised by how many individuals wanted to leave the public

Table 7.4: Federal Government Employment by Occupational Category, 1990–1998

Category	1990	1991	1992	1993	1994	1995	1996	1997	1998
Executive	4,775	4,313	4,117	4,155	3,878	3,735	3,399	3,258	3,203
Scientific and professional	23,682	24,060	25,077	25,551	25,745	25,671	24,161	23,574	22,630
Administrative and foreign service	65,189	67,351	72,064	73,803	74,318	75,359	71,670	70,430	72,816
Technical	26,232	25,794	26,353	26,925	26,489	26,007	23,933	18,504	16,180
Administrative support	62,689	61,875	62,190	73,865	67,673	63,307	56,771	53,920	49,721
Operational	35,205	33,761	33,171	36,162	33,296	31,540	28,043	24,708	22,633
Total (PSC data)	218,328	217,818	223,598	n.a.	n.a.	n.a.	n.a.	n.a.	n.a.
Total (TBS data)	231,221	234,334	235,343	240,461	231,399	225,619	207,977	194,394	187,183

Note: Employment figures were published by the Public Service Commission until 1993, when the Treasury Board became the sole agency providing these data. Treasury Board data are somewhat higher because they include employees hired for terms of less than six months. Also, these data differ from the Statistics Canada definition of federal employment (presented in Chapter 1) because they exclude members of the armed forces and the RCMP.
Sources: Public Service Commission, *Annual Reports*, various years; Treasury Board, *Employment Statistics for the Federal Public Service*, various years.

service. On the other hand, given the subsequent actions of the Liberals, it could be argued that the suspension of the WFAD was just a first step in a larger plan to remove the RJO guarantee.

Downsizing proceeded largely through the threat and use of the government's legislative powers. That is not to say the process was entirely unilateral. Consultation, informal negotiation, and joint co-operation occurred along the way. It is remarkable how few people were laid off. Treasury Board data indicate that between 1 April 1995 and 31 March 1998, 11,307 accepted the ERI, 11,519 opted for the EDI, and 5,599 accepted the Civilian Reduction Program (the Defence Department predecessor to the ERI/EDI programs). When combined with natural attrition and 9,784 jobs that were devolved with the incumbents, it turns out that only about 500 were actually laid off, and the number of employees on surplus status fell by more than half to 814 employees (Treasury Board, 1998: 56–72). That is not to say that everyone who accepted a buyout did so willingly; in many cases, particularly in the early stages of the downsizing exercise, employees felt they had no choice but to accept an ERI or EDI.

The downsizing proceeded smoothly because the buyout packages were generous. The Auditor General (1998: 1-20–1-23) determined that the average EDI and CRP payment exceeded $40,000, while the average ERI payment was about $32,000 plus the value of the pension penalty waiver. Although the numbers appear high, it must be remembered that these allowances are subject to tax, so the net cost to the federal government is somewhat lower.[30] Once the government opened up the program to allow for job alterations from non-surplus employees, the number of employees willing to leave exceeded the number of vacancies by more than three to one. Low morale and high workloads resulting from years of restraint and the denial of collective bargaining undoubtedly contributed to the large numbers who volunteered to leave the public service.

The work of the Joint Adjustment Committees also helped to ease the transition. Although their effectiveness varied across regions, both union and management viewed these interdepartmental committees as valuable in facilitating job swaps. In addition to their primary labour adjustment function, the JACs provided important venues for ongoing union-management interaction and co-operation at the regional level. If anything, their significance was magnified by the suspension of collective bargaining. A reformulated JAC structure will become a permanent fixture in the public service as a result of the most recent round of WFAD negotiations.

Other Conditions of Work

It should also be recognized that many other less visible forms of consultation/negotiation on human resource issues were occurring simultaneously. Both the Conservative and Liberal governments have involved public-sector unions to some degree in important issues such as pension reform, health benefits, and reclassification.

The National Joint Council became an extremely important forum due to the suspension of formal collective bargaining during much of the 1990s. As stated by some interviewed at the Treasury Board, it essentially became 'the only game in town'. NJC outcomes that have been viewed as fairly successful by both the government and the unions include the creation and operation of the JACs and the negotiation of health and dental plans and travel benefits. According to one union respondent, negotiating these micro-level benefits centrally, rather than at individual bargaining tables, saves both sides time and money. More importantly, the NJC has 'put money into the [union] members' pockets', because these negotiated benefits have not been used as a trade-off for other compensation in regular collective bargaining negotiations.

Feedback varied somewhat on the assessment of the nature, form, and degree of influence of the parties in consultation processes in issue areas outside of the NJC process. Union respondents claimed that the PS2000 and La Relève[31] initiatives failed to involve labour representatives in human resource issues, which cannot be satisfactorily addressed by management alone. They argued that discussions of morale, and of the quality and functioning of the public service, should involve unions. Employer respondents generally view these initiatives as relating to management and public service employees more broadly, outside of the more traditional vehicles of labour-management representation and negotiation.

The consultation process surrounding creation of the new Universal Classification System (UCS), which will merge and simplify occupational groups and subgroups within the public service (affecting classification and rates of pay), was also contentious. While there has been substantive union consultation on UCS, many argued that this arose largely because of pressure from the Auditor General to seek such input. Union respondents also noted that decisions made by management and executive committees undermined the functioning of the UCS consultation groups. Substantive disagreements remain over the weighting scheme for job elements (affecting job rankings), the timetable for introducing the new system, and whether management's greater use of deployments in a streamlined system will dilute the merit principle.

The parties were more positive about the consultations related to public service pension funds and human resource management in science and technology. Most respondents described the Pension Advisory Committee created by the Public Service Superannuation Act as a joint labour-management process, with significant union participation and input. This committee produced a report in December 1996 for the reform of the superannuation plan, including the recommendations for future investment of pension funds in capital markets and the creation of a joint union-management board. A Consultation Committee on Public Service Pension Reform was established by Treasury Board President Marcel Massé in February 1998, with plans for reaching a pension deal by the end of the year. The most difficult outstanding issue, however, who 'owns' the current pension fund surplus, led to an impasse. Then, in early 1999, the government proposed legislation that would not only give all of the surplus to the government but also remove union representation from the new pension management board (May, 1999a). The bill became law in September 1999. These developments obviously altered the unions' previously favourable views towards the pension consultation process.

There was significant union involvement in the shaping and implementation of the 1996 Science and Technology Management Framework, an initiative aimed at having science-based departments rethink science and technology activities, priorities, strategies, and operations, including human resource issues (Natural Resources Canada, 1996). The impetus for the initiative came from the 1994 Auditor General's Report, as well as from the pressure for budgetary and policy refocusing arising from Program Review. There was union participation on the senior-level Steering Committee, and in working groups on classification, rewards and incentives, and other issues. One union respondent cited direct influence in reorienting budget rules for conferences, so that conference travel could be considered part of training for scientists, and in removing promotion quotas that previously set a 25 per cent threshold for scientists classified at upper levels.

While respondents generally acknowledged that working-group and committee involvement fostered interpersonal relationships and joint efforts to address issues of concern, it is the implementation of results from the consultation process that ultimately indicates the influence of the parties. One union official claimed that consultation works best when there is a balance of power between parties, which has not been the case in recent years. Without such conditions, consultation becomes purely process-driven and does not lead to any action. This situation is amplified during periods in which collective bargaining is suspended, as many of these issues require formal negotiation.

Alternative Service Delivery

The delivery of public services outside of the more traditional forms of the public sector is perhaps one of the more significant and recent human resource challenges for federal public-sector unions. The move towards alternative service delivery, with delivery agents including parapublic, non-profit, private-sector, and mixed partnerships, accelerated in the 1990s. In virtually all cases, the union representing those employees retained its jurisdiction with the new employer, at least for a certain period of time. However, the number of employees involved may be so small that the union cannot effectively service these members. Given the restraint among union organizations in response to falling dues revenues at least in real (if not nominal) terms, bargaining and administering contracts for these separate employers spread union resources thin. As one union interviewee put it, only half jokingly, this proliferation of employers and contracts is the 1990s way of breaking a union. However, another union official argued that employees of separate employers are much easier to mobilize because the issues on the bargaining table apply directly to them. Finally, in the case of the Canada Customs and Revenue Agency, the unions involved are concerned that management used alternative service delivery as a convenient justification to reduce employee rights. This agency became a separate employer under the PSSRA on 1 November 1999. The unions must still contend with more restrictive bargaining than under the Canada Labour Code, while the employer is excluded from the Public Service Employment Act, removing employees' current rights to appeal staffing actions (Government of Canada, 1998).

Gilles Paquet (1997: 49) has predicted that the downsizing and the creation of alternative service delivery would transform the relationship between the government and the federal public-sector unions, given the decline in their membership and relative bargaining power. While it is impossible to disentangle the effects of the collective bargaining suspension, downsizing, and the move towards alternative delivery during the 1990s, taken together these initiatives have adversely affected the strength, bargaining power, legitimacy, and credibility of the federal unions.

There are differing opinions as to whether the move to alternative service delivery and the accompanying decline in the federal public service have stabilized or will continue. Long-time public servant and federal adviser Arthur Kroeger (1990) predicted a much smaller 'core' federal public service by 2000,[32] and while the focus of public service reform has not been size, the concept of the 'core' public service has been reiterated in many central agency publications. Others suggest, and federal budgets seem to support this view, that the large-scale alternative delivery initiatives are over because politicians are not interested in the process.[33] Either way, unions are attempting to ensure successor rights and similar wages and working conditions for the transferred employees, to prevent development of a dual labour market in which core workers are covered by strong collective agreements while those outside the core are largely unprotected.

Feedbacks

Labour relations processes and outcomes do not exist in a vacuum, and they clearly affect the evolving environment. Our discussion of the relationship of the Public Service Alliance and the Treasury Board with regard to the Workforce Adjustment Directive is a crucial case in point. From the Treasury Board perspective, on three different occasions the Alliance walked away from a reasonable compromise that their leadership participated in negotiating. We repeatedly heard that the Alliance board was only concerned with grandstanding and being politically correct. For many managers, the Alliance's behaviour left no alternative for the government than to legislate changes. On the other hand, interviewees from the Alliance stated that their members would bear the biggest share of the pain from government restructuring and the union was not going to concede the job security it had gone on strike for in 1991. They denied that real negotiations ever occurred, because the employer threatened legislation if the parties did not reach an agreement, a view reinforced with every successive legislative action taken by the government. That is why the recent WFAD could be significant. Instead of simply legislating, the government was prepared to negotiate a separate arrangement through collective bargaining. Likewise, the Alliance leadership opted for a pragmatic approach that led to slightly better job security provisions for their members. Both parties must be applauded for attempting to break the vicious cycle that had developed over the past decade.

Conclusions and Implications for the Future

If the restructuring and downsizing of the federal public service were evaluated solely from the perspective of outcomes, given the government's objective of deficit reduction, it could be judged as being reasonably successful. Layoffs were minimized, departure incentive packages were relatively generous, wages were not reduced, and although federal job security is no longer ironclad, many measures can be taken to facilitate employment security.

If, however, one were to evaluate federal labour relations in the 1990s from a 'process' perspective, a favourable interpretation of events would be more difficult to support. Collective bargaining was suspended for six years, the government frequently resorted to legislating agreements, and unions and management did not bargain as 'equal' partners. In addition, the suspension of collective bargaining made it extremely difficult for union leaders even to justify their mandate and legitimacy to members. The only bright spot concerns the recent workforce adjustment agreement between the Treasury Board and the Alliance, and even this has been negated somewhat by the Liberals' use of back-to-work legislation in 1999.

With the deficit eliminated and the government beginning to see fiscal surpluses, collective bargaining has resumed in an environment where concessions are not necessary. Yet, broader factors seem to work against a positive prognosis about the future of bargaining at the federal level. Over the past decade it has become clear that none of the political parties likely to form a government views collective bargaining as a basic democratic right. In fairness, they can point to poll results demonstrating that the public is not concerned about this issue. As one interviewee candidly stated, at the political level 'federal collective bargaining is like the monarchy: outdated (if not irrelevant), but too much trouble to be removed by statute.' In general, managers expressed the view that collective bargaining would be tolerated as long as it did not interfere with more important government policies (i.e., cutting the deficit). When such a conflict does arise, the government would not hesitate to use its legislative clout to impose a solution.

How should the unions respond in such an environment? Is it better to take a standard adversarial approach to bargaining and risk even harsher treatment under legislation or to come to terms with the situation, recognizing that consultation and negotiation under the threat of legislation is superior? Federal unions have been actively involved in consultations with government for many years, given the limited scope of bargaining in the PSSRA. In certain areas (such as the new classification standards) the unions have been successful in chang-ing employer positions, but at what point do the unions become irrelevant to their constituents if they can never negotiate as an equal?

During a period in which the long-time Clerk of the Privy Council, Jocelyn Bourgon, has spoken of the 'quiet crisis' in the Canadian federal public service, documented by numerous studies indicating low morale, lack of opportunity for advancement, and, by some, a sense that the federal civil service is 'in decline', public service renewal is indeed a challenging task. Yet it appears that the link between human resources management and the collective bargaining system has not been made. It is difficult to envision successful results from ongoing initia-tives to promote the quality and morale within the federal public service with-out the ability of federal civil servants, through collective bargaining, to have real influence over their wages, standards, and conditions of work.

If the parties are committed to maintaining a well-functioning labour-man-agement relations system in the federal public service, all efforts should be taken to avoid the use of legislation. Both management and unions must be prepared to endure what is often a difficult, lengthy, and frustrating process and to reject symbolic bargaining positions in favour of flexibility and pragmatism.

The National Joint Council and the Joint Adjustment Committees helped to ensure a smoother process and transition for downsizing in the last decade, despite the parties' unequal negotiating power. There is every reason to believe that the use of such fora to deal with specific issues in more decentralized insti-tutional settings, could supplement and enhance future collective bargaining.

Finally, federal unions must be assured more than token involvement in cur-rent and future management initiatives, such as La Relève and pension admin-istration. Without such participation and input, many recommendations for change will face barriers to implementation.

Notes

In the course of researching this paper the authors conducted approximately 25 interviews with senior officials of management and unions. We thank them for their time and candour. All interviewees were assured confidentiality, thus, no statements are attributed to individuals unless they were made publicly and reported in the media. We would also like to thank Richard Harkin of the Public Service Staff Relations Board library for all his valuable assistance.

1. For an in-depth discussion of how the NJC functions currently, see Sulzner (1998a).
2. Indeterminate employees are not hired for a limited term of appointment and constitute the 'permanent' workforce of the federal public service.
3. For a discussion of Public Service 2000, see Swimmer, Hicks, and Milne (1994).
4. These somewhat vague promises were made in response to questions sent out by the PIPSC and the Alliance. For example, Chrétien stated that the Liberals could not commit to rescinding Bill C-113 (the legislation suspending collective bargaining),

but that they were fully committed to the collective bargaining process. He also wrote, 'Any changes to the Workforce Adjustment Policy would be best arrived at through the negotiations process' (Chrétien, 1993).

5. Many of the union people commented that, in retrospect, the Tories were easier to deal with. According to one person: 'They didn't like unions and at least we knew where they stood. The Liberals were constantly talking one way, and behaving the opposite way.'

6. The Civilian Reduction Program (CRP) became the basis of later 'special negotiations' between the parties, when the staff reductions in other departments began to take effect. This program did not remove any guarantees under the WFAD. For a description of the CRP, see Lee and Hobbs (1996: 344–54).

7. For in-depth descriptions and analyses of the Program Review process, see Armit and Bourgault (1996) and Paquet and Shepherd (1996).

8. Each component typically represents all the Alliance members working in a specific government department, regardless of their occupational grouping.

9. Between the time of the budget and this announcement, the Alliance was gearing up for a work-to-rule campaign.

10. Statistics Canada had earlier developed a 'no layoff' policy as part of its career development program, which also included specialized training for employees. The Chief Statistician was unwilling to risk losing the organization's human capital investments through job alternations.

11. The federal experience stands in direct contradiction with that of a number of provinces, including Alberta and Ontario, where government used reorganization of services and/or fiscal responsibilities as a way of pitting unions against one another, thus weakening the chances of a co-ordinated union dissent to their policies.

12. For example, PIPSC leaders wanted to avoid a repetition of the National Energy Board situation, where the employees transferred to this new agency were left without any labour agreement.

13. One of the union negotiators referred to the three transition types as 'we like you, we just about like you, we don't like you'.

14. It must be remembered, however, that the WFAD was only supposed to be temporarily suspended, but it has been permanently modified. In early 1999, the government announced its intention to continue the suspension of arbitration for the next bargaining round. See May (1999a).

15. As a rough guide, note that between 1993 and 1996, when federal salaries were frozen, private-sector salaries and the consumer price index increased by 1.4 per cent annually, while other public-sector salaries increased by 0.4 per cent to 0.7 per cent per annum. See Table 7.2.

16. Section 13 of the Public Sector Compensation Act attempts to limit increases that can be realized upon exit from the restraint legislation.

17. The government's generous interpretation of what was allowable catch-up eventually extended to the military and RCMP, all of whom received increases substantially above the 2 per cent per year guideline. Interestingly, neither group has access to union membership or collective bargaining.

18. The six groups are: clerical and regulatory; secretarial, stenographic, and typing; educational support; library science; data entry; and hospital services.

19. On 19 October 1999, the Federal Court unequivocally rejected the government's pay equity appeal (LeBlanc, 1999), which led to an agreement between Treasury Board and the Alliance on the size and timing of pay-outs, settling the case.

20. Many members of the seven bargaining units covered by this agreement, which were unaffected by pay equity, received an additional increase through the elimination of the first increment step (those employees who were not at the top increment level moved up one step).

21. In a rare procedural move for an NJC agreement, the PIPSC sent the proposal to its members for ratification, where it was supported by a majority of those voting.

22. In addition to the five bargaining tables that negotiate for specific subgroups, a separate bargaining table was established to address common terms and conditions for all Alliance members. This was the venue where the parties reached agreement on a new WFAD.

23. Some leaders of other unions are dismayed that Treasury Board has rewarded the Alliance for rejecting the previously negotiated NJC package that they agreed to. There is pressure on the government to extend these two 'sweeteners' to all federal public employees.

24. The SSEA strategy assumed that the Treasury Board would bring up the issue in the next bargaining round, but, by then, interest arbitration would have returned. In that case, the union could refuse Treasury Board's offers, knowing that an arbitrator would not have the jurisdiction to address the workforce adjustment issue. Unfortunately for the SSEA, the government extended the arbitration ban for the next round (see May, 1999a). In February 2000, the SSEA and Treasury Board reached a new collective agreement that included acceptance of the 1998 WFAD amendments, removing the guaranteed RJO.

25. In both disputes the Treasury Board continued to meet with the Alliance and, for the blue-collar group, agreed to a deal superior to the imposed settlement.

26. The executive and perhaps the operational categories are the only exceptions.

27. One unintended by-product of the downsizing was the greying of the federal public service. Between 1986 and 1997 the median age of federal public-sector employees increased from 36 to 41 years old. For additional information on the gender and demographic effects of public service downsizing, see Peters (1999).

28. In some cases these jobs and their incumbent employees were transferred to another employer rather than being removed altogether.

29. The only exception was for employees represented by the SSEA, until February 2000.

30. It must also be understood that the pension penalty waiver was financed by the pension surplus, which could have been considered as belonging to the employees rather than the employer.

31. La Relève is the current initiative, undertaken through the Clerk of the Privy Council, aimed at countering the negative effects of downsizing and creating a renewed federal public service. La Relève is an acronym standing for 'leadership, action, renewal, energy, learning, expertise, values, and excellence'.

32. Kroeger predicted a 'core' public service of only 100,000 employees by 2000. While this reduction did not materialize, the concept of core indeterminate employees, surrounded by contract, term, and private-sector employees, remains important.

33. A number of those interviewed felt that politicians wanted to have a hands-on role in delivery of government services. The main transfers have involved food inspection, navigation and transportation systems, parks, and revenue/taxation services, and this process is nearing its end.

References

Advisory Committee on Senior Level Retention and Compensation (Strong Committee). 1998. Treasury Board Secretariat, Jan.

Armit, Armelita, and Jacques Bourgault, eds. 1996. *Hard Choices or No Choices*. Toronto: Institute for Public Administration in Canada.

Auditor General of Canada. 1998. 'Expenditures and Work Force Reductions in the Public Service', *Report of the Auditor General of Canada to the House of Commons* (Ottawa: Public Works and Government Services), 1-1-1-33.

Canadian Human Rights Tribunal. 1998. 'Decision of the Tribunal—Phase II', 29 July.

Chrétien, Jean, Leader of the Opposition. 1993. personal correspondence addressed to Iris Craig, president of PIPSC, 15 Sept.

Corcoran, Terence. 1996. 'Canada's Ugliest Privatization', *Globe and Mail*, 1 Nov., B2.

Date, Patrick. 1995. 'Public Service Unions to Help Find Jobs', *Ottawa Citizen*, 3 May, A1.

Government of Canada. 1996. Budget Implementation Act, Chapter 18, 20 June.

Howard, Frank. 1994. 'Public Service Cuts: Union Fears for 41,000 Jobs', *Ottawa Citizen*, 28 Jan., A1.

Kroeger, Arthur. 1990. Notes to speech presented to APEX, 18 Jan.

———. 1998. 'The Central Agencies and Program Review', in Peter Aucoin and Donald Savoie, eds, *Managing Strategic Change: Learning from the Program Review* (Ottawa: Canadian Centre for Management Development), 11–38.

LeBlanc, Daniel. 1999. 'Civil Servants Win on Pay Equity', *Globe and Mail*, 20 Oct., A1.

Lee, Ian, and Clem Hobbs. 1996. 'Pink Slips and Running Shoes: The Liberal Government's Downsizing of the Public Service', in G. Swimmer, ed., *How Ottawa Spends 1996–97: Life Under the Knife* (Ottawa: Carleton University Press), 337–78.

McKenna, Barrie. 1996. 'Nav Canada sets pay sweetener to have wage freeze lifted in privatization', *Globe and Mail*, 20 Mar., B1.

May, Kathryn. 1994a. 'Public Service Job Security Under the Gun', *Ottawa Citizen*, 24 Sept., A1.

———. 1994b. 'Public Service Going Private?', *Ottawa Citizen*, 26 Nov., A1.

———. 1996a. 'Public Service: Government puts Job Security on the Table', *Ottawa Citizen*, 28 Jan., A1.

———. 1996b. 'Government ends freeze on PS Wages: Workers Must Give Up Rights in Bargaining', *Ottawa Citizen*, 8 Mar., A1.

———. 1999a. 'Liberals "steal" from pensions, unions charge', *Ottawa Citizen*, 16 Feb., A3.

———. 1999b. 'PSAC calls federal back-to-work law heavy-handed', *Ottawa Citizen*, 23 Mar., A3.

Natural Resources Canada. 1996. *The Science and Technology Management Framework.* Ottawa, Mar.

Paquet, Gilles. 1997. 'Alternative Service Delivery: Transforming the Practices of Government', in Robin Ford and David Zussman, eds, *Alternative Service Delivery: Transcending Boundaries* (Ottawa: KPMG/IPAC).

——— and Robert Shepherd. 1996. 'The Program Review Process: A Deconstruction', in G. Swimmer, ed., *How Ottawa Spends 1996–97: Life Under the Knife* (Ottawa: Carleton University Press), 39–72.

Peters, Joe. 1999. *Statistical Profile of Employment in Government.* Ottawa: Canadian Policy Research Networks.

Public Service Staff Relations Board. 1990–7. *Annual Report.*

Sulzner, George. 1998a. 'The National Joint Council of the Public Service of Canada: A Vehicle for Bargaining and Dispute Resolution', *Journal of Collective Negotiations* 27, 4: 331–46.

———. 1998b. 'The Implementation of the Labor-Management Sections of the 1992, Public Service Reform Act and the Future of Federal Labor-Management Relations in Canada', *Journal of Collective Negotiations* 27, 2: 131–48.

Swimmer, Gene. 1995. 'Collective Bargaining in the Federal Public Service of Canada: The Last Twenty Years', in Gene Swimmer and Mark Thompson, eds, *Public Sector Collective Bargaining in Canada* (Kingston: IRC Press), 368–407.

———, Michael Hicks, and Terry Milne. 1994. 'Public Service 2000: Dead or Alive', in Susan Phillips, ed., *How Ottawa Spends 1994–95: Making Change* (Ottawa: Carleton University Press), 165–204.

——— and Kjerstine Kinaschuk. 1992. 'Staff Relations Under the Conservative Government: The Singers Change but the Song Remains the Same', in Frances Abele, ed., *How Ottawa Spends 1992–93: The Politics of Competitiveness* (Ottawa: Carleton University Press), 267–312.

Treasury Board Secretariat. 1996a. *Treasury Board Manual and Amendments: Human Resources,* 16 July.

———. 1996b. *Work Force Adjustment Directive,* 16 July.

———. 1998. *Employment Statistics for the Federal Public Service—April 1, 1997 to March 1998.* Ottawa: Minister of Public Works and Government Services.

Treasury Board Secretariat, Human Resources Branch. 1995a. 'Manager's Guide to Employment Adjustment', Mar.

———. 1995b. 'Proposed Early Departure Incentive', Apr.

———. 1995c. 'Proposed Early Retirement Incentive', Apr.

Chapter 8

Public Employment Relations: Canadian Developments in Perspective

Roy J. Adams

The past few decades have been hard ones for working people and for their unions nearly everywhere. It has generally been a time of union decline and management assertiveness, with the result that job security and conditions of work have become generally more precarious (ILO, 1997). The public sector has been no exception, as the chapters in this book clearly demonstrate. In this chapter I will place Canadian developments in a broad historical, comparative perspective and attempt to draw out lessons from the case studies.

Industrial Relations and the Changing Socio-economic Environment

Labour emerged from World War II strong and recognized as an essential actor in the economically advanced countries (Clarke, Bamber, and Lansbury, 1998). After an economic rebuilding period the economies of the West became overheated, primarily as a result of US involvement in Vietnam and the oil crises of the 1970s. In a milieu of inflation and rapid economic growth, labour became very assertive. Union membership grew rapidly and strikes and other forms of conflict were common. Many governments sought to negotiate wage restraint in return for tax and social program concessions (Banting, 1986). As a result, big gains were made in wages, worker participation and influence, and social security programs. The Great Recession[1] of the early 1980s, precipitated by a move towards monetary conservatism first in the US and the UK and then generally across the industrialized, market economies, brought that period to an end and ushered in an entirely new, economically conservative milieu (Clarke, Bamber, and Lansbury, 1998).

Unemployment shot up dramatically in the 1980s, greatly weakening unions.[2] Labour weakness led, in turn, to a deterioration in conditions of work for many workers. Precarious employment became more common, as did job insecurity.

International competition grew more intense due to the liberalization of trade and the growing competitiveness of Japan and the Asian Tigers. Private-sector reorganization and downsizing resulted in significant employment reductions, especially in manufacturing, and thus in the membership in private-sector unions, which were historically the backbone of the labour movement, in many countries.

During this period neo-liberal philosophy gained ascendency with its anti-*dirigiste* message of market ascendancy. This development, combined with employer demands for more freedom to deal with enhanced competition, produced pressure for the deregulation of markets in order to provide employers with more flexibility and freedom to meet the challenge.

These developments also had a significant effect on the public sector. During the labour insurgency period of the 1960s and 1970s several countries moved to establish genuine collective bargaining in the public service (Ozaki, 1987). The Great Recession of the early 1980s, however, led to a rise in budget deficits as government revenues fell and demands on government resources rose in many countries as a result of huge increases in unemployment (Tabatoni, 1985). This led to pressures for public-sector cutbacks, but those pressures dissipated with the revival of economies by the mid-1980s (OECD, 1995). A new recession in the early 1990s revived forces for restraint. In Europe, the move towards monetary union required the nations involved to meet tough debt and deficit targets.

One of the tenets of neo-liberalism is the proposition that the private sector is able to produce goods and services more efficiently and effectively than the public sector. This philosophy was championed in the 1980s by leaders such Margaret Thatcher in the UK and Roger Douglas in New Zealand (Peters and Savoie, 1998). In both of those countries major efforts were made to reorganize and reduce the size of the public service as part of a strategy designed to reinvigorate the economy. Both cases came to be regarded as models inspiring other countries to follow suit.

Complementing political initiatives were the development of academic ideas about how government bureaucracies could be reorganized to make them not only more efficient but also more responsive to their clients. The proposition that governments ought to concern themselves primarily with policy and strategy and leave implementation to the private sector helped fuel initiatives towards privatization, out-sourcing, decentralization, and downsizing. This philosophy was crystallized in terms such as 'new public management' and 'reinventing government' (Osborne and Gaebler, 1992; Pollitt, 1993; Boston et al., 1996).

In the United States Vice-President Al Gore undertook a major campaign to reform the US government by initiating the National Performance Review in 1993. By 1998 the program was reporting savings of $137 billion, and across the United States experiments were being undertaken at the state and local levels with the goal of making government do more with less (Borins, 1998; National Partnership for Reinventing Government, 1999).

In the 1990s the Organization for Economic Co-operation and Development (OECD) also began to proselytize public-sector reform. Noting an 'upward creep' in the 'ratio of revenues, spending, or the deficit to GDP', it called on member governments to 'strengthen the control and management of public expenditure' (OECD, 1995: 14). Towards that end it began to issue periodic reports on developments in several countries (OECD, 1995, 1997). Among nations engaging in serious public-sector reforms, besides Britain, New Zealand, and the US, were France, the Netherlands, and all of the Scandinavian countries (see, e.g., Peters and Savoie, 1998). The Germans closely watched the developments but proceeded more cautiously (Naschold and van Otter, 1996). However, by the early 1990s nearly all OECD countries were experimenting with some version of public-sector reform.

In some countries these initiatives resulted in substantial declines in the size of the public service. For example, Boston and his colleagues found that the number of permanent staff employed by the New Zealand government fell from 66,102 in 1983 to 34,505 in 1994 (Boston et al., 1996: Table 3.4). In the United Kingdom 'since Thatcher's accession to power in 1979, the number of public servants has fallen from 735,400 to 499,000'. (Peters and Savoie, 1998: 5). However, despite all of the hype about privatization and out-sourcing and a retreat of the public sector to the performance of core functions, government employment relative to total employment, as indicated in Table 8.1, has remained fairly steady.

Public-sector reform, however, was not limited to the OECD. The Great Recession of the early 1980s had a particularly devastating impact on the economies of nations in the developing world. Many of those countries had over-borrowed during the 1970s as banks sought to recycle oil dollars. In 1982 the Mexican currency crashed, and this was followed by a general Third World currency crisis. In order to qualify for needed assistance from international agencies such as the IMF and the World Bank many of these countries had to engage in severe spending cutbacks, including drastic reduction of their public sectors (Marinakis, 1992; Rose, Chaison, and de la Garza, forthcoming).

Canadian Developments

During the general labour insurgency of the 1960s and 1970s Canadian public-sector labour organizations, consistent with developments in many other developed countries, became more militant and successfully demanded the introduction of bilateral decision-making (Ponak, 1982; Rose, 1995).[3] The paternalism of previous governments, which had established terms and conditions of government employment by fiat, sometimes after consulting more or less formally with government employee associations, gave way to a collective bargaining process that was not much different from the one employed for decades in the private sector.

By the end of the 1970s Canadian public-sector employees were, for the most part, in a position that many considered enviable. They had a high degree of job security—a traditional aspect of public-sector employment—as well as good benefit plans, including pension schemes. And, as a result of public employee militancy, their wages had jumped from traditionally low levels to a plateau higher than their private-sector counterparts (Gunderson, 1995). Their fortuitous situation set them apart from their American colleagues, whose conditions of employment during the period fell to levels below comparable workers in the private sector (Doeringer et al., 1996). Although there was an upsurge of union membership and collective bargaining in the US public sector, the American unions were unable to win concessions equivalent to those in Canada. In the federal government, for example, the American unions were not permitted to negotiate over wages (ibid.).

In Canada, the Great Recession of the early 1980s had a tremendous impact on industrial relations in the Canadian private sector (Adams, 1995). Union membership fell significantly. Massive restructuring led to smaller factories and smaller unions. Labour organizations dug in their heals and adopted the battle cry of no give-backs.[4] Subsequent to the Great Recession there was little thought of making significant new gains. Labour found itself in a defensive position from which it has not yet been able to recover fully. Although the economy snapped back quickly a new outlook and strategy had been adopted by economic policymakers. Consistent with international developments, the first order of economic business in the new era was price stability. That policy kept inflation in check and stock markets rising but it also kept unemployment at high levels, which contributed to union weakness.

The federal government, in reaction to the Great Recession of the early 1980s, pushed for wage controls in its 6-and-5 program, which it argued should become a public-sector restraint model for the rest of the country (Swimmer, 1984). By the mid-1980s, however, the economy was again doing well, government revenues were up, and the conditions of public-sector workers under regularized collective bargaining appeared to be in good shape. Throughout the decade they maintained their wage advantage over their private-sector counterparts and union membership continued to expand. During the decade the major unions representing provincial and municipal employees grew by over 50 per cent, in stark contrast to the stagnation in the private sector (Rose, 1995; Gunderson, 1995).

Of the cases reported here the one government that adopted a seriously confrontational approach to its employees during the 1980s was Social Credit in British Columbia. However, as Mark Thompson notes in this volume, that approach led to a strong public-private alliance that forced the government to relent.

Several factors helped to change this generally rosy picture. First, neo-liberal philosophy matured and specific strategies for its implementation in the public sector began to be refined. By the 1990s, as noted above, Britain and New Zealand had been through massive changes and Roger Douglas, an architect of those changes in New Zealand, was globe-trotting to spread his philosophy of how to do it. As Reshef points out in his chapter on Alberta, during this period Douglas was a not infrequent visitor to western Canada and clearly had an influence on the policies adopted by the Klein government. It has also been suggested that his ideas had an impact on the Harris government in Ontario (Warrian, 1996). Of particular relevance, as Reshef notes, was the notion of making massive cuts quickly before the opposition could organize significant resistance.

Second, the new public management philosophy began to influence the thinking of more government leaders. It seems to have had a major impact on the reforms in several Canadian jurisdictions and especially, as the chapters in this volume suggest, in Alberta, Ontario, and the federal government.

A third factor driving change in Canada was the recession of the early 1990s, which brought about both a reduction in revenues and a rise in government welfare expenditures. Inevitably, deficits and debts rose, and thus attracted a lot of press attention. Concern about deficits and debt in many countries had risen in the wake of the Great Recession of the early 1980s as governments attempted to maintain social services without unacceptably raising taxes. In Europe these concerns accelerated after the nations of the European Union decided that the move towards a common currency involved macroeconomic convergence criteria as a requirement for participation. Italy, especially, had to make major cutbacks in government spending to qualify for inclusion.

Among Canadian governments the debt problem by the end of the 1980s was especially problematic at the federal level. The federal government had been running deficits since the 1970s and the continually growing debt began to enter the Canadian psyche as a critical problem that had to be dealt with. The situation in the provinces, however, was quite varied. In Ontario, for example, as figures by Rose in this volume indicate, debt as a percentage of GDP fell between 1985–6 and 1989–90. Interest paid on the debt as a percentage of revenue was lower in 1990–1 than it was in 1985–6. As late as 1988 Alberta had no debt and by 1993 its debt was still less than 10 per cent of GDP. Even in Manitoba and Nova Scotia, where the debt was over 20 per cent of GDP, it appeared to be falling and thus under control prior to the early 1990s recession.

The recession had the most drastic effect in Ontario. It hit just as the newly elected NDP government was about to implement an expansionist policy consistent with its program and values (Rae, 1996). The result was an alarming increase in debt just at a time when the public was becoming increasingly conscious about the consequences of the government's balance sheet. There is little indication that the Ontario NDP government was influenced by the ideology of neo-liberalism, Rogernomics,[5] or the new public management philosophy inherent in the reinventing government approach. Instead, its reaction to the rising indebtedness appears to have been entirely pragmatic. According to Bob Rae, premier at the time: 'Given depth of the recession, and the problem that uncontrolled debt would cause for key social programmes, it only seemed reasonable to ask public-sector workers to share in the solution' (Rae, 1996: 203).

As part of its strategy the Ontario government initially attempted to negotiate constraint with the public-sector unions, but it was unsuccessful in doing so. It then put into effect a policy of unilateral constraint in marked contrast to the policy of its sister NDP governments in British Columbia and Saskatchewan. The result was a disaster. It alienated much of the labour movement and resulted in several unions withdrawing their support from the New Democratic Party. In the next election, the party was soundly defeated.

Although not inconsistent with developments elsewhere, Canadian public-sector cuts in the mid-1990s were more severe than in most other countries. The reduction in federal government expenditures was steeper than in other G-7 countries (OECD, 1998). This was accomplished in part by reducing transfer payments to the provinces, which placed pressure on them to either raise taxes or cut their own programs.

Whereas Canadian governments tended to impose conditions unilaterally, undermining the process of collective bargaining, several European countries during this period moved away from unilateralism towards negotiation (Ozaki, 1993; Ferner, 1994; Beaumont, 1996). In the US federal government, where employee organizations still do not have the right to bargain over wages and have no right to strike, the huge reorganization exercise labelled the National

Table 8.1: General Government Employment as a Percentage of Total Employment, G-7 Countries

	1979	*1988*	*1993*	*1996*
US	17.1	14.4	14.4	13.4
Japan	8.8	6.4	5.9	6.0
Germany	14.7	16.0	14.9	15.4
France	19.9	23.0	24.3	24.9
Italy	15.8	15.5	16.1	16.1
UK	21.2	21.2	19.3	14.1
Canada	19.5	19.4	20.7	19.6
Unweighted average	16.7	16.6	16.6	15.6

Note: According to the OECD, 'General Government Employment covers the standardized institutional sector used in the System of National Accounts (SNA). General Government includes: the public authority and its administration at all levels: central or federal, regional (state or provincial), local, and social security funds; public services provided by the government (at all levels) on a non-market basis (e.g. public schools, hospitals, welfare services); non-profit institutions providing services on a non-market basis which are controlled and mainly financed by the public authority; social security funds imposed, controlled or financed by the public authorities for purposes of providing social security benefits for the community, which are separately organized from the other activities of the public authorities and hold their assets and liabilities separately from them.

'General Government does not include public enterprises. Such enterprises provide goods and services on a market basis but are controlled by public authorities. Therefore, the General Government sector is not equivalent to the concept of the larger public sector, which includes public enterprises, often used in the context of evaluating public sector borrowing requirements. Unfortunately, available data on public enterprises is insufficient for comparative purposes' (http://www.oecd.org//puma/stats/window/glossary.htm#General Government).
Sources: 1979: Oxley (1990); 1988–96: *OECD in Figures: Statistics on the Member Countries* (Paris: OECD).

Performance Review was, from its inception, managed by a National Partnership Council on which key union representatives had a seat (Kettl, 1994). Its entire tenor, contrary to that of most Canadian governments considered in this volume, was co-operative rather than adversarial.

Issues Raised by the Cases

Were These Actions Necessary, Desirable, and/or Ethical?

The initiatives reported in this volume have resulted in a significant deterioration in the conditions of work of government employees. Their job security has been weakened and their relative wages have deteriorated. There is also evidence that, although civil relations have been restored or maintained in some provinces (Nova Scotia, Manitoba, British Columbia), in most of the cases the labour relations climate has been negatively affected by the changes of the 1990s. Where evidence is available (Nova Scotia, Alberta, Manitoba, and the federal jurisdiction), public employee morale appears to be low and the attractiveness of a civil service career seems to have been substantially reduced. In short, there has been, to some extent, demoralization that may be producing a deterioration in the quality of government services.

Was the government action that led to this situation called for by economic circumstance? Did the Canadian governments that drastically cut back on employment have little choice? Or, alternatively, were the initiatives driven by opportunism?

As Phillips and Stecher note in their chapter on Manitoba, while the largest component of public service expenditure is wages, most of this wage bill is spent on employees in the health, education, and social service sectors. The wage bill for government employees in the narrowly defined public service (the focus of this volume) is a relatively small part of the overall public budget. Thus, cutting the wages and conditions of employees in this sector contributes only marginally to deficit and debt reduction. Neither British Columbia nor Saskatchewan[6] cut back on government employment in pursuit of fiscal responsibility, although Saskatchewan is generally considered to have successfully achieved that goal.

So, why have some governments considered it necessary to make sharp public-sector cutbacks? Rose (1995: 48) notes that many governments feel that they must act equitably, as suggested by Bob Rae's comment above. They cannot credibly make budget cuts that are likely to affect others without also cutting back on their own. Even if the contribution to the overall goal is relatively small, every little bit counts and symbolically the cutbacks are important.

An alternative explanation is that the debt/deficit situation was a convenient excuse for engaging in ideologically driven reform. Blais, Blake, and Dion's (1997) research on the relationship between political parties and public-sector reform is telling. They found that over a three-decade period parties of the right in Canada, the US, Britain, and France have been hard on public-sector employees. They were more likely to cut back on employment, hold down wages, and restrict or override collective bargaining than parties of the left. Generally, that is the case in this sample.

Right-wing governments in Alberta and Ontario were the toughest on their employees; left-wing governments in BC and Saskatchewan treated them the best. The Ontario government of Bob Rae was somewhat out of character, but Rae believed it was better to share the burden than to dump it entirely on a smaller group who would, alternatively, have had to have been laid off (Rae, 1996: 215). Blais, Blake, and Dion (1997: 44) find that Canadian federal Liberal governments, compared to Conservative governments, 'were more inclined to increase public employment and wages'. The current federal Liberal government has moved sharply away from that historical propensity.

If they were not economically necessary one may ask whether or not the cuts were in the general public interest.[7] If a less expensive public service has been achieved at the expense of the quality of services delivered, that might be a very false economy. It is not easy to sort out results of such reforms because of a complexity of variables affecting public-sector performance. However, according to Whetten, Keiser, and Urban (1995: 283), research on the impact of downsizing in the private sector suggests 'a dismal success rate'. The authors review survey research suggesting that reductions in morale, trust, and productivity are frequently associated with layoffs. Insecurity resulting from layoffs also increases stress and reduces the probability that employee involvement programs will be successfully introduced and sustained (Pfeffer, 1994; Kochan and Osterman, 1994).

In addition, many private-sector corporations have overshot their mark in their downsizing exercises and there is evidence that some of the most zealous governments in this sample have done the same. In March 1999 the Ontario government admitted that its policies had resulted in hospitals letting go far too many nurses and gave approval for the new hiring of some 7,700 registered nurses and 2,541 practical nurses (Boyle, 1999). Quite clearly, governments need to think carefully about the long-term implications of their actions on the morale of the civil service and on the relationship between civil service morale and the effective provision of government services. They also need to consider carefully their international legal and ethical obligations.

Canada is a member of the United Nations and a signatory of the UN's Covenant on Economic, Cultural and Social Rights. Canada is also a member of the International Labour Organization and has committed to follow the requirements of membership in that organization. Actions taken by several of the governments in this study are contrary to those international obligations.

All signers of the UN's Covenant on Economic, Social and Cultural Rights, including Canada and all of the provinces, have committed to respect the freedom of association of all workers and to promote collective bargaining (Adams, 1999). These obligations also exist for all members of the ILO. During the summer of 1998 the ILO passed a 'solemn declaration' reaffirming the commitment of all of its members to 'respect, promote and realize in good faith' a set of core labour rights held to be fundamental human rights. Included in the core was 'freedom of association and the effective recognition of the right to bargain collectively' (ILO, 1998: 14). Canadian representatives were among the 273 delegates who voted in favour of the declaration. Although there were some abstentions, no one voted against it.

Over the years the ILO's Committee on Freedom of Association, which investigates complaints regarding the application of the principle, has worked out a detailed jurisprudence on the issue (ILO, 1994; de la Cruz and von Potobsky, 1995). With respect to governments as employers, the jurisprudence holds that governments have a responsibility to recognize and negotiate with representatives freely chosen by all of their employees except for the military and the paramilitary. Unilateral action overriding collective bargaining is permissible only in situations of real crisis, such as periods of war or runaway inflation.[8] Unions in at least two of the case studies reported here (Manitoba and Nova Scotia) filed complaints with the ILO with respect to the unilateral overriding of collective bargaining. In both cases the ILO investigators found that the government involved was not abiding by its international obligations and asked it to refrain from the offending action. In both cases the request was ignored.

This contempt for international standards is not new. Indeed, in the past two decades there have been more complaints issued against Canadian governments for offending freedom of association and collective bargaining norms than against any other G-7 nation (Panitch and Swartz, 1993). What is new is the emergence of a heightened international consensus that core labour rights should be regarded as fundamental human rights, as indicated by the reaffirmation of support for these rights by numerous international bodies in the 1990s.[9] At the same time Canada has attempted to pursue an international policy as a champion of human rights by, for example, playing a leading role in the development of international commitments against the use of landmines. These two policies are obviously at loggerheads. By continuing to offend against the human right to bargain collectively Canada compromises its credibility as a leader in the cause of human rights compliance on the world stage.

In the cases reported here the offending behaviour is all the more objectionable in that there is little evidence to suggest it was necessary in order to achieve the desired fiscal ends. The ILO's Committee on Freedom of Association tends to be conservative and sympathetic to government arguments that intervention was critical in the pursuit of the overall public interest. Thus, an opinion of that committee that an action by government was impermissible is good evidence that, in its judgement, effective alternatives were available.

Evidence in this study supports the proposition that it was not necessary for these governments unilaterally to override collective bargaining to achieve their ends. Hard bargaining, as practised in Saskatchewan and Alberta, for example, while perhaps slower and more likely to produce overt conflict, was as effective in achieving the desired end as unilateral determinism. Canadian governments of both the left and the right have been entirely inconsistent in their stance towards public-sector collective bargaining. Thus, although the government in Saskatchewan chose not to override collective bargaining while pursuing its fiscal restraint goals in the mid-1990s, it passed legislation ordering the end to a legal strike by nurses during negotiations in 1999 (O'Hanlon, 1999).

Beyond hard bargaining, considerable research points to the fact that adversarialism produces inferior employment outcomes. The most positive results are achieved by labour-management co-operation (Adams, 1995; Pfeffer, 1994; Kochan and Osterman, 1994). Consistent with the general evidence, the chapters here indicate that co-operation has produced positive results in British Columbia and more recently in Saskatchewan. The United States' partnership approach, which seems to have accomplished quite a bit, stands in sharp contrast to that of the harsh and adversarial policies followed in several of the cases reported here. Co-operation, however, requires a willingness by both sides to compromise and respect the interests and needs of the other. Ontario's Social Contract disaster must be seen as the result not only of bad judgement by government, but also of unbending union intransigence. Co-operation is a win-win game, but only if both sides fully participate.

Are Canadian Taxes Really Too High?

As noted by several authors of chapters in this volume, one of the factors giving rise to the cutbacks documented here was a judgement by Canadian governments that the budget deficits of the 1990s could not be effectively addressed by raising taxes because Canadians were suffering from tax fatigue. The belief seemed to be that any attempt to meet budget requirements by raising taxes would be met with serious political resistance. Whatever the truth or falsehood of that belief, hard data suggest that Canadians, despite some significant increases in the 1980s (Swimmer and Thompson, 1995), are not inordinately burdened by taxes.

Table 8.2 provides OECD data on current tax rates in several highly developed countries. Canadian taxes are about average. Many other countries at the same level of economic development have much higher tax rates. It is mostly much poorer countries that have significantly lower taxes. If Canadians consider themselves to be overtaxed they are wrong.[10] However, as the US situation illustrates, political attitudes with respect to taxes are not necessarily grounded in hard data. Americans are one of the lowest-taxed peoples in the developed world but resistance to tax appears to be very high. Our understanding of this phenomenon would certainly benefit from some carefully targeted research.

Is There a Level of Government Debt/Deficit Compatible with Fiscal Responsibility?

Since the growth of debts and deficits was supposed to have been the prime motivation behind the government initiatives in several of the cases reported in

Table 8.2: Total Tax Receipts as a Percentage of GNP, 1995

Canada	37.2	Austria	42.4
France	44.5	Mexico	16.0
Italy	41.3	Turkey	22.5
Netherlands	44.0	Korea	22.3
Sweden	49.7	US	27.9
Japan	28.5	UK	35.3
Germany	39.2	G-7	36.3*
OECD	37.4*	European Union	41.8*

* Unweighted averages.
Source: OECD (http://www.oecd.org); G-7 average calculated by author.

this volume, one may ask if there are some parameters within which any government should be expected to remain. Is there an acceptable level under which any government might be said to be within responsible bounds? If so, it is hard to see any pattern in Canada. In 1996 the federal debt approached 70 per cent of GDP. Across the provinces variation ranged from 7.87 per cent in Alberta to 78.35 per cent in Newfoundland. When the Klein government began its program of drastic cutbacks in 1993 the provincial debt stood at less than 10 per cent, a level lower than any of the other jurisdictions save BC.

No doubt there is some level of debt that would fatally constrain any government. Financial institutions are wary of loan recipients with big debts and so charge them higher interest or, in extreme cases, withhold loans altogether. But since Newfoundland and the federal government are still functioning and appear to be in no immediate danger of bankruptcy, levels under 70 per cent would seem to be manageable.[11]

In short, the drastic policies undertaken by several governments in this study were the result either of overreaction, given the facts of the situation, or of choice justified by ideology or political calculation.

What Can Unions Learn from These Episodes?

Few of the labour organizations discussed here were notably successful in developing a strategy capable of turning back a government determined to make major changes to employment conditions. The most notable instance of success was that of the British Columbia labour movement in countering the thrust of the Bennett Social Credit government in the early 1980s by forming a broad coalition with a range of non-governmental organizations.

On the other hand, labour has survived the move to fiat and, in essentially all of the jurisdictions, collective bargaining has been restored as the primary method for establishing terms and conditions of employment. Is there anything the unions might be able to do to ensure that future governments do not again renege on their commitment to collective bargaining? As noted above, even though the judgements were in their favour, the filing of complaints with the ILO had little immediate effect on governmental behaviour.

Nevertheless, the globalization of trade has heightened international sensitivities around the concept of human rights in employment. The basic proposition, as suggested by the ILO's recent declaration, is that a core of labour rights should be enjoyed by workers everywhere and this core includes the right to bargain collectively. That collective bargaining is considered by the international community to be a human right equivalent to protection against child labour or discrimination in employment is not very well appreciated in Canada. Efforts by social movements in the 1950s, 1960s, and 1970s produced social and legal forces that make it nearly impossible for any employer, including governments, to discriminate on the basis of creed, colour, or ethnicity. More recently, action by non-government organizations has produced substantial pressure on multinational corporations, especially those in the apparel industry, to conform to human rights in employment (see, e.g., Varley, 1998). Now would appear to be the time for public-sector unions in Canada to begin to pursue strategies designed to make it difficult for governments to engage in unilateralism in future. Towards that end proselytizing collective bargaining as a human right is one strategy that they might profitably consider.

Conclusion

Although collective bargaining is still alive, a major conclusion of this study must be that collective bargaining in the Canadian public sector is not well. While the thesis of Panitch and Swartz that Canadian governments have systematically sought to undermine collective bargaining would seem to be too severe, nevertheless, the cases reported here clearly demonstrate that Canadian governments have adopted the attitude and policy that they may engage in bargaining or suspend it whenever they find that course of action to be convenient. The evidence in this study does not support the proposition that bargaining suspension was essential in pursuit of fiscal restraint. Moreover, since collective bargaining has been loudly hailed internationally—with the full support of Canadian governments—to be a fundamental human right, the casual suspension of bargaining cannot be morally justified. From a human rights perspective, it is tantamount to the circumstantial toleration of racial discrimination, forced labour, or the exploitation of children. In a nation respectful of fundamental human rights norms, governments must be willing to forgo policies and actions that were considered legitimate in less enlightened times. The only reasonable interpretation of the international consensus would seem to be that the suspension of collective bargaining for public employees is only acceptable in circumstances far more critical than those reviewed in this study.

Notes

The author would like to thank Joe Rose, Graham Lowe, Gene Swimmer, and two anonymous referees for helpful comments on an earlier draft of this chapter.

1. The recession of the early 1980s deserves the designation of Great Recession because, from an industrial relations perspective, it marked the end of one era in labour-management relations during which labour insurgency was ascendant and the onset of a new era that has seen business aggressiveness and the recession of labour power and influence.

2. From 1979 to 1983 the rate of unemployment went from 4.5 to 11.3 per cent in the United Kingdom, from 5.8 to 9.6 per cent in the United States, and from 6.2 to 9.9 per cent in Australia. For the OECD as a whole the rate went from 5.4 to 8.9 per cent.

3. In Canada strikes and lockouts as a percentage of working time went from 0.12 per cent in 1963–5 to a peak of 0.55 per cent in 1976, falling to 0.19 per cent in 1983 (Adams, 1985: Table 2).

4. As noted by Kumar (1993: 92), Canadian unions were 'convinced that concessions were damaging to the interests of their members, and the working class generally, and would in the long run adversely affect the fundamental nature and purpose of trade unionism.'

5. Rogernomics is the name given to the economic policies introduced by Roger Douglas, New Zealand treasury minister in the 1980s. According to Dannin (1997: 30), 'In practice, Rogernomics included restrictive monetary policy to engender recession and restore profitability; dismantling social services; high unemployment; tax reductions as part of supply-side economics; privatisation; deregulation; and limiting state responsibilities.'

6. In Saskatchewan, although there was no cutback between 1991 and 1996, there was a reduction in the size of the government service in 1997.

7. I mean only to suggest that the evidence is weak in support of the contention that cutbacks in government employment were economically necessary.

8. For example, an ILO investigation into the federal government's 6-and-5 wage restraint program of the early 1980s found that it was justified as a temporary measure to contain inflation (Panitch and Swartz, 1993: 51).

9. Among the international bodies that have indicated their support during the 1990s for core labour rights as human rights are the OECD, the World Trade Organization, and the International Organization of Employers, which put forth the proposal that resulted in the ILO's Declaration on Fundamental Principles and Rights at Work (Adams, 1999). It should be noted that, despite this consensus, Canada is not the only OECD country that fails to live up to international human rights obligations with respect to collective bargaining for government employees. For example, several US states unilaterally impose conditions of employment while forbidding their employees to engage in collective bargaining. In addition, the governments of both Japan and Germany, while recognizing the right of their employees to organize in order to represent their interests,

refuse to enter into collective agreements with public-sector employee organizations. On the other hand, as noted by Ozaki (1990: 230), 'in the large majority'
of industrialized market economy countries 'the bulk of public employees enjoy
the right to participate in the determination of their employment conditions
through some form of collective bargaining.' Moreover, contrary to developments in Canada but consistent with the development of the international
moral consensus, the trend over the past few decades has been towards the
extension of more rather than fewer bargaining rights to government employees
(Ozaki, 1993; Ferner, 1994; Beaumont, 1996).

10. Subjectively, the feeling of being overtaxed or undertaxed depends on one's
    comparison group. Because of Canada's proximity with the United States there
    may be a natural tendency for Canadians to compare themselves with their
    neighbours to the south, where taxes are, in fact, lower.

11. The Maastricht convergence criterion for participation in the common European
    currency requires an annual deficit lower than 3 per cent and a debt below 60
    per cent of GDP.

References

Adams, Roy J. 1985. 'Industrial Relations and the Economic Crisis: Canada Moves Towards
    Europe', in Juris, Thompson, and Daniels (1985).
———. 1995. 'From Adversarialism to Social Partnership: Lessons from the Experience of
    Germany, Japan, Sweden, and the United States', in Adams, Gordon Betcherman, and
    Beth Bilson, *Good Jobs, Bad Jobs, No Jobs* (Toronto: C.D. Howe Institute).
———. 1999. 'Collective Bargaining, the Rodney Dangerfield of Human Rights', *Labour
    Law Journal* 50, 3: 204–9.
Banting, Keith, ed. 1986. *The State and Economic Interests*. Toronto: University of Toronto
    Press.
Beaumont, P.B. 1995. 'Canadian Public Sector Industrial Relations in a Wider Setting', in
    Swimmer and Thompson (1995).
———. 1996. 'Public Sector Industrial Relations in Europe', in Belman, Gunderson, and
    Hyatt (1996: 283–307).
Belman, Dale, Morley Gunderson, and Douglas Hyatt, eds. 1996. *Public Sector Employment
    in a Time of Transition*. Madison, Wis.: Industrial Relations Research Association.
Blais, André, D.E. Blake, and Stéphane Dion. 1997. *Governments, Parties and Public Sector
    Employees: Canada, United States, Britain and France*. Montreal and Kingston: McGill-
    Queen's University Press.
Borins, Sandford. 1998. *Innovating with Integrity*. Washington: Georgetown University
    Press.
Boston, Jonathan, John Martin, June Pallot, and Pat Walsh. 1996. *Public Management: The
    New Zealand Model*. Auckland: Oxford University Press.
Boyle, Theresa. 1999. 'Nursing ranks to be restored', *Hamilton Spectator*, 15 Mar.
Dannin, Ellen. 1997. *Working Free*. Auckland: University of Auckland Press.
de la Cruz, H.B., and G. von Potobsky. 1995. *International Labour Law*, 2nd rev. edn.
    Deventer, Netherlands: Kluwer.
Doeringer, P.B., Linda Kaboolian, Michael Watkins, and Audrey Watson. 1996. 'Beyond the

Merit Model: New Directions at the Federal Workplace?', in Belman, Gunderson, and Hyatt (1996: 163–200).

Ferner, Anthony. 1994. 'The State as Employer', in R. Hyman and Ferner, eds, *New Frontiers in European Industrial Relations* (Oxford: Basil Blackwell).

Fryer, John L. 1995. 'Provincial Public Sector Labour Relations', in Swimmer and Thompson (1995).

Gunderson, Morley. 1995. 'Public Sector Compensation', in Swimmer and Thompson (1995).

—— and D. Hyatt. 1996. 'Canadian Public Sector Employment Relations in Transition', in Belman, Gunderson, and Hyatt (1996: 243–82).

——. 1997. *Industrial Relations, Democracy and Social Stability*. Geneva: International Labour Office.

——. 1998. 'Clearing the Final Hurdle, ILO Conference adopts Rights Declaration, seeks end to child labour abuses', *World of Work* #25 (June-July).

ILO. 1994. *Freedom of Association and Collective Bargaining*. Geneva: International Labour Office.

Juris, H., Mark Thompson, and Wilbur Daniels, eds. 1985. *Industrial Relations in a Decade of Economic Change*. Madison, Wis.: Industrial Relations Research Association.

Kettl, D.F. 1994. *Reinventing Government? Appraising the National Performance Review*. Washington: Brookings Institution.

Kochan, Thomas A., and Paul Osterman. 1994. *The Mutual Gains Enterprise*. Boston: Harvard Business School Press.

Kumar, Pradeep. 1993. *From Uniformity to Divergence: Industrial Relations in Canada and the United States*. Kingston, Ont.: IRC Press.

Marinakis, A. 1992. *Public Sector Employment in Developing Countries: An Overview of Past and Present Trends, Interdepartmental Project on Structural Adjustment*. Occasional Paper #3. Geneva: ILO.

Naschold, Frieder, and Casten van Otter. 1996. *Public Sector Transformation, Rethinking Markets and Hierarchies in Government*. Amsterdam: John Benjamins Publishing.

National Partnership for Reinventing Government. 1999. Summary of Accomplishments 1993–1998. http://www.npr.gov/accompli/

OECD. 1995. *Budgeting for Results: Perspectives on Public Expenditure Management*. Paris: OECD.

——. 1997. *Trends in Public Sector Pay in OECD Countries*. Paris: OECD.

——. 1998. *Outlook*. Paris: OECD, June.

O'Hanlon, M. 1999. 'Saskatchewan nurses vow to continue illegal strike', *Globe and Mail*, 10 Apr.

Osborne, David, and Ted Gaebler. 1992. *Reinventing Government: How the Entrepreneurial Spirit is Transforming the Public Sector*. Reading, Mass.: Addison-Wesley.

Oxley, H., et al. 1990. *The Public Sector*. Paris: OECD.

Ozaki, M. 1987. 'Labour Relations in the Public Service', *International Labour Review* 126, 3 and 126, 4.

——. 1990. 'Labour Relations in the Public Sector', in R. Blanpain, ed., *Comparative Labour Law and Industrial Relations in Industrialized Market Economies*, 4th edn (Deventer, Netherlands: Kluwer).

———. 1993. 'Labour Relations in the Public Sector', in R. Blanpain and C. Engels, eds, *Comparative Labour Law and Industrial Relations in Industrialized Market Economies*, 5th edn (Deventer, Netherlands: Kluwer).

Panitch, Leo, and Donald Swartz. 1993. *The Assault on Trade Union Freedoms*. Toronto: Garamond.

Peters, B.G., and D.J. Savoie, eds. 1998. *Taking Stock: Assessing Public Sector Reform*. Montreal and Kingston: McGill-Queen's University Press.

Pfeffer, Jeffrey. 1994. *Competitive Advantage Through People*. Boston: Harvard Business School Press.

Pollitt, C. 1993. *Managerialism and the Public Services*, 2nd edn. Oxford: Basil Blackwell.

Ponak, Allen. 1982. 'Public Sector Collective Bargaining', in John Anderson and Morley Gunderson, eds, *Union-Management Relations in Canada* (Don Mills, Ont.: Addison-Wesley).

Rae, Bob. 1996. *From Protest to Power*. Toronto: Viking.

Rose, Joseph. 1995. 'The Evolution of Public Sector Unionism', in Swimmer and Thompson (1995).

———, G.N. Chaison, and E. De La Garza. Forthcoming. 'A Comparative Analysis of Public Sector Restructuring in the United States, Canada, Mexico and the Caribbean', *Journal of Labour Research*.

Swimmer, Gene. 1984. 'Six and Five: Part grandstanding and part grand plan', in A. Maslove, ed., *How Ottawa Spends* (Toronto: Methuen).

———. 1995. 'Collective Bargaining in the Federal Public Service of Canada: The Last Twenty Years', in Swimmer and Thompson (1995).

——— and Mark Thompson. 1995. 'Collective Bargaining in the Public Sector: An Introduction', in Swimmer and Thompson (1995).

——— and ———, eds. 1995. *Public Sector Collective Bargaining in Canada*. Kingston, Ont.: IRC Press.

Tabatoni, Pierre. 1985. 'The Market Economies Tack Against the Wind: Coping with Economic Shocks 1973–1983', in Juris, Thompson, and Daniels (1985).

Varley, Pamela. 1998. *The Sweatshop Quandary*. Washington: Investor Responsibility Research Center.

Warrian, Peter. 1996. *Hard Bargain: Transforming Public Sector Labour-Management Relations*. Toronto: McGilligan Books

Whetten, David A., John D. Keiser, and Tom Urban. 1995. 'Implications of Organization Downsizing for the Human Resource Management Function', in G.R. Ferris, S.D. Rosen, and D.T. Barnum, eds, *Handbook of Human Resource Management* (Cambridge, Mass.: Basil Blackwell).

Contributors

Roy J. Adams is Professor (emeritus) of Industrial Relations at the DeGroote School of Business at McMaster University.

Sandra Bach is a doctoral candidate in Public Policy at Carleton University.

Paul Phillips is Professor of Labour Studies and Economics at the University of Manitoba.

Yonatan Reshef is Professor of Strategic Management and Organization at the Faculty of Business, University of Alberta.

Joseph B. Rose is Professor of Industrial Relations at the DeGroote School of Business, McMaster University.

Carolina Stecher is a graduate student in Labour and Workplace Studies at the University of Manitoba.

Gene Swimmer is Professor of Public Administration at Carleton University.

Mark Thompson is the William M. Hamilton Professor of Industrial Relations at the Faculty of Business and Commerce, University of British Columbia.

Terry Wagar is Professor of Industrial Relations at the Department of Management, St Mary's University.

Index